The Most Memorable Games in

GIANTS

HISTORY

The Most
Memorable Games in

GIANTS
HISTORY

*The Oral History
of a Legendary Team*

JIM BAKER AND BERNARD M. CORBETT

BLOOMSBURY

NEW YORK   BERLIN   LONDON

Published by Bloomsbury USA, New York

All papers used by Bloomsbury USA are natural, recyclable products made from wood
grown in well-managed forests. The manufacturing processes conform to the environmental
regulations of the country of origin.

Library of Congress Cataloging-in-Publication Data

Baker, Jim, 1941–
The most memorable games in Giants history / The Oral History of a
Legendary Team Jim Baker and Bernard Corbett. — 1st u.s. ed.
p. cm.
Includes bibliographical references and index.
ISBN 978-1-60819-068-3 (hardback : alk. paper)   1. New York Giants
(Football team) — History.   I. Corbett, Bernard.   II. Title.
GV956.N4B35 2010
796.332'6407471—dc22
2010021088

ISBN 978-1-60819-068-3

First U.S. Edition 2010

1 3 5 7 9 10 8 6 4 2

Typeset by Westchester Book Group
Printed in the United States of America by Quebecor World Fairfield

From Jim Baker:

To Sid Ringel, a great Giants fan and a great man.

From Bernard M. Corbett:

To my late father Mitchell; he began with Huff and ended with Strahan and never recognized the existence of the AFL in our suburban Boston home. Thank you for all those shared Sundays in front of the TV, living and dying with our beloved Big Blue.

CONTENTS

CONTENTS

Philadelphia Eagles vs. New York Giants
November 19, 1978

Dallas Cowboys vs. New York Giants
December 19, 1981

Denver Broncos vs. New York Giants
SUPER BOWL XXI
January 25, 1987

New York Giants vs. San Francisco 49ers
NFC CHAMPIONSHIP GAME
January 20, 1991

New York Giants vs. Buffalo Bills
SUPER BOWL XXV
January 27, 1991

Minnesota Vikings vs. New York Giants
NFC CHAMPIONSHIP GAME
January 14, 2001

New York Giants vs. New England Patriots
SUPER BOWL XLII
February 3, 2008

Acknowledgments

The Voices

Index

Introduction

The seed for this book was planted in the week immediately following the Giants' stunning upset of the Patriots in Super Bowl XLII. Many
think this was the best Super Bowl ever—and some even argue it was the
best *game* ever—but from a longer view, it was merely the latest contribu-
tion to NFL history from one of the league's most storied teams.
Through the years, the Giants had been chronicled in highlight reels,
photos, and newspaper clippings, but it seemed to us that something
was missing: the real stories of these games, told by the people who
lived and played them, in their own words.

Through 2009, the New York Football Giants have engaged in over
twelve hundred regular and postseason games. They have, in the
course of their eighty-five seasons in the National Football League,
produced some of the most fascinating contests the game has ever
known—for better and worse. An unending parade of championships may have been a delight to fans, but football is about more than
just that. No, part of the fan experience is sticking with a team
through its near misses and lean stretches, and we have included those
here, too.

Not all of these are necessarily the Giants' most successful games, although some would make that list: They are what we believe are their
most memorable games. And, as everyone knows, memories are not
always pleasant. That is why the Giants' record in this book is a mere
9–4—not a great season, but in most years, good enough to be playoff
worthy—and two of those four losses are as humiliating as any team
has ever suffered. Every team has its highs and lows, but the Giants

have pushed the envelope in both directions like few others. And the grimmer moments from team history remind us just how exhilarating the highs, however fleeting, can be.

In this book you will find a forgotten gambling scandal to rival the Black Sox, the most dramatic kick in NFL history, the highest-scoring game ever, with its bizarre and improbable final play, and, arguably, the lowest point to which any NFL team has ever fallen. But we're reporters, not monsters—rest assured that when you finish this story, you'll be left with a happy sight: a certain wide receiver, ball pressed against his helmet, crashing to the ground without losing control.

Conspicuous by its absence is the so-called "greatest game ever played," the 1958 NFL championship between the Colts and Giants. How, you might ask, can a book like this not contain that contest? There are some very good reasons. Most importantly, this game has been given plenty of attention throughout the years, most recently in fine books such as *The Glory Game* and *The Best Game Ever*. ESPN also pulled out all the stops in producing *The Greatest Game Ever Played*, an entertaining and comprehensive study of the '58 championship made in conjunction with its fiftieth anniversary. Frankly, we didn't think there was a pressing need to revisit a contest that has been so thoroughly and eloquently covered in the recent past.

Besides, we already had four Giant losses in our book! Instead we chose a game from that same season with a happier outcome for New York, a game without which there would have been no "Greatest Game Ever." It's a game filled with forgotten stories, high drama, and an incredible ending—and that's what this book is really all about.

We hope you enjoy it.

Jim Baker
Bernie Corbett

The Giants' Most Memorable Games

1925–1945

Most of the key moments in football history took place after World War II, but in truth there were glory days before the glory days. Indeed, the Giants were playing outstanding games almost from the moment of their establishment in 1925. The contests described here include their greatest and most significant games of that period.

December 6, 1925: Chicago Bears 19, Giants 7 This was the day Red Grange, the first bona fide gate attraction in the NFL, came to town. It is sometimes referred to as the game that saved the Giants franchise from dying on the vine, as a reported seventy thousand or so turned out at the Polo Grounds to see the recent Illinois star run wild on the locals. It was, without a doubt, the signature event of the early days of the NFL.

One would assume that New Yorkers, who were accustomed to having Babe Ruth on hand for seventy-seven games a year, wouldn't have been so star struck, but seeing Grange and the Bears was the thing to do in the America of late 1925. The problem with player-as-gate-attraction, of course, is that he has to play. Bears coach George Halas held Grange out of about half the game, owing to a grueling schedule that saw Chicago playing ten games in the span of about three weeks. Grange did not break loose for any 70-yard touchdown runs, the likes of which had made him a household name while playing collegiate ball, but he did make some pivotal plays in the game, including a key block on Joe Sternaman's second touchdown and a game-sealing 35-yard pick-six in the fourth quarter.

November 27, 1927: Giants 13, Chicago Bears 7 The Giants were successful on the field in their first two seasons and by year three were one of the top teams in the league. And this may have been New York's most significant game yet. The G-men entered play with a record of 8–1–1 while the Bears were 7–2–1. With the season winding down, a Giants loss would have put the two teams in a tie for first. In the days before standardized scheduling and a formal playoff system, winning a game like this was of paramount importance. Early on, New York made a goal-line stand, an achievement of much greater importance in those days when a single score was the league average. Rather than punting the ball out of the end zone, which was standard operating procedure at the time, back Hinkey Haines took the snap instead of punter Mule Wilson and threw the ball over the center of the line to Chuck Corgan, who ran it to the Giants' 30. Although this drive did not result in a score, it took a great amount of pressure off the Giants' defense. In the low-scoring, positional football of the twenties, a play like this was a difference maker.

Opening the second half of a very physical contest, the Giants marched down the field to the Bears' 2, where Chicago nearly duplicated New York's goal-line stand of the first period. Instead, Jack McBride powered through the line on fourth down, getting into the end zone to give the Giants a 6–0 lead. New York scored again on their next possession when they took a punt to the Chicago 30 and ground their way home, finishing the drive with another plunge by McBride, who stayed on the field and kicked the extra point for a 13–0 lead. In the fourth quarter, the Bears got on the scoreboard when Laurie Walquist hit Joe Sternaman for a touchdown with ten minutes to go. The action heightened from there and the Giants ultimately held fast. When they beat their tenants, the Yankees, in a snowstorm the following week, the championship was officially theirs.

December 14, 1930: Giants 22, Notre Dame All Stars 0 The great college football coach Amos Alonzo Stagg once opined that "A real man would never turn to professionalism." While one might assume from this comment that the immortal Mr. Stagg worked pro bono during his college coaching days—volunteering at Yale, for instance—the truth is he was once paid to coach football by two colleges simultaneously. What Stagg really meant was that college football was the best thing around. A decade into the existence of the National Football League, it was still a widely held opinion that there was something quite substandard about the pro game. Knute Rockne, the storied Notre Dame coach, was another loud proponent of the superiority of amateur over pro. After the 1930 season ended, he gathered together a team of Notre Dame alumni—those Notre Dame alumni, that is, who had not sullied themselves by playing pro ball—to play the Giants in a charity game in which he hoped the Irish would teach the pros the virtues of not getting paid. Rockne rounded up a who's who of recent Irish players, including the famous Four Horsemen: Jim Crowley, Elmer Layden, Don Miller, and Harry Stuhldreher (who themselves were not complete amateurs: Layden—three games—and Stuhldreher—one—had brief NFL experience and both played for the Brooklyn Horsemen of the upstart American Football League).

The result seems obvious in hindsight. The Giants overwhelmed the Irish line throughout the game and romped, 22–0. The pros even pulled a number of their starters in the second half. (Was it because, as Giant coach Benny Friedman would have it, Rockne came to him before the game and begged him to go easy?) Jack Elder of Notre Dame blamed the debacle on a lack of conditioning, noting that the team had been together for less than a week. The Giants, meanwhile, had recently completed a 13–4 season, good for second place in the NFL. The All-Stars tried nine passes and none of them connected. The rout, however it may have come to pass, went a long way toward hushing the notion that the quality of college football was somehow better than the pros.

December 9, 1934: Giants 30, Chicago Bears 13 This game appeared, on paper, to be one of the great mismatches ever in an NFL final (Vince Verhei in *Pro Football Prospectus 2008* has calculated that the Giants had only an 11 percent chance of winning going in) as the Bears were undefeated and the Giants had lost five times. It turned out to be one of the league's most memorable games, mostly because of some serious weather. In addition to the disparity in their records and point differentials, the Giants were contending with the unavailability of future Hall of Famer

Red Badgro, although the Bears were missing Beattie Feathers, their star rookie halfback. On top of that, the game was played in a steady freezing rain, wreaking havoc on the field and leaving thousands of seats in the stadium empty.

The Bears, who had not lost in their last seventeen regular season games, took a 7–3 lead in the second quarter on a 1-yard rush by Bronko Nagurski. Jack Manders put them up 10–3 with a field goal, and that's how the half ended.

Since three hours before game time, though, the Giants had been attempting to secure basketball shoes for their players. The New York captain, Ray Flaherty, had been at Gonzaga in 1925 and his team had worn them to good effect in similar conditions in a victory over the University of Montana. In 1933, the University of Washington had used them on a frozen field in a charity game against the Seattle All-Stars and scored a preposterous 69 points in the first half. Giants player Bill Morgan had witnessed that game and recounted how Washington loaned their opponents sneakers for the second half and there was no further scoring. The Giants finally secured the shoes of the Manhattan College basketball team and came out with them for the second half.

The effect was not felt right away, as Jack Manders knocked home a 23-yard field goal to put the Bears up 13–3. With the field as it was, and facing a Chicago defense that had allowed just under 7 points a game, that 10–point lead looked fairly insurmountable with just fifteen minutes left on the clock. It was then, though, that the sneakers began to make a difference. Perhaps all the slipping and sliding on the icy field was wearing down the superior Bears; not so the comfortably shod Giants. Whatever the case, the Giants took control in the fourth quarter.

In a sequence of scoring that is forever etched in Giants lore, New York put up 27 unanswered points in the final quarter. Wide receiver Ike Frankian wrestled a pass away from defender Carl Brumbaugh to make it 13–10. After stuffing a Bears drive, the Giants put the ball in the hands of Ken Strong, who ripped off a 41-yard run and kicked the extra point to put them ahead. Strong scored again on an 11-yard run off the right end. The extra-point attempt resulted in a blocked drop kick. Ed Danowski closed out the scoring for New York. Masked by its moniker as "the sneaker game" is the fact that it remains one of the great upsets in league history.

4

December 3, 1939: Giants 9, Washington Redskins 7 For four straight years in the late 1930s, an extraordinary thing occurred in early December: The title of the NFL's Eastern Division came down to the final game of the season, and each time it involved the Redskins visiting the Giants. Here are the standings heading into the last game of the 1936 through 1939 seasons (ties were not counted in figuring winning percentage by the NFL until 1972):

1936	W	L	T
Boston	6	5	0
New York	5	5	1

1937	W	L	T
Washington	7	3	0
New York	6	2	2

1938	W	L	T
New York	7	2	1
Washington	6	2	2

1939	W	L	T
New York	8	1	1
Washington	8	1	1

The first three of these showdowns were not especially close. In 1936, the Redskins prevailed 14–0 in conditions of unimaginable depravity. Rain, fog, and acres of mud made for a sloppy and injury-riddled game. The next season, the Redskins—now relocated to the nation's capital after generating little interest in Boston—triumphed again, this time by the score of 49–14. In 1938, it was the Giants who rolled, 36–0. By 1939, this was no mere coincidence: It was obvious that the schedule makers were contriving to get this showdown game in place in the stadium where the gate was bound to be a good one.

The '39 versions of these two teams provided easily the best matchup of the four years in question. It also produced the closest and most memorable game of this run, one that had a little bit of everything in it. Washington was favored heading into the game mostly because they

5

were mashing their opponents, while New York was more economical in its victories. Earlier in the season, they had tied 0–0 in Washington, so the anticipation going into the game was huge. The second-largest crowd ever to see a professional football game was on hand for the opening kickoff. The throng of over sixty-two thousand—one in five of whom had come up from Washington to root on the Redskins—had been topped only by Red Grange's visit to New York in 1925.

It was a brutal day for the Redskins as star players Sammy Baugh, "Anvil" Andy Farkas, Charley Malone, and Turk Edwards all ended up on the bench nursing injuries. The Giants slowly built a 9–0 lead on two field goals from Ward Cuff and one from Ken Strong. In the fourth quarter, Frank Filchock got the Washington offense moving. He had struggled earlier, throwing, among his many interceptions, one to Tuffy Leemans in the Giants' end zone. (Throughout his career, Filchock was no stranger to interceptions, as we will see in the next chapter.) Late in the game, he had the Skins moving. Washington would gain 164 yards in the air to New York's 47. With less than six minutes to go, the Redskins got on the board when Filchock hit Bob Masterson on a 20-yard touchdown pass. The Giants went out quickly and Dick Todd returned the ensuing punt 30 yards, giving the visitors excellent field position to start their money drive.

Once again Filchock drove his team down the field. With under a minute to play, they were at the 5-yard line. They took a delay-of-game penalty, backing them up to the 10, and making it a 15-yard field-goal attempt for Bo Russell. As Arthur J. Daley wrote in the *New York Times*: "Back went Russell's right foot as it swung in the arc that meant triumph or defeat. Through the early darkness of a dreary day the ball spun in its lazy flight. Higher and higher it rose until it fell with a sodden thud in the mud in front of the clubhouse."

Referee Bill Halloran saw it as something less poetic than did writer Daley, ruling it wide. Redskins coach Ray Flaherty, late and great of the Giants, protested strenuously as the Giants ran out the clock. That's when things really heated up. As the Associated Press reported, "Immediately after the gun sounded, Flaherty and some of the Washington players dashed out after Halloran again. They followed him off the field and toward the dressing rooms. As they neared the exit, Ed Justice,

the two-hundred-pound Redskin halfback, was seen to swing a punch at the official. Flaherty grabbed him and pushed him away before he had a chance to do any more."

SIGNIFICANT, IF NOT NECESSARILY MEMORABLE

October 11, 1925: Providence Steam Roller 14, Giants 0 The very first regular-season Giants game took place in Rhode Island on a day when the New York sports news was crowded with descriptions of the funeral of the great pitcher of one of the other New York teams to bear the name Giants, Christy Mathewson. The new NFL franchise shared its name not only with the longtime New York baseball team but with a soccer team as well, so finding space on the city's sports pages was going to be a struggle unless they impressed early. The defeat was followed by two losses to the Frankford Yellow Jackets on consecutive days, first in Philadelphia and then at the Polo Grounds. These were followed by . . .

November 1, 1925: Giants 19, Cleveland Bulldogs 0 This was the first Giants victory ever and it took place in front of an impressive home crowd of eighteen thousand. After their slow start, they released the aging Jim Thorpe and things began to pick up. New York crammed seven games into November that first season and won them all.

December 12, 1926: Giants 31, Philadelphia Quakers 0 Unable to negotiate partial ownership of the Bears for his client, Red Grange, C. C. Pyle took the star to New York and they formed their own league, the first of four loops to use the American Football League moniker. The league title was won by the Philadelphia Quakers, who arranged to play an exhibition against the Giants. Sometimes half-jokingly called "the first Super Bowl," it served notice that the AFL level of play was no match for the NFL. The field at the Polo Grounds was covered in snow and mud, but five thousand were on hand to watch a closely fought first half in which the Giants managed only a field goal. Talent would out in the second half, though, as New York went up 17–0 and could have had more, except runs of 65 and 52 yards were nullified by penalties. The

final two scores came when both Jack McBride and Tillie Voss intercepted George Sullivan passes and returned them for touchdowns.
Much is made of the fact that the Giants "only" finished seventh that
year, but it was a very strong seventh: They went 8–4–1 and outscored
their opponents 147 to 51. Still, it was a sound repudiation of the new
league, which folded thereafter.

September 29, 1929: Giants 0, Orange Tornadoes 0 This game is significant only in that it represents the first time the Giants would play a
regular-season game on the sovereign soil of New Jersey, the state they
would make their permanent home forty-seven years later. The closest
anyone came to scoring was on the last play of the game, when Benny
Friedman tried a field goal but Orange knocked it down as time expired. The Giants had played in New Jersey not too long after they
were founded, beating the Newark Red Jackets in a preseason exhibition game in Newark, 3–0, on September 27, 1925.

November 24, 1929: Green Bay Packers 20, Giants 6 The Packers
came to town sporting a 9–0 record, while the Giants were 8–0–1. New
York managed to do something that only four other teams did against
Green Bay in 1929: score. Benny Friedman engineered a 70-yard drive
in the third quarter to make the game 7–6, but he was harried by
a strong Green Bay rush and was picked off twice, including once in
the red zone. The Packers went on from there to finish at 12–0–1 while
the Giants won their last four to end up at 12–1–1, making this game the
difference in the standings.

December 7, 1941: Brooklyn Dodgers 21, Giants 7 This contest is known
more for what was happening half a world away than for what was trans-
piring on the field. New York had already locked up the Eastern Division
title and was just playing out the string. The Dodgers carved up the Giants, who avoided being shut out only with a last-moment touchdown.
Meanwhile, word was spreading throughout the crowd that something
was amiss in Hawaii. The Japanese attack on the American naval base at
Pearl Harbor had begun before the game started, so some in attendance
knew and some found out as the game progressed. For fifty-five thousand

people, the answer to the famous question "What were you doing when you found out about Pearl Harbor?" was "Watching the Giants and Dodgers at the Polo Grounds."

December 12, 1943: Giants 31, Washington Redskins 7 After seven weeks of the 1943 season, the fate of the NFL's Eastern Division seemed pretty well assured. The Redskins were cruising at 6–0–1, the only gray mark on their record a 14–14 tie against the Eagles-Steelers combo team that operated that wartime season. The Giants, meanwhile, were muddling along at 3–3–1, interweaving nice efforts with blowout losses, as .500 teams often do. In week eight, the Redskins finally lost while New York won their second in a row, downing the Cardinals. In the short, ten-game wartime schedule, they still had a chance to catch Washington if they could sweep the home-and-home series against them on the final two Sundays of the season.

On December 5, they were trailing 10–0 in the third quarter when Bill Paschal scored the first of two touchdowns. The second came with under five minutes to go and pulled New York to within one game of Washington. The following Sunday found them at Griffith Stadium. Slingin' Sammy Baugh had one of his more forgettable efforts, throwing five interceptions and having a punt blocked that resulted in the Giants covering it in the end zone for their first of four touchdowns. The victory completed New York's comeback and forced a playoff game against the Redskins. Unfortunately, the rebound ended there, as the Giants were blanked 28–0. It marks the only time in NFL history that two teams have met three consecutive times.

Chicago Bears vs. New York Giants

NFL CHAMPIONSHIP GAME
December 15, 1946

	1	2	3	4	F
Chicago Bears	14	0	0	10	24
New York Giants	7	0	7	0	14

Try as we might, it is nearly impossible to picture the events surrounding the 1946 NFL championship game in anything other than black-and-white. It is a film noir played out in the nightclubs and back rooms of New York City. The cast of characters, although real, fit cinematic types familiar to the genre: the small-time hood, the puppet masters for whom he works, the femme fatale in his employ, the handsome athletes reduced to pawns in a larger game. It is that rare instance in league hisory where the story behind the game may well be better than the game itself.

Which isn't to say the '46 title contest wasn't memorable: It was.

Indeed, Bears quarterback Sid Luckman, veteran of more than 130 professional games, called it "the most vicious football game" in which he had ever played. It was a struggle featuring the two most successful franchises of the two-division era that had begun in 1933, one of which was shorthanded owing to injuries and a suspension.

And yet the story behind the game remains mostly buried in the vaults of time.

Baseball's most famous betting scandal, the 1919 White Sox World Series fix, generated a best-selling book (Eliot Asinof's *Eight Men Out*) and a big studio movie based on that book. That particular scandal continues to resonate today because, in some quarters, it is still believed that star White Sox outfielder Joe Jackson belongs in the Hall of Fame despite the fact that he consorted with and took money from fixers. If nothing else, this ongoing debate has given the Black Sox scandal a longer shelf life than might have been expected. The 1946 NFL championship game has had far less staying power in the American sports pantheon. Yet it was every bit as stunning and every bit as salacious.

Don Pierson: It wasn't until the early nineteen eighties when the NFL began including it in their official history in their media guide every year. Growing up as a fan in Ohio, coming to the *Tribune* in the sixties, I never remember reading anything about it.

Dan Daly: I only saw it mentioned, very briefly, in a single sentence in a book that the *Sporting News* had come out that just summarized the various Super Bowls and NFL championship games. It had some scoring summaries and a little brief synopsis of each one of the games, and it just happened to mention that a couple of New York Giants players had been caught in this betting scandal.

Jack Clary: When I started covering sports back in the fifties and into the sixties, nobody ever talked about it. When you talked about gambling in sports, there might be an oblique reference.

One of the main reasons the game has not resonated through the years is that the NFL was tipped off beforehand and was able to do damage control. Another is that it came at a time just before the league really burned itself into the national consciousness. By 1919, the World Series was an American institution. In 1946, the NFL championship game was not. Yet another reason is that—unlike baseball, whose history has always been the bailiwick of outsiders—the NFL has been in the unique position of being the purveyor of its own official story and was not always quick to recount the tale of what could have been one of its darker moments.

Through the research of men like Pierson, Daly, and Clary and a feature done by NFL Films, however, the game's background is now, at least, better known. It still does not rival the Black Sox scandal (which, evidence suggests, was just the tip of the iceberg of baseball's gambling problems throughout the early 1900s), but it remains the closest thing to a fix that big-league professional football has experienced.

Heading into the 1946 NFL championship game, the Giants were a 10-point underdog to the Chicago Bears. Wanting to ensure that a bet on Chicago went their way, certain New Jersey gambling interests made covert and not-so-covert inquiries to two key New York players, fullback Merle Hapes and, more importantly, quarterback Frank Filchock. They tempted them with offers of cash, cushy jobs, and, most conspicuously, nights on the town with companionable young women.

THE TEAMS

Neither the Bears (8–2–1) nor the Giants (7–3–1) of 1946 were teams for the ages. While Chicago led the league in scoring, four teams (out of ten) allowed fewer points. Meanwhile, New York scored the fourth-most points and allowed the third fewest. The Giants broke the 20-point barrier in just five of their games but did pitch four shutouts, one of them accounting for the Bears' worst defeat of the season, 14–0, on October 27.

Chicago failed to break 20 points only on that and one other occasion, when they beat the Green Bay Packers the next week, 10–7. They scored 87 points in their two games against the 1–10 Lions and held the very weak Packer team to 14 points in two games.

New York's three losses were by 10 points each, coming at the hands of the Eagles, Redskins, and Rams, newly relocated to Los Angeles. Although it was a game they did not lose, the Giants' worst showing of the season was probably their outing against the Boston Yanks, who came into New York on November 17, sporting a 0–7 record, and played the home team to a 28–28 tie.

Upton Bell: The league was struggling. It struggled for a long time. The New York Football Giants, the Washington Redskins, and the Chicago Bears really dominated pro football. And of course my father came up with the amateur draft to try and help the lower teams, which it did to a degree. But still, those three teams had the most money—and the Packers had a little bit. It reflected the power in the league: New York, Chicago, and Washington.

The head coaches in the game had six championships between them. The Giants' Steve Owen had been with the team since 1931 and had won it all in 1934 and 1938.

George Franck: When I got to the Giants as a number-one pick with a big college reputation, I had a big, fat mouth. There was a lot of animosity with veteran players. They had three All-Pros on the line and I had to learn to stop my mouth from bubbling over. Tuffy Leemans told me in the huddle to "do what I say," and I remember an end run and a clear-out for a touchdown. Steve Owen only knew how to coach linemen and didn't like backfield coaching. He had no idea how to coach speed, and I was a speed guy.

The Bears were coached by George Halas, already something of a living legend a quarter of a century into the league's history. He had guided the team since its inception as the Decatur Staleys and brought them the title in 1921, 1933, 1940, and 1941.

Ed Sprinkle: We were in a meeting and Halas was making a talk during my first training camp there. He said, "You All-Americans still have a chance of making this football team, along with all the rest of you." He was trying to play down the fact that we came out of college with some great reputations. He was hard-nosed. When he was there, he demanded—he was like a tyrant. You played football for *him*. If you goofed off, you didn't play.

I loved the man. I got along well with him. He really respected me and I respected him. A lot of people said he was cheap. He wasn't like some of the big-money guys who owned the Giants or Washington or whatever. When he started out, he got the Bears franchise for three hundred dollars.

The Bears' standouts were Hall of Famer Bulldog Turner and Ken Kavanaugh, both All-Pros in 1946 (when there were only twelve named

13

by the Associated Press, in a league with thirty times that many players). Their quarterback was future Hall of Famer Sid Luckman.

Ed Sprinkle: Sid Luckman was a great quarterback. He wasn't the outstanding passer that Sammy Baugh was. I thought Sammy Baugh was the best passer I'd ever seen. Sid would throw sidearm. He was great. He got the ball there.

The Giants were led by All-Pro quarterback Frank Filchock and fellow All-Pros Jim White and Jim Poole.

Jim Keane: In 1946 we had clinched the Western Division with two weeks to go. The Giants were fighting it out with Washington in the east. They had shut us out earlier in the season. I think Luckman had one of his toughest days ever. We still wanted to play the Giants, though. The championship game was scheduled to be played in the east. The players' share would be paid based on the gate. We didn't want any part of Washington. We knew playing in New York at the Polo Grounds would be a much bigger crowd—more money for us, win or lose. The Bears' players sent postcards to the Giants encouraging them to beat Washington. They said, "Get your asses in gear," and we mailed them [back] to the Polo Grounds hoping we would be playing there again.

FRANK FILCHOCK

The Giants' quarterback in 1946 was Frank Filchock, a former All-American from Indiana who had been drafted by Pittsburgh and then traded to the Washington Redskins in 1938. In the summers of the early parts of his career, he played professional baseball in the Class C Kitty League. He hit .280 for Fulton in 1939 and .335 the next year before abandoning the diamond for good.

With Washington he was "Flingin' Frank" to Baugh's "Slingin' Sammy." While never one of the game's elite quarterbacks, there can be no doubt that he was a superb athlete, the sort of which the modern game's specialization rarely allows. (See "The Double Threats," page

32.) Consider all the different functions he performed in the 1946 title game:

- Passing
- Rushing from both the quarterback position and taking handoffs as wingback
- Returning punts
- Returning kickoffs
- Returning a field-goal attempt
- Punting
- Playing defensive back

A fixer who could reach a player with this many different responsibilities would be giving himself the best chance of guaranteeing an outcome. Filchock liked the nightlife, and it was this passion that made him an easy mark for a fixer on the make.

Monk Edwards: Filchock was a loose, easygoing guy. Very likable.

Jim Keane: He was a good guy and a great competitor.

George Franck: He and Hapes were going to the Copacabana with gamblers.

Hapes was a less obvious target. Among the thirty or so non-tailbacks who had at least four rushing attempts per scheduled game in 1946, he was the only one who did not average at least 3 yards per carry. He had only three receptions all year, too. He was, however, the man the Giants often relied upon to bull his way into the end zone on short yardage attempts. An intentional fumble in that situation would go a long way to ensuring that the fixers got what they wanted.

THE FIX

In spite of their blanking of the Bears earlier in the season, the Giants were installed as seven-point underdogs. The depletion of their backfield was one of the reasons for this, as was the fact that they had had to play a meaningful game the week before while the Bears had already clinched the Western Division title with two games to go, permitting them to relax through the rest of the schedule. The spread soon rose to 7½, and there was money pouring in. It then went to 10. Research suggests that, in some circles, it got up to 14 points within forty-eight hours before the game, a sure sign that more money was being dumped on the Bears than the Giants.

When we think of gambling fixes, we usually think of the favorite being approached to either lose the game outright or to make it closer than it should be. This was the case in the 1919 World Series and the infamous college-basketball point-shaving scandals, when players on the defending national champion CCNY basketball team accepted bribes to ensure they would not beat spreads. In popular culture it's always the favored boxer who is asked to take a nap so that the fixers can clean up on the underdog.

In this case, however, the schemers were going for what can only be characterized as a "cincher fix": that is, a bet where the underdog ensures, through poor play, that the favorite will cover the point spread.

Filchock and fullback Merle Hapes were befriended by Alvin Paris, a businessman who always seemed to have access to good-looking women. He had promised Hapes and Filchock jobs in his gift business, jobs that paid more than the rather pedestrian salaries even the best NFL players got at the time.

THE FIXERS

In reality, Paris was a front for a gambling syndicate headed by Harvey Stemmer and David Krakauer and was slowly feeling out the players about taking a powder in a contest in exchange for payment. Stemmer had made some headlines the previous year when he attempted to bribe the Brooklyn College basketball team to throw their January 31, 1945, game against the University of Akron. He had been sentenced to a year in prison and was fortunate not to be serving a longer sentence, since the laws against bribery considered it a felony only if the attempt was made on professional athletes. Such was the perceived sanctity of the amateur athlete at that time that those who wrote the legal code never conceived of something so heinous as someone approaching one with the idea of throwing a game.

Stemmer was able to continue his nefarious activities because, owing to a manpower shortage during the war, prisoners were made trustees at area hospitals. Because of this orderly gig, Stemmer had access to telephones and used them to quarterback the Giants' bribe attempt. He was not a gangster of the traditional sort but a "blue-collar worker" before he drifted into the darker side of sports gambling. In his book *Sports Heroes Fallen Idols,* Stanley H. Teitelbaum—who had firsthand knowledge of him as a neighbor—describes Stemmer as a "likeable man, friendly, extroverted and unassuming." The policeman who tapped his conversations (which were not taped, but transcribed live in those days) described his voice as being rough with an unsteady lisp, while Krakauer's was "strong and rough."

Paris, twenty-eight, was from a felonious family. His father, Sidney, had done a federal bid for mail fraud in the 1930s, while his stepfather was the New Jersey racketeer Eddie Ginsberg. Eddie's brother Matty was convicted of bookmaking at the same time Paris was schmoozing Filchock and Hapes.

Paris, along with Filchock and Hapes—both of whom were married—hit many of the city's nightspots in the company of some very beautiful women. Most prominent of these female inducements—and the one for whom there exists a photographic record—was Ida McGuire. She was a would-be actress who had been introduced to Paris by his stepfather and who later appeared briefly in two major studio movies that were shot on location in the northeast: *Miracle on 34th Street,* in which she played a drum majorette in the Thanksgiving Day parade scene, and *Boomerang!* She was uncredited in both films.

McGuire later admitted that she had had a few dates with Hapes and had met both players at a cocktail party hosted by Paris, but she denied ever hearing any talk of gambling, let alone of a fix.

Paris made numerous attempts to bribe Hapes and Filchock to ensure the Bears would cover the spread and win by at least 10 points. He later testified that he gave them each five hundred dollars, winnings from a bet he and his backers made on their behalf on the clincher against Washington. Both players insisted they knew nothing about the bets and didn't take the money. Still, though, they stayed in touch with Paris, even after he offered them both a thirty-five-hundred-dollar package to throw the game. Inexplicably at the time, Coach Owen moved the pre-championship practice to Bear Mountain, New York, miles outside the city. Paris pursued them there, going so far as to drive Hapes's family to see a practice.

George Franck: We thought that Hapes might have been throwing games earlier in the year against Washington; our best guy inside the ten-yard line losing the ball at the five-yard line? I felt sorry for him having to apologize for keeping the score down.

Dan Daly: You've got the guy who is sort of the front man for the bookmaker, Alvin Paris, showing up in Bear Mountain for a Giants practice session a couple of days before the championship game. He's physically present at one of their practice sessions. They had telephone conversations in the days leading up to that game. The week of the game, you've got Filchock actually sitting down in a luncheonette in downtown New York and actually meeting with Paris a few days before the game. I mean this was no little brief flirtation. There was a lot of stuff going on there.

George Franck: The Thursday before the championship game, I told somebody to bet on the game. I wanted them to give me the ball. I felt there was no way the Bears would beat us. I told a friend of mine who was a bookie, don't take the points—bet the odds [five to one], make five thousand dollars [on a one-thousand-dollar wager]. I didn't know what had gone on until later on, after it was over. All he told me was lay off the bets.

What Paris didn't know was that his phone had been tapped by the police. The night before the game, he was arrested, and Hapes and Filchock were brought before New York mayor William O'Dwyer. Hapes confessed that he had been offered the bribe while Filchock did not. With game time looming in twelve hours, Commissioner Bert

Bell needed to decide their fates quickly. Bell had been the former owner of the Eagles, and his role as the league's leader was still being defined.

Upton Bell: The league was looking for somebody who was one of their own, who understood the problems in the league and maybe would be able to guide it in a different way. And so they chose him because he was an owner, a coach—he played in college but he really owned a team in the league. He knew their problems—he knew what it was like to survive.

In some ways, they probably didn't realize it at the time, but it was the ultimate choice. I really believe that without him—and certainly with the help of George Halas and George Preston Marshall and Art Rooney and people like that—pro football would not be around today. They mainly chose him, I think, because he knew the problems of survival; he knew the bad situation they were in.

In the wee hours of game day, Commissioner Bell decided that Hapes should sit and that Filchock would play. Ironically—and this is sure to have fed into his thinking—benching Filchock would have played into the designs of the gamblers. Without his one-man offense, the Giants would have been hard-pressed to stay competitive at all with the Bears.

Don Pierson: I think it was a pretty strong reaction given the circumstances. I think in retrospect, he probably shouldn't have allowed Filchock to play either. Hapes at least admitted it. Filchock lied. But he probably shouldn't have allowed either one of them to play.

Jim Keane: We found out about the Giants' gambling situation the night before at the hotel. Hapes was suspended and Filchock was going to play.

Bob Margarita: It didn't bother us because we weren't involved.

Jim Keane: As far as the gamblers in Chicago . . . Halas kept the security around our team pretty tight. He had the old Cubs trainer check the rooftops of the buildings around Wrigley Field for spies. The bookies were always trying to find an edge. There must have been thousands of them in Chicago then.

One linemaker even had the audacity to send a wire to Bell, asking whether or not the point after touchdown would be attempted in the event the championship game went into overtime and was won by a touchdown. He wanted to know so he could better set the spread.

Bob Dobelstein: The gamblers? Hapes and Filchock got hoodwinked by them.

Monk Edwards: As for gamblers, we were not admonished to stay away from them. It was expected that we would know better than to even be seen with those guys.

Bob Dobelstein: There wasn't much of that crap going on at that time. That really opened things up, unfortunately.

THE GAME

The field at the Polo Grounds was in appalling condition at the start of the 1946 NFL championship game. It was barely lined and looked as though it had hosted a recent cavalry attack, so churned was the turf. While the *New York Times* characterized it as a "good field," the cinematic record seems to suggest otherwise. Carved up by cleats and weather, it is testament to the less-demanding groundskeeping standards of the day that this was considered a decent stage for a championship game by the paper of record.

George Franck: Bill Paschal was injured, and without Merle Hapes at fullback, we had to move Frank Reagan, a tailback who only weighed a hundred and seventy pounds, to fullback. He just bounced off the Bears' big ends. Hapes was a much better blocker and we really missed him in that game.

Ed Sprinkle: That was the first game that I played that I started at right end. They moved George Wilson to left end. That was my first starting job with the Bears, in the championship game! The Bears had Ken Kavanaugh and Jim Keane as offensive ends and I played defensive end.

After Hall of Famer Ken Strong's opening kickoff went out of bounds, Bill Osmanski took the rekick from the 12 to the 35. On the first play from scrimmage, Jim Poole dropped Osmanski for an 8-yard loss and the Bears soon had to punt the ball to New York. On second and 10 from their own 24, Filchock handed off to Franck, who rumbled to the 32 only to cough up the ball. Loose on the field for a moment, it was smothered by the Bears' Stu Clarkson, and Chicago gained possession. A few plays later, on first and 10 from the 21, Luckman found Ken Kavanaugh for a 21-yard score.

Later in the quarter, the Giants' Len Younce dunked Luckman for a 15-yard sack, forcing the Bears to punt. Luckman, this time in the game as punter, boomed a 47-yarder that was deadened on the New York 27. On third and 13, Filchock took the snap and dropped back.

Ed Sprinkle: I hooked Filchock with my left arm. He was passing. I really, really hit him. I broke his nose. I hit him as he threw the ball up in the air and Dante Magnani intercepted it and just like walked in for a touchdown. They didn't have any face masks or anything back in those days. I hit him. I didn't try to be dirty or anything. I just jumped over the blocker and made a wild swing and that was it. Filchock was a tough football player. I respected him. I was just fortunate, I guess, that I got in and hit him.

You had a lot of rapport and respect for other players, and I had a lot of friends that I made with the other teams after it was over, but when I was on the football field I didn't have any friends out there. I liked to hit them.

As Bears back Hugh Gallarneau told Richard Whittingham in *What Bears They Were*, "We just beat Filchock to a pulp that day; we were all so mad at him about what he brought down on the game. We broke his nose and just generally beat the hell out of him."

Ed Sprinkle: Halas gave an interview one time, and they asked him, Who was the toughest Bear that he had coached? He said Ed Sprinkle. I felt that was quite an honor for him to respect me that much. But that game I had a great game.

Eight minutes into the game, the Bears had bruised their way to a 14–0 lead, much aided by Filchock's flailing interception. And the crunching continued on the very next series. On a Filchock keeper, the Bears were called for roughing, putting the ball across midfield. Rookie Mike Jarmoluk—at six five, 232 pounds, one of the bigger players on the field—smashed into Frank Reagan on the next play and fumbled. Gallarneau fell on it, once again securing a Bears turnover. But New York's mighty defense held and Filchock struck back, finding Frank Liebel for a 38-yard scoring strike to make it 14–7.

The second quarter, though it involved no scoring, was even more brutal than the first. Reagan had to leave the field with a broken nose while Franck was sent to the hospital with a separated shoulder. In the third quarter future Giant head coach Jim Lee Howell recovered a Bears fumble at the Chicago 20. New York tied the game when Filchock and Steve Filipowicz hooked up on a 5-yard scoring pass.

Later in the quarter, the Giants were faced with a punting situation near midfield. With Franck and Reagan injured and Hapes suspended, the Giants were without any of the men who had done their punting that season, so the duty fell to Howie Livingston. He shanked a 16-yarder. So instead of being buried deep near their own end zone, the Bears had the ball at their own 29.

Luckman responded by driving his team down the field, aided in no small part by an unnecessary-roughness penalty on the Giants, which gave the Bears the ball on the New York 19. Luckman then made the offensive play of the game.

Ed Sprinkle: The Bears had a play we called "bingo, keep-it"— everybody would go one way and the quarterback would run a reverse.

He faked to the halfback, Gallarneau, but kept the ball himself, exploiting a hole in the left side of the New York line. Luckman raced to the 5, dodged two tacklers, and continued into the end zone to make it 21–14. It was a big play by any standard, breaking a tie in the waning moments of the championship game; but all the more impressive was the fact that Luckman almost never moved his feet. (Indeed, a somewhat dubious article in the *New York Tribune* claimed it was his first rush from scrimmage all season.) Still, Luckman found his way to paydirt and the Bears took command of the game.

New York could not counter and, this time, Coach Owen called on Len Younce, another nonpunter, to boot the ball away. He was more successful than Livingston, but the Bears drove once again. This time they stalled and settled for a 26-yard field goal by Frank Maznicki. Filchock desperately tried to rally the Giants downfield, but his last pass of the day was intercepted by his opposite number, Luckman, making the final score 24–14.

Bob Dobelstein: That championship game set a record for attendance and a record for the players' take from the game. I think we got about two thousand dollars a man. That was pretty good considering that nobody was making more than four to five thousand at the time.

Jim Keane: In the '46 game, we were only focused on winning. That extra money was all the motivation we needed.

Ed Sprinkle: The game itself was a highlight of my career. I enjoyed it.

SIX INTERCEPTIONS
So did Frank Filchock throw the game? Consider two pieces of information:

1. Filchock was offered a bribe.
2. He then threw six interceptions in the game he was requested to fix, and his team lost.

What is your natural conclusion?

While it should never be said that six interceptions in one game is not a lot, some historical light needs to be shed on what Filchock did in the '46 championship game. In the National Football League of 1946, one out of every eleven passes thrown was intercepted. In 2007, the figure was closer to one out of thirty-three. During the regular season, Filchock threw 169 passes and was picked off 25 times. Among the regular and near-regular quarterbacks in the league that year, he was easily the most often intercepted. (See "1946 NFL Interception Percentage," page 32.)

In the modern game, only a very small percentage of quarterbacks will have interception rates higher than the man who had the *best* percentage in 1946, Paul Governali (who, incidentally, was one of the men who replaced Filchock in the New York backfield in 1947 and 1948). Bill Dudley of Pittsburgh, the league MVP for 1946, was in double figures at 10 percent, as was future Hall of Famer Sammy Baugh of Washington at 10.6 percent. On average, Filchock threw a pick about once every seven passes, which often meant three or four per game. Given that he threw 26 times in the championship game, we could expect him to throw four interceptions at that rate. And facing one of the league's best teams, shorthanded by two running backs, throwing a couple of interceptions above average is not too surprising.

Remember, too, that the Redskins' quarterbacks tossed eight picks in their infamous 73–0 loss to the Bears in 1940, three of which were returned for touchdowns. Filchock himself, then a Redskin, was responsible for half of them. The great Luckman himself threw two picks in the 1946 championship game, and the Giants got their hands on three other balls that could have just as easily been intercepted. But for a matter of a few inches, the Bears' quarterback would have had a total of five interceptions, nearly matching that of Filchock's.

One more thing to consider: On what is perhaps the key play of the entire game, Ed Sprinkle broke Filchock's nose and Magnani returned the consequent interception for a touchdown. If Filchock were throwing the game, wouldn't that move be leaving a little too much up to chance? Wouldn't a better, not to mention easier, course of action have been to keep the ball and then fumble it backward when Sprinkle laid on the lick? After all, Filchock's blindly thrown ball might just as well have been caught by his own team. In fact, that throw—however ill-advised—may well have been a last-ditch attempt to save possession.

Jim Keane: I thought Filchock played fantastic. He ran, threw, kicked . . . if not for him, we would have won by three touchdowns.

Don Pierson: Everybody claims he played hard. He was hardly innocent looking back then because he did lie about the thing. I guess you have to give him the benefit of the doubt.

In his 1952 autobiography, *My Kind of Football,* Giants coach Steve Owen had this to say about Filchock:

One thing in [my football career] that made me mad, sick, worried . . . Neither boy was criminally involved. But, there was no doubt that Hapes had led Paris on by permitting the fixer to wine and dine him. Filchock was just plain foolish for not telling what he knew the minute he knew it . . . no one ever saw a boy give a more spirited and courageous performance on the football field. Honestly it choked you up knowing how hard he was trying. [We lost] . . . but it was not for lack of effort by Filchock. The boy's nose was broken early in the game, but he kept on fighting through every play with blood and mud coating his face and uniform.

CRIME AND PUNISHMENT: THE LEGACY

With the heat on him from the authorities, Paris copped a plea and sang like Edith Piaf. He sold out his string pullers and was given a relatively light sentence of one year. Predictably, there were death threats against him. Squealing on racketeers has that kind of effect. Immediately upon his arrival at Rikers Island, Paris's new fellow inmates made it clear that he was in serious trouble. Authorities transferred Paris to the Manhattan Detention Complex, known more popularly as the Tombs. Paris survived, though, and got out of prison on September 22, 1947, after serving nine months of a one-year sentence. Although not sentenced until April 7, he was given credit for the time he had been held since being arrested in December and also for good behavior.

While Filchock was never accused of actually agreeing to the gamblers' offer, Commissioner Bert Bell was not pleased that he did not make their advances known before the game. Ironically, it was the player who was truthful about being approached—Hapes—who was suspended for the championship game, while Filchock, who lied about his contact with the gamblers, was allowed to play.

Don Pierson: I'm sure neither one of them would have played today. Although I doubt it would have gotten that far today. What really interested me in reviewing the situation was how Filchock and Hapes had so openly consorted with these shady characters for a time before the bribe came to light. Today I don't think players can get away with anything. They can hardly brush their teeth without somebody knowing about it.

Joe Horrigan: It would be very different today. I guess the way you look at it is these were things that were not uncommon in sport, in the sense of I don't mean the controversy itself, but the way things were handled—there wasn't a huge media focus, particularly on pro football. Baseball, certainly at that time, was the sport that was most closely watched by the American public, and it was really only radio and print media, so we didn't have twenty-four-seven coverage of sport.

Commissioner Bell was just beginning to flex the muscle of centralized NFL control. The league was not long removed from its days as a league with no fixed schedule and teams that played or didn't play as much on whim as on conviction. The near fix afforded him an opportunity to show authority for the best interests of the game.

Upton Bell: My father found out about the plot because he was one of those people who had his ears to everything. He knew gamblers. Remember when he was a kid running around Philadelphia in his twenties, he knew everybody from Al Capone to every gambler around. He knew them even though he was from high society. He had something that no other commissioner had at the time. He had the ability to find out what was going on. The story broke, he found out about it, and immediately took action the night before the championship game by suspending Hapes and letting Filchock play in the game because Hapes had admitted initially that somebody did approach him about fixing the game. Filchock didn't. After the game, Filchock and Hapes were suspended for life. Filchock was reinstated, but it was years later.

Joe Horrigan: From what you can gather looking back through the print media of the day, it seems that Bert Bell handled it quickly and decisively and obviously had faith in what he was being told by Frank Filchock of his involvement or noninvolvement to the degree that he allowed him to play. The Bears did win, 24–14, which in the end was what the whole controversy would have been about had they lost. Bert Bell also realized, I think, there was also a little bit of a Solomon-like decision: We can't take away the quarterback of this club—who was telling me he's innocent—for failure to report the incident, which was really his crime. He suspended him as well as he did Merle Hapes.

Upton Bell: My father had great ability on the phone. He didn't write many letters. There was a lot of stuff done in the league in letter form but basically he believed in the telephone, and he was on the telephone night and day. In those days, there were no ex-FBI agents working for the league. After that there were; he proceeded to hire them over a period of time. There was no real policing of the game other than the owners or the commissioner.

The league became increasingly security conscious in the wake of the '46 championship game, developing investigative and protective systems that continue to evolve to this day.

Don Pierson: In 1970, right before Super Bowl IV, Lenny Dawson, the Kansas City Chiefs quarterback's name, came up in connection with an FBI gambling investigation. Commissioner Pete Rozelle was on top of it. He said his name had actually come up the year before. Dawson had passed a lie-detector test. The league has really been on top of these things probably since 1946.

Upton Bell: If that game had gone on and he hadn't taken the action or it had been fixed, I think you would have seen the end of the NFL. The confidence people had in the league—it was shaky to begin with even though they drew big crowds, particularly in New York and Chicago. I think with the new league coming along and all that, it would have finished all of them. None of them had that much money anyway.

Filchock headed to Canada to continue his pro football career. Bell eventually reinstated him and he appeared in one game for the ill-fated first incarnation of the Baltimore Colts, for whom he completed one pass in three attempts. After that it was back to Canada, where Hapes also found a second home.

Jim Keane: Let me tell you how I ran into Filchock. In 1952, Halas really stuck it to me and put me on waivers. I was getting freezed out. He wanted to keep me away from the Packers. So I decided to go play in Canada for the Saskatchewan Roughriders. I went up and played two games on a Saturday and a Monday. Well, we end up playing against the Winnipeg Blue Bombers. I had a great game. Caught six passes. I looked over and who was trying to cover me? Frank Filchock! He said, "Hey, Jim, you ran me out of one league—what are you trying to do, run me out of another one?"

In 1960, his playing career over, Filchock was hired to be the very first head coach of the Denver Broncos of the brand-new American Football League.

Dale Dodrill: My last year as a player was 1959. The Cowboys selected me in the expansion draft the next year. I didn't want to play in the heat so I retired. I went back to Colorado to my insurance business. I had started in the off-season as a player, since it was tough to get hired in the off-season. The Broncos had contacted me about coaching. I was hired to handle the defense. Frank Filchock was the head coach and he would handle the offense. The places Frank had coached before, there was always a lot of behind-doors politics. He talked about how staff members always had the switchblades out, always tried to cut his throat. I told him, "Look, Frank, I didn't apply for your job." We trained at the Golden School of Mines that first year. Frank didn't spend any time coaching. There were no meetings. We were always done by noon so Frank could go home and walk Suds, his dog. He loved that dog.

Dan Daly: When the AFL was starting up in Denver, I read the stories that were in the Denver papers about him being hired as the coach of the Broncos. They talked about his NFL career. They talked about his career in Canada and they talked about the fact that he coached up there and so forth. Absolutely no mention of the '46 event. Nowadays that kind of thing would get a paragraph in every story that was ever written about the guy for the rest of his life.

Dale Dodrill: I tried to have meetings with my defense as a group. Being an expansion team, we had a lot of castoffs. It gave us satisfaction from week to week to be prepared. Frank didn't believe in practice and details. I remember one game, the other team kept running around the end. We couldn't stop them. Frank finally asked me, "Whose fault is it?" I said, "The linebackers'." All Frank said was, "They're professionals. They should know what to do." He was never one to work on the details.

Once Filchock was reinstated, the primary legacy of the game was in the law. It led to a landmark legal decision in the use of wiretaps, still a fairly new technology at the time. Krakauer and Stemmer alleged that the wiretap evidence used against them was gathered illegally. The court of appeals in Albany unanimously reaffirmed their convictions in 1948, however. They clearly had resources at their disposal, as they took the case all the way to the Supreme Court in May of 1949.

Their convictions were upheld there, too, albeit on a tie vote with one abstention.

The 1946 championship was also the first major test for Commissioner Bell.

Upton Bell: A lot of things Bert Bell did will remain one hundred years later. First was the amateur draft, which he was behind when he was still an owner. Second was the injury report. Third was the hiring of ex-FBI agents in every city to report on any activities all the way up to game time.

Joe Horrigan: This was part of Bell's living legacy, if you will. He acted swiftly, and, frankly, football at the time paralleled baseball in the decisions that they made for the good of the game. I think Bert Bell made it a very important part of his commissionership to make sure that he had control of the integrity of the game and, in this specific instance we're talking about, removing the veil of potential influencing of results of games. He found obviously the league could not survive if the feeling was there that a game could be controlled by outside entities. It was really something that he focused on.

Upton Bell: I can remember as a kid, he had a separate phone line at the house. He was truly a twenty-four-hour-a-day commissioner. So that phone would ring all the way up to Sunday, right up to game time, and he would be getting tips from people. He went to his grave and we never found out who they were. They would tell him how the odds were going all the way up to game time. If there was a problem, he would call right up to the club that day and say, "What the hell is going on here, so-and-so? Steve Van Buren of the Philadelphia Eagles, is he playing? Because the odds on the game have changed."

And that's when he decided he wanted an injury report. That survived. The draft has survived to this day. Even though Pete Rozelle gets the credit, it was my father's TV policy that helped save the league.

Bell, while still a new owner of the Philadelphia Eagles, is credited with starting the NFL amateur draft in 1935. Seven decades later it has grown into a television spectacle.

Jack Clary: I thought [Bell] handled it very cleanly. He did what he had to do. He cooperated with the authorities. He let them take the lead on it. He backed them up. He exercised his powers as commissioner. Remember, he had been a former coach, so he was right in tune with the football aspects of the thing. The game was preeminent to him. He eliminated the problems and the game went on, and that was it.

For the NFL, avoiding a betting scandal at that moment in time was a major achievement. The rise of Babe Ruth is often cited as the key ingredient in keeping baseball fans' minds off of baseball's most notorious scandal, but the game was well entrenched by then. The NFL, still battling its college counterpart in popularity, might not have fared so well if it had not been able to act to stem the scandal before it took on a life of its own. Would it be too much to suggest that a black mark at that key juncture in history might have cost the NFL its place at the head of the groaning postwar table of disposable American income and the burgeoning phenomenon of television? Might it have given the upstart All-American Football Conference a chance to designate itself the "clean league" and put the NFL in a subservient role so that, when it came time to think merger a few years later, it was the AAFC that did the absorbing and not the other way around?

Instead, because of his swift actions, Bell earned even more respect and, ultimately, power. His contract was soon renegotiated upward, and he would be given a ten-year contract a few years later. Furthermore, it set the tone for making the commissioner's office a base of power from which Bell's successor, Pete Rozelle, could work the NFL into its current position as the most successful professional sports league the world has ever known.

APPENDICES

1946 NFL Interception Percentage
(Minimum 50 passing attempts)

Int. Pct.	Player, team (pass attempts)
14.8	Frank Filchock, Giants (169)
11.0	Dave Ryan, Lions (154)
10.6	Sammy Baugh, Redskins (161)
10.4	Jim Callahan, Lions (67)
10.1	Roy Zimmerman, Eagles (79)
10.0	Bill Dudley, Steelers (90)
8.7	Tommy Thompson, Eagles (103)
8.5	Irv Comp, Packers (94)
7.9	Paul Christman, Cardinals (229)
7.0	Sid Luckman, Bears (229)
6.8	Bob Waterfield, Rams (251)
5.2	Paul Governali, Yanks (192)

The Double Threats

In 1946, Frankie Filchock led the Giants in both passing yards and rushing yards. Taking that kind of double threat out of the equation would have been a boon for the fixers. In Filchock's day, it was much more common for a team's main passer to also be its leading rusher. This was for two reasons: Passing was far less common than rushing, and many more plays had the man who received the snap take off with the ball. As passing became more important, a quarterback's ability to run became a secondary consideration.

The evolution of the frequency of these double threats is this:

1932 to 1945: One team in seven
1946 to 1959: One team in eighteen
1960 to present: One team in 217

In fact, the double threat was pretty much extinct by the 1960s. It wasn't until lefty-throwing Bobby Douglass led the Bears in both departments in 1972 that another one showed up. Unfortunately for Douglass, his ability to run wasn't the only thing that was throwback about him; he also had a completion percentage that was reminiscent of the early days of the forward pass.

Then, once again, the double threat went into mothballs until Randall Cunningham came along. These are the men who led their teams in both categories since Filchock did it for the Giants:

Donovan McNabb (Philadelphia Eagles, 2000)
Randall Cunningham, four times (Philadelphia Eagles, 1987–1990)
Bobby Douglass (Chicago Bears, 1972)
Tobin Rote, three times (Green Bay Packers, 1951 and 1956; Detroit Lions, 1958)
Charley Trippi, two times (Chicago Cardinals, 1951–1952)
Joe Geri (Pittsburgh Steelers, 1950)
Johnny Clement (Pittsburgh Steelers, 1947)
Bill Dudley (Pittsburgh Steelers, 1946)

Cleveland Browns vs. New York Giants

December 14, 1958

	1	2	3	4	F
Cleveland Browns	7	3	0	0	10
New York Giants	0	3	0	10	13

Make a list of the most dramatic field goals of all time, and the one that decided this game had better be on it. It might even be argued that—taking into account all the factors involved—this game was decided by the single most dramatic kick ever made. When considering what was on the line, the conditions, the time left, and the distance, this one makes a very strong case for itself. Further adding to its cachet is the rivalry between the two combatants that existed at the time.

THE GIANTS
There is a neighborhood in Somerset, New Jersey, that bespeaks the fame of the Giants of the late 1950s. It contains streets named for Pat Summerall, Frank Gifford, Rosey Grier, Charlie Conerly, Emlen Tunnell, Mel Triplett, Jimmy Patton, Tom Landry, Vince Lombardi (the lone case where a first name is used), Don Maynard, and Allie Sherman, among others. Missing out on being so honored in this subdivision—but no less deserving of recognition—were Dick Modzelewski, Kyle Rote, Bob Schnelker, Jack Stroud, Jim Katcavage, and Ray Wietecha—which is not even mentioning Hall of Famers Sam Huff, Roosevelt Brown, and Andy Robustelli. They were, many of them, household names at the time or would go on to become as much later on.

Were some of these players more famous than they would have been had they played, say, in Pittsburgh? Almost certainly. But there was no denying their talent level, especially on defense. In the course of their careers, the team members of the 1958 Giants would make seventy Pro Bowls and be named All-Pro thirty-two times. Two years after humbling the Bears in the NFL championship 47–7, they allowed the fewest points in the league. On the other hand, they only outscored the Redskins, Eagles, and Packers.

LANDRY AND LOMBARDI

Cleveland head coach Paul Brown was a legend in his own time. Intelligently disciplined and creative, he was almost universally respected. By 1958, his innovations and the success of the Browns had elevated him to the top of the coaching elite.

Frank Gifford: Paul Brown bordered on genius. He was ahead of everybody in terms of head coaches. He was the first one to call the plays from the bench. They platooned a lot more than we did. Paul Brown wasn't popular with anyone.

Gifford was especially bitter toward Brown, since Brown had once faced the former USC star in a big way. At the Pro Bowl, he had sidled up to Gifford and told him he just might trade for him. Then, with the game being played at Gifford's "home" field, the Los Angeles Coliseum, Brown barely gave him any playing time. Gifford was embarrassed in front of his family and hometown supporters. He chalked it up to Brown's typical sense of gamesmanship.

Frank Gifford: They totally dominated pro football at that time. They were one of the teams that destroyed the All-America Football Conference because they never lost a game in it. It was Paul Brown's team. He handpicked them. He was so far ahead for his time. Paul Brown did everything. He coached the offensive line and the defense. He was brilliant.

But Brown was not the only legend coaching in this game—far from it. As good as the Giants teams of the late fifties were, as many household

35

names as they produced, they are perhaps best known as the final stage in the development of the two coaches who would dominate football's next era: Tom Landry and Vince Lombardi. It is to head coach Jim Lee Howell's unending credit that he not only understood their talents but gave them rein to exercise it without too much meddling. Howell is famous for saying he simply made sure the balls had enough air, but the ability to delegate should never be underestimated. Howell had the good sense to let Lombardi run the offense and Landry the defense when other men might have felt threatened by their presence.

Rosey Grier: Jim Lee was an ex-marine, and he gave these guys an opportunity to do their best. I think that Jim Lee Howell was the best coach—was the fairest coach I ever played for. There was no one that he favored over anyone else. Every guy had to do what he was supposed to do, otherwise he was gonna get on them. I appreciate the fairness of this man. I thought he, being from Arkansas, was never gonna be fair—particularly to black ballplayers—but he was.

Sam Huff: Jim Lee's pregame talk would be the itinerary of what time the bus left. What time the game would be over. Kick-off time at one o'clock—all this kind of stuff. He did very little coaching. But he managed. He had Lombardi and Landry. He managed the coaches, which I later learned that head coaches do. That's what Jim Lee Howell did. He was an administrator. That's why he moved into the front office when they lost Landry and Lombardi and worked in personnel. He knew better because he lost the two best coaches in the history of the NFL.

Landry insisted that his players trust in his system, something they—reliant on their individual talents—weren't always quick to do.

Alex Webster: Tom Landry was the key. He put in a defense that was just unbelievable and he stuck with it. It took the players a long time to learn his theory. The defense had the confidence in Tom. They believed in him and everything he said.

Rosey Grier: Tom Landry was the guy that came up with the inside-outside four-three. It was a great defense. It was really a pleasure to play for Tom Landry. I remember something he once said to me after I made an incredible play on a running play. He said, Nine times out of ten you'd miss that play. He said, You made a great play. So next time, they ran a similar play, and I could have made the same type of fantastic play. And I decided to let it go, see what happened. And I let the play go and someone else made the play big-time. And so I decided right then I'd play the defense that Tom Landry had set up. I was supposed to try to go out and take those big chances out there and make those big plays. I'd begin to play within the defense, and all those holes were taken care of. That's when I began to really trust his defenses and play my position and it worked out very well.

Sam Huff: I didn't realize at the time how close Landry and Lombardi were. They played off of each other.

Rosey Grier: Part of our defensive scheme under Tom Landry was to free the middle linebacker and the free safety. What we helped to do was keep people off of Sam. Sam was able to make a lot of tackles. But he would have made them anyway because he was a great ballplayer.

Al Barry: When I was on the offense I would sit on the bench when our defense was in and Tom Landry, he knew exactly what Paul Brown was gonna call. He did. He would call the play that they were gonna run. Because he studied the film so much, he felt like Paul Brown.

Pat Summerall: I remember my first day with the Giants, I was impressed with the intelligence of the other people, the other players. They didn't have much more physical ability than the Cardinals did, but I could see they were a lot more intelligent than the players we had on the Cardinals. So the first night I was there at training camp I remember distinctly that we had been out renewing old acquaintances and meeting new people and doing whatever, we were kind of raucous—we'd been drinking a little beer during the day. We went to a team meeting, and they were trying to call the roll. One of the assistant coaches was trying to call the roll. He couldn't get everybody quiet. So this guy walked in with the horn-rimmed glasses and the stocky kind of build and just cleared his throat and there was a quiet that fell over the room, almost a hush. And I said to the guy sitting next to me, "Who the hell is that?" and he said, "That's Lombardi. And you'll know soon enough." And believe me, I did soon enough.

Al Barry: Lombardi was a demanding guy, but he used to come out and warm up with us. Do the push-ups and the sit-ups.

Bob Schnelker: He could always fire a team up. He always knew the exact time to do it. Whether it was on a Monday at the first meeting after the game, on Sunday or Friday or pregame, whatever. He always knew the right time to get the guys jacked up, ready to play. I can remember the same thing when I went to Green Bay when he was the head coach and I was an assistant. He'd get these talks going, even as an assistant, you'd want to go out and play, you'd be all fired up. He had that knack. He had a very unusual voice. He had trained to be a lawyer. He had a great speaking voice, real deep. He had this presence even though he was short—he was a stout-looking guy. He believed in what he was saying.

Sam Huff: I could have gone back to West Virginia and made more money than what they offered me, so why did I have to put up with a guy yelling at me like Jim Lee Howell was: "You're not running fast enough. You're not doing this." I was depressed! So I said, "I don't need this." Don Chandler was from Oklahoma, and he was a punter, and he said the same thing. All of a sudden, I said to Chandler, "I'm out of here!" He said, "I am too." We got our playbooks and went downstairs. I wanted to hand it to Jim Lee Howell, but I didn't know where he was. We knocked on a coach's door, and it was Vince Lombardi who answered. Lombardi came to the door, and he said, "What the hell you want?" as only Lombardi can say it. I said, "Here's my playbook, and here's Chandler's. We're out of here. We're quitting." "What's wrong with you?" Lombardi said. "After all we've done for you! You're going to leave this training camp?" I said, "Yes. We're out of here." We went back to the room and Ed Coleman came to me. He was the offensive-line coach, and he was coaching me. I was an offensive guard at that time before Tom Landry moved me to defense. "What are you doing?" Coleman asked me. And I said, "I'm out of here. I can't take it anymore, Ed." He said, "Sam, you could be a great ballplayer in this league." And I said, "I can't take Jim Lee Howell. I'm first in everything that we're doing. Running and everything else—you know that, but he yells at me. Nobody yells at me." Even to this day, I don't allow anybody to yell at me.

Al Barry: I had just gotten traded from Green Bay and it was the last game before the regular season starts, so I had to really study my plays. The problem is, all my life, the thirty-eight is around the right end—the three back carrying around the eight hole, which is on the right-hand side. And twenty-nine would be to the left. Well, the Giants had a different system. With them, it was the opposite: The thirty-eight was around the left and the twenty-nine was around the right. So I pulled out in this practice game, I was going full speed, and I said to myself, "We're gonna go for a touchdown, no-body's out here!" And I looked over and I heard this big loud noise and they had tackled Gifford right in front of the Giants' bench. Next Tuesday, Lombardi says, "Watch Barry pull on this play." And he ran it about three or four times. "Let's watch that again." I never did that again.

Pat Summerall: I was amazed at his ability to control the group and his teaching ability and his presence and his vocal manner and ev-erything. I was so impressed by him. I knew he was something extra. It was a rude awakening but a pleasant awakening to find out that, number one, the Giants had some very intelligent people, and, number two, that they had Lombardi running the offense and Tom Landry was coaching the defense. Having played for both offense and defense, I went to both meetings on occasion when I could. I learned pretty quickly that they were something special, both of them.

Bob Schnelker: Lombardi was great at getting people ready to play more than Xs and Os. He had a knack for that, a very basic offensive plan. It always seemed to work because he had the confidence it would work and instilled that confidence in us. I can even remember playing big games, and this could have even been that Cleveland Brown game, where he'd put out a play on Friday morning for that Sunday's game and expect it to work. His philosophy was, if he thought it was good enough to put in on Friday, the players got to believe it will work, and it always did.

The Giants very nearly lost Lombardi to the Eagles after the 1957 season when they made him an offer to become their head coach. In the end, Lombardi decided to stay with New York for the time being, albeit as the game's highest-paid assistant coach. He would move on to helm Green Bay before the '59 season, and Landry would also leave a year later to take the reins of the fledgling Dallas Cowboys. This game, then, would prove to be the final regular-season contest of their partnership.

THE OPPONENT

In the history of American professional sports, there has never been anything quite like what hit the National Football League in 1950. No other league has experienced the intrusion of a new club that immediately began to dominate the way the Cleveland Browns did. From the first moment the Browns were merged into the NFL from the All-America Football Conference, Cleveland and their innovative coach, Paul Brown, served notice that they were the team to beat. It is quite unprecedented that, well into its history, the top league in its sport is visited upon by a superior force the likes of the Browns. In Cleveland's first game in the NFL, they outmatched the defending-champion Philadelphia Eagles. And just like that they were among the league's elite.

While Cleveland would have its problems in the playoffs, they were the top performer during the regular season for some time. In their first ten years in the National Football League, 1950 to 1959, they had the best overall record, going 88–30–2. Only two teams seemed to be able to stand up to the Browns with any regularity: the Lions and the Giants. Detroit beat them in all three of their regular-season meetings and took three of their four championship showdowns. In their own division, however, New York nearly played them to a standstill, winning nine of their twenty meetings with one tie. The Giants, at 76–41–3, had the second-best record in the NFL during this period. It can be argued that the team with the third-best record, the Bears, benefited greatly from being in the other division. In the days of the twelve-game schedule, teams played ten of their games within their division, and so teams often went years without seeing an opponent from the other division. From 1950 to 1959, Chicago played only two regular-season games against the Browns (both blowout losses) and one against the Giants—a 17–17 tie in 1956. From 1950 to 1959, the Browns and Giants accounted for all ten titles in their division. They finished tied for first twice, first-second four times, and first-third twice.

When the Browns finally did falter, going 5–7 in the 1956 season, they were fortunate to have moved up in the draft for an amazing onslaught of talent coming out of the college ranks. There were really no busts in the first round of the 1957 draft. Paul Hornung, John Brodie, Jim Parker, and Len Dawson are all in the Hall of Fame. Of the thirteen players taken in the first round that year, none played fewer than eight seasons and, on average, they played eleven years each. The Browns were rewarded for their 1956 downturn by getting the sixth pick, with which they chose a player you might recognize: a Syracuse running back named Jim Brown.

Dick Modzelewski: We're watching this game against Cleveland one time in a meeting, and Landry was our coach, and they just showed a pile of [Giants] on top of one human being and he's carrying all of us, and Tom said something like, "Can anyone tackle this guy?" And we said, "Hey, that's Jim Brown!" He said, "Okay." We called him Superman.

Frank Gifford: If Jimmy Brown played today, he would be a huge star. He was the only player I know of that I would get up off the bench and go over and watch when our defensive team was on the field. I was absolutely mesmerized by him. He did things that no one could ever do. He was two hundred and thirty pounds, about six two, and he could run a nine-eight, nine-nine hundred-yard dash. He didn't slow down when he put a football suit on, either.

Dick Modzelewski: He's no doubt in my mind the best running back God ever made. No one will ever compare to him. Nobody.

Sam Huff: I think, truthfully, Jim Brown was the best athlete this country has ever produced. He and I had a great matchup. That's one of the things that made pro football, was matchups like that.

Alex Webster: When we played Cleveland, Sam Huff was set up to get Jim Brown.

Dick Modzelewski: I always tell people I had both shoulders operated on and I got knee operations and a bad ankle—all from trying to tackle Jim Brown.

Rosey Grier: You'd raise yourself up to play the Cleveland Browns because they had a solid, good team, and they had one of the greatest backs to ever put on the shoulder pads. And when you played against Jim Brown you knew that if you missed him, he had six on you. We scouted him so well, we knew if Jim Brown was in one position he was going to do one thing, if he was a couple steps over he was going to do something else, and if he was in the back he was going to do something else. So we had him so focused, so down, that anything he did getting set we knew what he was going to do on the play. Whatever position he was in, our defenses could shift automatically. The hurry-up offenses they have today? Wouldn't have made any difference to us. And anytime they came up with something and we didn't know what it was, we were gonna blitz them. We were well ready for the Cleveland Browns that time.

Dave Anderson: Well, that rivalry started because they had to neutralize Otto Graham. That was what created the umbrella defense.

Landry created it as a player back in the early fifties. But then with Jim Brown—there was one season between Otto Graham and Jim Brown, 1956—and Brown became the new weapon in Cleveland. And if you didn't stop Jim Brown, you weren't going to beat the Browns.

Aside from Brown, Cleveland had added four other eventual Hall of Famers in 1957 and 1958: Henry Jordan at tackle, Gene Hickerson at guard, Bobby Mitchell at halfback, and Willie Davis at defensive end. Paul Brown had done an excellent job of finding talent to replace the first wave of Brown greats who had retired or moved on. In addition to these newcomers, ace kicker Lou Groza was still on hand, as was Hall of Fame offensive tackle Mike McCormack. Mitchell picked up 6.4 yards per carry in '58, a devastating second punch when Brown got a break. Cleveland was third in scoring and also allowed the third-fewest points.

By the time the two teams met on the final day of the 1958 season, there was no love lost between them. Dick Modzelewski's brother Ed played for the Browns, and their experiences as opponents sum up the rivalry.

Dick Modzelewski: We played the Browns one time—this was a different year—and we were beating them bad. We were in the huddle, and Sam Huff looked up and said, "Oh, my God, here comes the crowd onto the field." So Paul Brown took his team into the locker room and Andy Robustelli and I and a few of us took my brother Ed on the Giant bench and we covered him up with a Giant hood, took his helmet and hid it. When Paul Brown came out with the team, Ed took the Giant hood off and became a Cleveland Brown again. We still talk about that—laugh like hell. Rivalry is right! One time the Giants were playing in Cleveland, and the Browns were on our one-yard line, and I got into their backfield somehow and I tackled Ed for a loss and I turned around pretty happy—at that time nobody jumped around like they do now—Ed turned around and threw the ball, hit me in the back of the head with it. After the game's over, you got your brother back again, but on the field you're enemies.

HOW THEY GOT THERE

At 9–2, Cleveland had a one-game lead on the 8–3 Giants. A New York loss or a tie would give Cleveland the division title and a chance to meet the Baltimore Colts for the NFL championship. New York needed to be victorious to force a playoff game the following week.

Prior to the final game of the year, the Browns had scored at least 20 points in every game save for two—one of them a 21–17 loss to the Giants at home. For their part, the Giants would not have had a fighting chance at the division title that cold December day if not for a controversial play that took place the week before. In a maneuver that would be repeated fifty years later by Patriots coach Bill Belichick, Detroit coach George Wilson gave the Giants a chance to fight another day.

Detroit held a 17–12 lead with thirteen minutes to go when they found themselves with a fourth and 21 at their own 44. Wilson trotted out punter Yale Lary, who, instead of hanging the ball in the air to be kicked, tucked it under his arm and took off to his right. As Rosey Grier recalled, someone yelled, "Grab him! He's going to run with it!" The Giants were on Lary immediately and ran him out of bounds after a gain of only a yard. New York took over on downs and eventually scored on a 1-yard run by Frank Gifford.

For a league that was becoming increasingly attractive to gamblers, the fake had set off alarm bells. In the ensuing days, Commissioner Bert Bell was inundated with conspiracy theories and demands for an investigation into Wilson's curious decision to fake the punt on fourth and long.

"I don't think there was anything at all 'strange' connected with the game," Bell said. "George Wilson sent in that play. The team has been using it with success for several years. There was nothing new or strange about it."

"I called the play," Wilson said in his own defense. "You've got to gamble. That play has worked three times in three attempts in the last four years. If our right end had pulled out and blocked where he was supposed to, it would have worked this time."

In the wake of the 1946 championship bribe attempt, the NFL had stepped up security and was refining it to an art. Bell pointed out that the league had ex-FBI men on the ground in the six game cities every week, watching for indications of chicanery.

"We know everything that goes on in the league," he said. "We know every point spread and the day-to-day fluctuations. We know—knew at twelve thirty last Sunday afternoon—that the Giants closed favorites to win by four points. Our Detroit man reported nothing untoward last week."

Curious though the play call may have been, a lot had to happen in its aftermath for it to serve those who had gambled on the game. The Giants still had to come back and score—which they almost didn't. Then they had to hold their lead, which, if not for Harland Svare's block of a late Lions field-goal attempt, they would not have. Even with that, they ended up not covering the spread.

Whether the Lary play was a moment of destiny or just one of a hundred things that had to happen for the Giants to still have a chance, the stage was now set for a major showdown with the Browns.

SUMMERALL IN DOUBT

Unfortunately, it seemed the Giants were going to have to face Cleveland without the services of their placekicker, Pat Summerall. Throughout the week leading up to the game, he was gimping around with what some were calling a charley horse, although a strained knee sounds like a more professional diagnosis. Don Chandler, who had been a kicker in college and had a few professional extra points to his credit, was preparing to fill in for the injured Summerall.

Pat Summerall: I had gotten hurt the week before. I'd gotten hit on the kickoff against Detroit. I didn't really think during the week that I'd be able to kick. I told Don Chandler after the warm-up to stay ready because I wasn't sure I was going to make it.

Frank Gifford: He had been injured and there was some thought that I would have to do the kicking. I could kick the ball that far, but north and south wasn't my problem—it was east and west that was very difficult for me.

The kicking game in the NFL of the fifties was something of an afterthought to the point that it belied the very name of the sport. When a kicker is injured in modern times, a handful of free-agent replacements are brought in and asked to compete for the spot. Pulling someone from the existing roster for the chore is only done in the most extreme emergencies in the NFL of today. Even though Chandler would go on to fame in the next decade as the placekicker for the Packer dynasty, he was not a placement kicker by trade in 1958.

A great illustration of the general disregard for the kicking game in this era (and the restrictions that came with having much smaller rosters) comes from Summerall's earlier career with the Chicago Cardinals. For the last game of the 1955 season, Chicago was playing Cleveland and Summerall was injured. The Cardinals entrusted the kicking duty to position players. They scored four touchdowns yet missed every single extra point as quarterback Lamar McHan and halfback Dave Mann each took two shots at the 10-yard kick. Chicago blew a 10-point lead and lost to the Browns 35–24. The missed points ended up not making the difference, but the notion of a team missing one extra point in today's NFL—let alone four—stretches the credulity of the modern fan.

Al Barry: We worked on special teams usually on the last day of the week, like a Saturday or something.

Pat Summerall: Not very much time was spent on kicking practice. It was sort of an afterthought at that time. Although the time I spent practicing, Tom Landry was my kicking coach. And so we spent time every day on it. But at least with the Giants I had somebody to practice holding and somebody to practice snapping. And we had a chance to do the exercise. With the Cardinals, I had to do it on my own.

George Allen "Pat" (for "point after touchdown") Summerall was a fourth-round draft pick of the Detroit Lions out of the University of Arkansas, where he had played as a defensive lineman and tight end. His NFL destiny, though, involved his third position: placekicker. His first pro season was cut short by injury and, after playing in just two games for the Lions, he was shipped to the Chicago Cardinals after the 1952 season. It was a step down for Summerall, for, over his next five years in Chicago, the Cards would go 17–41–2 while the Lions would remain one of the dominant teams of the league. A step up in surroundings presented itself after the 1957 season, however.

On May 12, 1958, Summerall was traded to the Giants along with defensive back Lindon Crow in exchange for defensive back Dick Nolan and halfback Bobby Joe Conrad, whom the Giants had just taken in the college draft.

Pat Summerall: I'd been with the Cardinals and the Cardinals had changed from Ray Richards as the head coach to a guy named Pop Ivy, who I did not know. He was the new head coach after the season of 1957. So I wasn't sure, as anytime happens when you change head coaches—you're not sure what's going on. So I called Pop Ivy and asked him where I stood with him and with the team and so on and so forth, and he assured me that I was one of the building blocks, one of the keystone players, one of the players that they wanted to build the Cardinals' future about, and he told me that I was one of the places they started building. I was close to retiring, I had thought about retiring and not playing anymore after the desperate years with the Cardinals. Two weeks later after that conversation with Pop Ivy, I picked up a paper where I was living in Florida, and found out that I'd been traded to the Giants, which really shocked me after that conversation. But I knew the Giants to be a first-class organization run by the Maras [Tim, Jack, and Wellington Mara]. I knew they had a reputation as being great people, class people. Very religious. Good people.

Jack Cavanaugh: Pat's first year with the Giants, they had one of the best placekickers in the NFL. He made ten of twenty field-goal attempts that year. He made all of his extra-point attempts. He was a key figure. Pat did not have what they call a long leg. He was good from maybe up to forty, forty-five yards.

Long field-goal attempts in those days had an inherent and heightened drama due to prevailing conditions of the time. It is important to remember that what we consider routine in modern times was anything but in the 1950s. The advent of soccer-style kicking, the improvement of field conditions, specialization, the introduction of indoor stadiums—all of these factors ratcheted up the accuracy and length of kickers to the point that kicking stats of the fifties look absurd when taken out of context. Summerall, though inaccurate by today's standards, was one of the game's best.

THE GAME

By game time, Summerall was able to report for duty. From the looks of things, however, it was going to be a hard day to move the ball. The Giants' first series was three and out.

Pat Summerall: I don't know if it was the worst or not, because the field conditions were always bad. But that was pretty bad. It was muddy, snowing, what have you. It was pretty awful.

Jack Cavanaugh: The weather was horrendous. It was cold and snowing—the snow intensified as the game went on, and, as a matter of fact, by the last quarter the field was pretty much covered with snow. You couldn't even see the line markers. You couldn't tell the difference between the thirty- and the forty-yard line. It was snowing very hard.

Frank Gifford: It was cold—very cold. By the end, the field was obliterated by snow. I just wanted to go home. We were really frozen. The weather had been terrible that year.

Dave Anderson: That look that Yankee Stadium had in those years, especially late into the season and late in a game—it was dark, because they didn't start at one o'clock, the game started at two. So it was almost five o'clock when this happened. It was like the middle of the night. The lights would be on from the second half on. It was like playing a night game. And it was cold and icy, and, God, it was awful.

Al Barry: That was probably the coldest game I ever played in.

Bob Schnelker: As a player, it was sort of fun to play in games that were unusual like that, where there's a lot of snow or mud. You know, sometimes you got caught in rainstorms. It sort of made your outlook a little bit different. You had to be careful what you were doing. It was unusual, but it wasn't disastrous to play in it.

Dave Anderson: But that, to me, was the charm of pro football: the weather and the scene and everything. It was sunny and fairly warm when you kicked off, but by the fourth quarter it was like a freezer. Even the photos were dark. There was no sun—there were no shadows at Yankee Stadium in the fourth quarter. No warmth. Everybody was in their overcoats and earmuffs—it was awful. That was football. In a way I miss that. Everything is so antiseptic today, so perfect. The field, the Astroturf, the domes. That's not pro football. Pro football, to me, is what happened in the fifties and the sixties.

Then, as if to put the lie to appearances, on Cleveland's very first play from scrimmage, Milt Plum handed off to Jim Brown, who ignored the conditions and burst through the center of the Giant line. He didn't stop running until he was 65 yards away, standing in the New York end zone. He had pulled away from the last of the New York pursuers at the 15.

For the rest of the first half, Brown's gains were much more pedestrian. After that first long gain, the Giants held him to a very human 3.3 yards per carry on 25 tries. On their second possession, the Browns got to the New York 35 on a 43-yard completion from Milt Plum to Preston Carpenter. They stalled there, though, and Groza missed a 37-yard field-goal attempt. Charlie Conerly relieved Don Heinrich at quarterback and moved the Giants past midfield. Their progress stopped when Willie McClung put a lick on Alex Webster on third and 7 and Conerly's pass fell incomplete. Summerall came on to try his first field goal from the 46, but it fell short.

The Giants got excellent field position on their next possession after Don Maynard fell on a punt at the Cleveland 48. Conerly hit Webster down to the 33 for the first down. Three plays later, it was fourth and 1 at the 24. Howell went for it, but the Browns stepped up and jammed Mel Triplett at the line. New York got the ball back three plays later when Lew Carpenter fumbled and Jim Katcavage recovered it at the Cleveland 39. This time, Summerall was good from 46 yards out and the score now stood at 7–3. The Browns quickly answered with three points of their own and, by halftime, the score still stood at 10–3. Cleveland was in control, but their lead was by no means safe.

In the third quarter, neither team mounted much of a threat. Finally, with time becoming of the essence, the Giants called on their most versatile player to make something happen.

Frank Gifford: When I came out of USC, I was a single-wing tailback and I was more recognized by the pros at the draft as a running back. I had played quarterback in high school, so it wasn't that I didn't have the experience of throwing the ball. When I came to the Giants, Allie Sherman was an assistant coach. He was a former quarterback. I used to throw the ball to him a lot fooling around in practice. It was called the Lombardi forty-nine sweep, where I would throw the ball. We would pull two guards. It was like an old single wing to the right. We did it both ways. I'd switch sides and run it to the right or the left. They would pitch out to me. The forty-eight sweep was from the left halfback position, and Charlie would flip it back to me and I would go around the weak side.

Bob Schnelker: Well, Frank was a smart player and he could throw a football. He could do everything. He was an intelligent guy. He could read what was happening as he was running the option. We used it quite a bit because he could handle it. Not everybody does a good job with it. They're liable to throw an interception or whatever. Frank was very sharp about things like that.

Al Barry: Gifford was a great runner and a threat to pass. He'd stop, jump up, and throw the ball.

Bob Schnelker: Because of Gifford's ability as a runner, he could really sell that. When he'd start to sweep, the defense would react to that. You see the film of Frank and he'd really sell the run. He'd kind of jump up, almost like a jump pass. It worked in that game.

Frank Gifford: The first one was a long gain to Kyle Rote off of the forty-nine sweep—the guards pulled to make it look like I was going to run the ball, and then I pulled up and Kyle was open. He juked the defender and went about sixty yards. Kyle was a great running back at Southern Methodist University. He was a bonus pick after the 1950 season. His rookie training camp, he stepped in a gopher hole and tore his knee up. He was never the running back again after that knee surgery to repair that leg. They moved him to wide receiver and he had a really fine career. Had he never stepped in that gopher hole, he might be remembered as one of the great running backs of all time.

The Rote catch set up an even more important play, as the Giants went back to the well again.

Frank Gifford: This one we called Green Forty-eight option if it was to be a pass. Charlie Conerly pitched it out to me, I tucked it away like I was going to turn it upfield and run, the cornerback came to me, and Bob Schnelker broke behind him. It was really quite simple. It worked just like we'd drawn it up.

Bob Schnelker: I remember I just sneaked back into the back of the end zone and I just stood there. Frank threw it and I just sort of leaped up to make sure I caught it. There wasn't anybody around me. Frank read it perfectly. The fact that he was a good runner made the defense go for him and not worry about an option pass.

Gifford's passing had knotted the score at 10 with 4:40 gone in the fourth quarter, but the Giants needed to score again if they were going to force the playoff game with the Browns. (A month later, Gifford would repeat this two-throw feat in the Pro Bowl, setting up a field goal with a 22-yard toss to Schnelker and putting the East ahead 9–7 with a 40-yard TD strike to another Giant teammate, Alex Webster. The East would eventually win 28–21, and Gifford was named Back of the Game.)

New York held Cleveland after the ensuing kickoff, forcing a punt. They drove from their own 30 to the Browns' 25. They stalled there, so, on fourth down with five minutes showing on the clock, Summerall was sent in to break the tie. This kick was off-line, though, and so the two teams remained deadlocked at 10.

Once again the Giants' vaunted defense smothered the Cleveland attack for a three and out. Brown punter Dick Deschaine shanked his kick and the Giants were in business at the Browns' 44 with plenty of time to angle into field-goal range or to go all the way for a touchdown.

Jack Cavanaugh: The weather was bad. In bad footing like that, when it's snowing, the receiver has an advantage over the cornerback. The receiver knows where he's going. The defender in the secondary could be slipping and sliding all over the place—he doesn't know where the receiver's going. However, the ball was slippery and Conerly threw his first-down pass incomplete.

On second down, Alex Webster said to him, "Charlie, I can beat the cornerback on the left side. I know I can. I'm beating him all day and of course I've just been going down there as a decoy. I can beat him." So sure enough Alex shot down the middle, cut off to the left, and Conerly laid a beautiful forty-yard pass right into his hands— except that Alex dropped it. It was down on the ten-yard line and, had he caught it, he was going in the end zone for a touchdown.

Alex Webster: I dropped the damn thing. That was the most humiliating thing I can remember. It wasn't the snow, I just misjudged it. I felt so bad about that. It broke my heart because I thought the game was over with, but Summerall saved my butt.

On third and 10, Conerly hit Gifford at the 35. As he took his first step toward the extra yard that would give New York a first down, he was met hard and separated from the ball. Cleveland fell on the ball, taking over possession. Needing no more than a tie to win the division, they only had to sit on the ball for a few minutes and ride home victorious. The officials, though, saw it differently. They ruled the pass incomplete. With fourth and 10 and just over two minutes remaining, the next play call was an obvious one: a pass play to cover the distance needed to keep the ball in the Giants' possession.

THE KICK

That's not what happened, though. In spite of the miserable weather, in spite of the long yardage, in spite of Summerall's injury and his last miss, Coach Howell decided to kick for the win.

Pat Summerall: Everybody was sort of shocked when Jim Lee Howell called for the field goal. In fact, Lombardi didn't want to do it, and there was a little bit of argument between them. Jim Lee said, "Go ahead and try a field goal." So we did.

Jack Cavanaugh: Lombardi had a lot of input. Jim Lee would consult with Lombardi, but at crucial situations, Jim Lee made the decisions.

Sam Huff: I don't know how long the field goal was—even now I don't know how long the field goal was. It probably shouldn't even been tried. The field-goal team, and everybody, rushed on the field.

Pat Summerall: When I got in the huddle, Conerly, who was the holder, said to me, "What the hell are you doing here?" And I said, "We're trying a field goal."

Alex Webster: We all shook our heads and just looked at him.

Jack Cavanaugh: Charlie didn't think too much of the idea, since he expected to pass on fourth down.

Rosey Grier: When I looked at where he had to kick it, I would rather him have to kick back the other way. It seemed as though that was way down there. Snow was falling. It looked *waaaay* down there. You see those two sticks sticking up out of the ground and you say, "How in the world is he going to make that?"

Jack Cavanaugh: Charlie cleared a little spot in the snow. Charlie was a great holder—one of the best in the business—always had the laces facing forward. Pat got back five yards, where Charlie was.

Pat Summerall: So they lined up and he gave me what was a good hold and got a good snap from center from Ray Wietecha.

Sam Huff: I blocked my man and Summerall kicked that thing. It looked like it was going up into the stands.

Pat Summerall: It behaved as a kick does when you hit it a particular way when you're a straightaway kind of kicker—the kind of kicker that doesn't exist anymore. When you hit it solid, it behaved like a knuckleball, and I wasn't sure if it was going to break through the goal post. You don't know how it's going to behave. When it broke through the goal post, I knew it was going to be good. I never thought it was going to be far enough when I first hit it.

Dick Modzelewski: I was on the field-goal team, and when I heard that ball go thump, I just knew it was going the distance.

Pat Summerall: I could see it through the snow, I could see it going through.

Rosey Grier: And he kicked that ball and we heard that crowd and they were yelling and yelling and then they went crazy.

Pat Summerall: When I came off the field everybody was celebrating because we were ahead, 13–10. I couldn't kick off, because of the injury, so I stayed on the sideline. Lombardi grabbed me and hugged me. I thought he was going to say "nice game," or some congratulatory sort of words. Instead he said, "You son of a bitch, you know you can't kick it that far."

Alex Webster: I used to say to him, "Thank God I dropped that pass—I made you a hero." And Pat would say, "Yeah, I guess you did."

Rosey Grier: I realized: We've done what we came to do. We won this game. We get to play them in a playoff game to see who plays in the finals.

There were still two minutes left to play, and all the Browns needed was a field goal to keep the tiebreaker game off the schedule. When Jim Brown returned the ensuing kickoff out to his own 45, they were in an excellent position to make that very thing happen. Plum hit Ray Renfro for a 14-yard gain, but was then sacked for a huge loss. Cleveland got back past midfield, but just barely. Just like that, it was fourth and 10 with just twenty-five seconds left to play. Could there be two miracle kicks in one game? Paul Brown sent in Lou Groza in the hopes that it could happen, but he was bucking a headwind and had a longer field than did Summerall. Groza, the preeminent kicker of his era, set up at his own 45 and let fly, but it fell short.

Not that it really matters, but there is much disagreement about how far Summerall's game winner actually had to travel to be good. It officially went in the books as a 49-yarder, although it stands to reason there would be some confusion, given that snow was obscuring the field.

Jack Cavanaugh: Who knows? Kyle Rote always insisted he was standing on the fifty-yard line on the sideline and that the ball was beyond the fifty, like maybe fifty-two yards back.

Dave Anderson:. Everybody always wonders how many yards Summerall kicked it for the field goal. People say forty-eight and fifty-two and whatever. I can tell you exactly because at the *New York Journal-American*, Dave Eisenberg was the beat writer, and I was there doing sidebars. Our seats in the old press box at Yankee Stadium—the old football press box, which hung down from the mezzanine halfway down the left-field line—split the fifty-yard line if we looked straight ahead at the field. As I looked straight ahead, there was Summerall. People can say whatever they want, but as far as I'm concerned, it was a fifty-yard field goal.

THE LEGACY
It's no great leap to say that, without the Summerall kick, there would have been no Greatest Game Ever. The Giants shut down the Browns the following week (actually, Paul Brown limited Jim Brown to just

seven carries and the Giants' defense throttled him on all but one of them), and New York prevailed 10–0. The '58 championship game, credited with launching the modern NFL, would never have happened if Summerall had slipped, if he'd undershot by just a yard, or if any other detail had been out of place.

Dave Anderson: When Wellington Mara was the Giants' president for all those years, behind his desk he had the team photos of all the championship teams—even if they just won the division or the conference. They didn't have to win the Super Bowl or the NFL championship, and there was like thirty pictures there, at least. But the only action photo in his office was Summerall kicking that field goal. It was across from his desk. It was on a table so if he sat at his desk he could see it. The team photos were all up on the wall behind him. He always said that was his favorite photo and also one of the most important field goals not only in Giants history, but in NFL history.

Jack Cavanaugh: Next to Bobby Thomson's home run in '51 that won the pennant for the Giants, I think the Summerall field goal was the most dramatic moment, the most dramatic occurrence, at a sports event in New York City. There was nothing else comparable. Oh, sure, Mickey Mantle hitting the tape-measure home runs, five hundred feet or so, but never at such a climatic moment as Summerall's. And as I said before, the fact that Summerall did it—and he never kicked one longer, even on the brightest day, and on the best possible field, than he kicked it that day. As he told me, he said sometimes when the adrenaline flows you do things you don't think you're capable of. And it was, I think it was in a class with Thomson's home run. Probably not quite, because of what Thomson's home run meant. That meant the pennant, whereas for the Giants it only meant they won the conference . . . not won it, but tied the Browns for the conference championship. Not quite the same.

Dave Anderson: It's probably the most important field goal in history. Sure, Adam Vinatieri won two Super Bowls with field goals, but those just won a game—this one kind of turned history. Created it, really. Without it we wouldn't have had the Colts and the Giants' overtime game. Everything just kind of flows from that. I mean, the American Football League was inspired by that game—that overtime game inspired Lamar Hunt to start the AFL. A lot of people don't even realize that.

Within a few months of Summerall's kick, Hunt, unsuccessful in his attempts to buy the Chicago Cardinals and move them to Dallas as well as convincing Commissioner Bell to expand the NFL, was convening a meeting of prospective team owners in a new league venture. They would play their first game within two years of the end of the 1958 season.

APPENDICES

Who had a harder job after leaving the Giants, Lombardi, who took over a Packers team that went 1–10–1, or Landry, who started from scratch with the expansion Cowboys? The record indicates it was Landry, whose charges managed just one tie their first year while Lombardi's team went 7–5 and was in the NFL championship in his second season. By way of comparison, the league's other expansion team of the period, the Minnesota Vikings, struggled early, too. They became respectable faster than Dallas, but Dallas became very good faster than Minnesota. Landry had a disadvantage that neither Lombardi nor the Minnesota Vikings had to contend with, though: The Cowboys got a late start in 1960 and did not participate in the college draft.

> 1959: Giants 20, Packers 3 (Landry as defensive coordinator vs. Lombardi as head coach)
> 1960: Packers 41, Cowboys 7
> 1964: Packers 45, Cowboys 21
> 1965: Packers 13, Cowboys 3
> 1966: Packers 34, Cowboys 27, NFL championship
> 1967: Packers 21, Cowboys 17, NFL championship
> 1969: Cowboys 41, Redskins 28
> 1969: Cowboys 20, Redskins 10

The Longest Field Goals, 1951–1960

There were only seventeen field goals in the 1950s longer than Summerall's game winner against the Browns. All but two came fairly early in the season or in a mild climate, further emphasizing the degree of difficulty of what Summerall did amid the elements. Those seventeen field goals of 50 or more yards (about one every forty-three games on average) were kicked by these nine men.

56   Bert Rechichar, Baltimore Colts vs. Chicago Bears, September 27, 1953

53   Lou Groza, Cleveland Browns vs. Los Angeles Rams, NFL championship, December 23, 1951

52   Lou Groza, Cleveland Browns vs. New York Giants, October 12, 1952

Bert Rechichar,* Baltimore Colts vs. Washington Redskins, October 25, 1953

Bert Rechichar, Baltimore Colts vs. San Francisco 49ers, November 27, 1955

Jim Martin, Detroit Lions vs. Baltimore Colts, October 23, 1960

51   Lou Michaels, Los Angeles Rams vs. Baltimore Colts, October 16, 1960

50   Pat Summerall, Chicago Cardinals vs. New York Giants, October 17, 1954

George Blanda, Chicago Bears vs. Dallas Texans, October 12, 1952

Lou Groza, Cleveland Browns vs. Pittsburgh Steelers, November 22, 1953

Dick Bielski, Philadelphia Eagles vs. Cleveland Browns, October 9, 1955, and October 30, 1955, vs. Pittsburgh Steelers

Bert Rechichar, Baltimore Colts vs. Washington Redskins, October 23, 1955

Ben Agajanian, New York Giants vs. Washington Redskins, October 13, 1957

Jim Martin, Detroit Lions vs. Green Bay Packers, October 4, 1959

Lou Michaels, Los Angeles Rams vs. San Francisco 49ers, October 2, 1960

Bob Khayat, Washington Redskins vs. New York Giants, October 16, 1960

*Also had a 52-yarder in the 1957 Pro Bowl.

It's interesting that Vince Lombardi would tell Summerall that he couldn't kick a ball that far when he already had when playing for the

Cardinals—against the Giants, no less—and not once, but twice! He also had a 49-yarder against New York on November 1, 1953.

The Deciders

Nobody had more late deciding kicks in the 1950s than Pat Summerall. In addition to his spectacular game winner against Cleveland in 1958, he had three other fourth-quarter field goals that proved to be the game icers. Three of these kicks make the list seen here, the longest deciders (fourth-quarter field goals that either won games or created ties) of the decade 1951–1960.

49   Pat Summerall, New York Giants vs. Cleveland Browns (13–10); December 14, 1958
      George Blanda, Chicago Bears vs. San Francisco 49ers (20–17); November 2, 1952
47   Lou Groza, Cleveland Browns at New York Giants (6–3); September 29, 1957
46   Sam Baker, Washington Redskins vs. Baltimore Colts (27–24); November 8, 1959
43   Bob Khayat, Washington Redskins vs. Pittsburgh Steelers (27–27); October 23, 1960
37   Pat Summerall, New York Giants vs. Pittsburgh Steelers (27–24); November 13, 1960
32   Les Richter, Los Angeles Rams vs. Pittsburgh Steelers (27–26); October 2, 1955
28   Pat Summerall, New York Giants vs. Baltimore Colts (24–21); November 9, 1958
28   Nick Bolkovac, Pittsburgh Steelers vs. Chicago Cardinals (31–28); October 11, 1953
25   Bobby Layne, Detroit Lions at Los Angeles Rams (10–7); October 13, 1957

Summerall's other decider was an 18-yarder against the Rams in Los Angeles on September 26, 1959. It came with less than two minutes to play and the Giants trailing 21–20. The only other kicker with more than one was Groza, who, in addition to his Giant killer listed above, tied a game at 30 for the Browns against the Redskins on November 17, 1957, with a 23-yarder with just thirteen seconds to go.

The Fastest Team to 100 Wins

Before the Browns happened along, the team that had enjoyed the most early success after joining the NFL was the Giants. The Browns would end up breaking the Giants' very own record for fastest team to one hundred wins in the NFL.

138 games   Browns (1950 to 1961)
155 games   Giants (1925 to 1936)
157 games   Packers (1921 to 1934)
158 games   Bears (1920 to 1931)
165 games   Chiefs (1960 to 1971)

The AFPA (pre-NFL, 1920 and 1921) and AFL (1960–1969) were counted here, but the AAFC (1946–1949) was not. If Cleveland's dominant 47–4–3 record prior to coming to the NFL were allowed, they would have reached one hundred wins in just their 119th game, a 41–10 shellacking of the Packers in week five of the 1955 season.

Washington Redskins vs. New York Giants

October 28, 1962

	1	2	3	4	F
Washington Redskins	7	6	7	14	34
New York Giants	7	14	21	7	49

Has any player in Giants history had more of an impact in a shorter time with the team than did Yelberton Abraham Tittle? Separately, Tittle and the Giants were each good; together they were great. Tittle had the first-, third-, and fourth-best passer ratings of his career in his first three years in New York, starting at the age of thirty-five in 1961. He helped prolong a golden age for the Giants. (See "The Best Three-Year Runs in Giants History," page 104.) He remains an iconic figure in team lore, not to mention that of the sport entire. His legend is still vibrant fifty years after he was referred to in football circles as "an old man."

His greatest day as a Giant—and, arguably, the most productive passing day a quarterback has ever had (see "The 500 Club," page 80)— came in week seven of his second year with the team. First, though, fate had to deliver him to Yankee Stadium.

THE COMING OF Y. A.

For all the success of the Giants of the late fifties, there were seasons where the defense was carrying a much greater load than the offense. From 1956 to 1960, the Giants finished fifth, fifth, ninth, second, and sixth in points scored. They were higher than fourth in total yards just once, finishing second in 1959, and finished tenth out of twelve teams in 1958. Their passing attack was inconsistent from year to year. They finished eighth, second, eleventh, third, and fourth in aerial yardage during that period. Given that they appeared in three championship games in those five years, these are perhaps only cosmetic blemishes, but with the exception of a peak season at the age of thirty-eight in 1959, quarterback Charlie Conerly was never one to put up gaudy passing numbers. Furthermore, he was at the age at which he was being asked about retirement in every interview.

"We had too big a gap between Conerly and Lee Grosscup," Wellington Mara told *Sports Illustrated,* referring to their backup, the team's number-one draft choice in 1959. "You can't expect Charlie, at his age, to play fourteen games in a season, and Grosscup isn't ready to take over yet. We needed someone to fill in that gap." So the Giants looked to the trade market.

Fortunately for New York, San Francisco 49ers coach Red Hickey was trying to revolutionize his offense. In 1960, he sprang the shotgun on an unsuspecting Colts team and upset them 30–22. For 1961, his plan was to fully commit to the shotgun offense while every team but the Cardinals was still using the standard T formation. Aside from Tittle, San Francisco was already in possession of quarterbacks John Brodie and Bob Waters, and then Hickey added Billy Kilmer, an extremely mobile quarterback from UCLA, in the 1961 college draft. Alfred Wright described the trio this way in *Sports Illustrated:* "Brodie is a splendid passer and can run a little if he has to. Kilmer is a wonderfully brave and deceptive runner but completely unpredictable and an uncertain passer. Waters is fast enough to be used as a defensive back. He can also throw a good pass and is self-assured enough to have earned the nickname 'Cool' Waters." Once in operation, Hickey's shotgun rotated the three men on every play.

And it looked as if Tittle was the odd man out.

Y. A. Tittle: He was using the shotgun offense. The quarterback became a deep tailback, and they were just throwing like they do today with third down and long yardage. He decided to use it every down, and chunk the T formation. The quarterback became a tailback and ran the ball more than he threw it, and I was not cut out for that. Certainly not at my age.

Clearly there was no room for the thirty-four-year-old Tittle in this mix. Still, though, Mara played it close to the vest when he approached the 49ers about Tittle's availability. He described the situation this way: "You don't go to another owner and say, 'We want so-and-so.' What you do is say, 'You can't use four quarterbacks. Who do you want to trade?'"

It's one thing to be traded for high draft picks or another established star, but when Hickey told Tittle he had been traded to New York for guard Lou Cordileone, the veteran replied, "Who?"

Cordileone was equally nonplussed. "Me?" he said. "Me? For Y. A. Tittle? You gotta be kidding?"

Y. A. Tittle: I was sort of surprised to be traded because I already played many years in the NFL, and I thought I would be ending my career in San Francisco. When I was traded to New York, I had mixed emotions at first because I wasn't finished in San Francisco. Then, after going home and talking to my wife, she was eager to see Broadway. She wanted to see the bright lights. I was thinking of retiring at that point.

Frank Gifford called Tittle to welcome him to the team and assured him there would be plenty of playing time for him.

Y. A. Tittle: The first question I asked the Giants when they traded for me was if I was going to back up Charlie Conerly. Was I going to receive an equal shot at the job—to have the best-man-wins competition? They told me I'd be given equal opportunity. Charlie started most of the exhibition games and the first couple of games. Then I got into a game and did extremely well and finally got the job.

Alex Webster: Charlie was our leader. Then, when Tittle came in, we'd never seen anything like him before. He was such an enthusiastic guy. He was always pushing; a real leader. Charlie turned to Sherman and said, "That's it," and he stepped down. I always thought he was a man's man to do that.

Rosey Grier: When we played Y. A. when he was with the 49ers, I thought he was the greatest quarterback in the world. And then to come and be with the New York Giants! Realizing what an incredible guy he was, how he could stand back there and get those passes off—not that Charlie Conerly wasn't a great quarterback for me—but Y. A. Tittle had the ability and he had the receivers to do all kinds of things. He was an incredible quarterback. I really love Y. A. Tittle.

Frank Gifford: Y. A. couldn't run that well, but he could get out of the pocket. He was very smart. We were one of the first few teams that put the patterns in so he could have a quick read to recognize the defense and he could go to the first receiver, then the second receiver, and, possibly, the third receiver quickly. He could do that better than anyone in the game.

Alex Webster: He was a great play faker. He had this one play where he would roll out and sprint like he was going to run all the way to the sideline. Then he would fall down, get up, and throw to the opposite side of the field. It was a screen pass, but the longest screen pass you ever saw. And it worked. He had such a good imagination. He and Allie Sherman communicated well, too.

Del Shofner: What made him as good as he was, I think, is that Y.A. got as excited about a pass when he was that age as he was when he first came into pro football. I don't think he ever lost his youth as far as football was concerned. He thought young and he played young. He and I were roommates on trips together. The only thing we ever talked about was football. Y.A. had really a super football mind. He knew what defenses were and he knew what he wanted to throw against them. He really studied the game.

Tittle felt like an outsider at his first Giants camp, but he worked hard at winning over his new teammates and soon developed a great camaraderie on the offensive unit.

Greg Larson: Y. A. was just a fabulous guy for his linemen. Every Saturday whether we were on a road game or at home, he would take us over to a local restaurant and we'd have meatball sandwiches and beers and play liar's poker and he picked up the tab for everything. I just loved that man. He never complained or yelled at anybody, he just was the sweetest guy.

Dick Modzelewski: Y. A. said, "You guys give me the ball and I'll score as much as I can for you."

Tom Scott: He'd get in the huddle and say, "Listen up, you bastards"— something like that. That would shock their ears and make them listen.

Greg Larson: I think bringing in Y. A. was Allie Sherman's brightest moment. I think Y. A. should be regarded as the best screen passer— his technique was so dang good.

Y. A. Tittle: I made a very good decision. I decided to come back and give it another go, and we won the Eastern Conference championship.

And as for Red Hickey's shotgun? It was fun while it lasted, but it only lasted while it was fun. After rolling up huge scores to open the 1961 season 4–1, the 49ers were the talk of the NFL. They had scored at least five touchdowns in each of their victories and were basically terrorizing the league. The Bears put an end to that, however, when they moved Hall of Fame linebacker Bill George up on the line. Having an extra man to hurry the quarterback undid the shotgun and the Bears humbled the 49ers, 31–0. Hickey scrapped the 'gun and went back to the traditional T, and the 49ers went 3–4–1 the rest of the way (although they did avenge their loss to Chicago later in the season). After a 6–8 season in 1962 and a rough start to 1963, Hickey resigned and eventually became a scout for the Cowboys. His legacy does survive, however, as Tom Landry reintroduced his shotgun with Dallas in 1975, albeit as a formation alternative rather than a basis for the entire offense. It was oft imitated and remains in wide use today throughout the league.

More important for Giant fans, though, was that without Hickey's innovation, Y. A. Tittle would never have ended up in New York.

Y. A. Tittle: I think the New York Yankees' success in baseball paved the way for a lot of our success, and then when we became good and idolized like the Yankees, it really did help our morale. I think it was good for the National Football League, too. Frankly, in my opinion, I think it's always good for New York to have a good sports team because of the media concentration there. When New York has a good team, it really helps the league.

TITTLE'S TARGETS ARE ASSEMBLED

The Tittle trade wasn't Wellington Mara's only astute move before the 1961 season. The Giants needed a receiver with big-play potential. Mara's eyes fell on Del Shofner of the Los Angeles Rams.

Y. A. Tittle: Right after I got traded, they asked me about Del. I said that I had seen him a lot when I was with the 49ers, and I said he had great speed and tremendous hands. When I got to the Giants, they had receivers with good hands but nobody with Del Shofner's speed. Frank Gifford was a great player, but even he didn't have Del's speed. I said to get him because he'd give us diversity on our passing offense.

Defensive back Dick Lynch was also consulted. "I couldn't cover him man-on-man in 1958 or 1959," Lynch said. "I couldn't cover him in 1960 either. He's as good as he ever was."

Lynch was differentiating the years because, after finishing first and second in receiving yards and being named an All-Pro in both 1958 and 1959, Shofner's production had dropped to almost nothing in 1960. He had gone from being an All-Pro to the forgotten man of the Rams offense.

Del Shofner: I had some recommendations by a couple of the Giants' defensive backs at the time, Jimmy Patton and Dick Lynch. They said that they couldn't believe that I'd fallen off from where I was a couple of years before. So they were a big factor in it, and Y. A. definitely went to bat for me, and he was one of the reasons that I went to New York.

While still handling the bulk of the punting chores for the Rams, he caught only 12 passes in 1960, down from 51 and 47 the previous two seasons. Mara wanted to know what the problem was.

Del Shofner: Basically, I had ulcers all the time that I played. It's one of those things—I was just sick nearly all of the year and I didn't produce very much and they were willing to trade me. I was awfully sad to go, and it took me probably a couple of months before I realized how lucky I was. Later on, the ulcers reared up on me one time when I was with the Giants and I had to be put in a hospital for a while. I don't know whether we knew what I had or not, but it just got to the point where I had gone to sleep on the bench during a ballgame. I was so weak I just couldn't stay awake.

Jack Cavanaugh: The Rams thought that he was nearing the end of his career. They thought that he had slowed up. The guy was tremendously fast; he'd been a great sprinter at Baylor.

Mara still had his doubts. "But you've got to take a chance," he told *Sports Illustrated.* "You can't think the guy I'm giving up may come back and beat me. If Shofner played back to his '58 and '59 form we wanted him badly." Despite having become persona non grata in the plans of Rams head coach Bob Waterfield, Shofner still cost the Giants a heavy price. On August 28, 1961, New York traded two draft picks—a first-round pick in 1962 and a second-round pick in '63—for the twenty-six-year-old receiver.

Rosey Grier: They could really score then with Shofner and all those guys. They could really play. We were so happy when we had that kind of team, and it just made all the difference in the world for us.

Del Shofner: It's no question that a receiver would like to go to a football club that likes to throw the ball first and run second. And there for a while that seemed like everything we did with the Giants.

Another receiver who would figure prominently in Tittle's big day was tight end Joe Walton, a man known to a later generation of New

York football fans as the Jets' head coach for most of the 1980s. Walton was acquired from the Redskins in a trade that turned out to be fairly lopsided in New York's favor. Their greatest loss in the three-way trade was Dave Whitsell, a defensive back who went on to a long career and who led the league in interceptions in 1967. They also surrendered two kickers, John Aveni to Washington and Allen Green to Dallas. Green was just 5 for 15 in field-goal attempts in 1961, but Aveni was a staggering 5 for 28. It was the last year in the NFL for both.

Joe Walton: When I was traded, I was disappointed. Why? For two reasons. In those days, if you got traded you felt like you failed—you hadn't done a good job. The second reason was I married my wife, Ginger, in June of 1961. She was a former Miss Washington, D.C., and we had already started looking for places in Washington. That's where she was from. All of a sudden we come back from our honeymoon and I had been traded to the Giants. I thought to myself, This is not good. Well, it turned out to be the best thing to happen in my life. I didn't realize it at the time. Not only did I go to a great team that went to three championship games, I got my coaching career started there.

Frank Gifford: Joe Walton got more out of less ability than anyone I have ever met in my life. He was a great competitor and great teammate.

Alex Webster: Joe wasn't a big guy for a tight end, but he was a tough kid and could get open.

Del Shofner: He wasn't tall like a lot of the receivers are now that play tight end, but he was a very adequate blocker. I tell you what, he really did have a good pair of hands on him and he really caught the ball well.

Y. A. Tittle: Joe had the confidence of an eagle. He just believed that he could do anything. Sure enough, if it was third down and nine yards to go, if you needed a first down, you might as well call Joe's number. He'd *want* you to call it. He'd say, "I'll be open." He was a very smart guy who used that intelligence when he became a head coach. He was very helpful. We had a good combination of receivers. Joe Walton's brains . . . Del Shofner's speed . . . Kyle Rote before he retired . . . and Frank Gifford. Boy, those teams couldn't get us out!

Joe Walton: The Giants carried themselves like champions. It was a revelation to me. I was very impressed. I felt like I was on a pretty classy football team.

THE GIANTS

The additions of Tittle, Shofner, and Walton put the Giants' offense on a higher plane in 1961. Scoring jumped by 4 points a game from 1960 to 1961 and another 2 points per game in 1962. Only the Packers outscored the Giants in 1962 (although the upstart Cowboys matched the Giants' 398 points). Kyle Rote retired after catching 53 passes for 805 yards in 1961, but Frank Gifford *un*retired and helped make up for Rote's absence with 39 catches and 796 yards of his own.

Y. A. Tittle: Frank Gifford had won the championship earlier in New York. Because of that, I think he gave us the belief that we could do it, too. I won't say he was a spiritual leader, but some of us hadn't gone to a championship game. We didn't know if we were good enough to do it. Some of the guys on our team had been there before, and I think that was very helpful for us.

That year, running back Alex Webster's yards per carry dropped off, but he nearly doubled the number of passes he caught out of the backfield from 26 to 47. Pat Summerall hung up his cleats after 1961, but punter Don Chandler did double kicking duty and would set a team record with 104 points (breaking the mark established by Gene Roberts in 1949). Along with Tittle and Shofner, the Giants placed three other offensive players in the Pro Bowl. All were linemen: Roosevelt Brown, Darrell Dess, and center Ray Wietecha.

As the offense zoomed, the defense was no longer quite so resolute. While Jimmy Patton, Erich Barnes, and Jim Katcavage were all named to the Pro Bowl, New York surrendered a third again more points than they had in 1961. Even with that, their record improved from 10–3–1 to 12–2 as they won six games by less than a touchdown.

Because it was rightfully presumed that the Yankees would be in the World Series every year, the Giants spent most of the early parts of their seasons on the road, leaving Yankee Stadium free for its main tenants. In 1962, the Giants' first four games were away, but they emerged from their exile 3–1. The only loss was in the opener in Cleveland, when Tittle was picked off three times: The Browns prevailed 17–7. Wins in Philadelphia, Pittsburgh (in which Tittle threw for 332 yards and 4 touchdowns), and St. Louis followed. When the Giants finally came home to Yankee Stadium, they were downed by the Steelers, 20–17, as Gene "Big Daddy" Lipscomb and Ernie Stautner harassed Tittle all day, sacking him four times. It would be their last loss of the regular season.

They bounced back to beat the Lions 17–14. The Detroit defense, one of the best in the NFL, punished Tittle repeatedly. One of the hits he took caused blood to drain into his elbow, the sort of thing that keeps one from combing one's hair, let alone throwing a football. Tittle was doubtful right up until game time the next week against Washington. New York started the day 4–2, sitting in second place, ahead of the 3–2–1 Cowboys and trailing the 4–0–2 Redskins.

THE OPPONENT
The Washington Redskins of 1960 and 1961 were as bad a football team as you're likely to find in NFL annals. In those two seasons, they were 2–21–3. It was even worse than that, though. Both wins and one of the ties came against the expansion Cowboys. From week five of 1960 to week nine of 1961, the Redskins went 0–17. Included in that span was a crushing 53–0 loss to New York on November 5, 1961, in which they surrendered six touchdowns on defense while the offense was chipping in 11 points to the New York cause by giving up a pick-six and getting nailed twice in the end zone for safeties.

The Redskins were very late to integration, which hurt them, although they were clearly not rounding up competent Caucasians, either. There was no clearer indictment of the absurdity of their institutional racism than watching integrated teams run circles around the Redskins every week. They finally got with the program in 1962 when future Hall of Famer Bobby Mitchell was brought in from Cleveland. By 1963, when *Ebony* magazine did an overview of African-Americans in the NFL and AFL ranks, they listed Washington with five. This was still less than a lot of teams, but more than others and equal to the number the Giants had at that moment.

Mitchell made an immediate and important impact on the Redskins' fortunes. He scored three touchdowns in their opener, including a 92-yard kickoff return and a score that was part of a late, two-touchdown comeback to tie the Cowboys 35–35. More late heroics followed the next week in a victory over his old team, the Browns. The maturation of quarterback Norm Snead in his sophomore year and the presence of Mitchell were at the root of the Redskins' surprising 4–0–2 record. (Snead's rating in his rookie year had been just 51.6. Through the first six games of 1962, it was 85.6.) At that point in the season, Mitchell had 34 catches, over half the Redskins' receiving yards, and all eight of their touchdown receptions.

The signs were there, however, that, while the Redskins were light years ahead of where they had been the previous two seasons, they were not quite all their record indicated. For one thing, they had been outgained in four of their six contests. Overall, their opponents had 500 more yards than they did—a rate that is simply not sustainable if a team hopes to compete for a title in a seven-team conference. They had very little going for them on the ground, either. Their 144 rushing yards against the Rams in week four would be one of only two times they cracked three figures on the ground all year, and they would finish last in rushing in 1962. At 2.9 yards per attempt, they were the only team in the league to average under 3.5 yards per carry.

Most telling was their pass defense, however. Through week six, they were averaging around 260 air yards allowed per game. This was almost 70 yards above league average and easily the worst in the NFL.

THE GAME

Joe Walton: Yankee Stadium had a magic to it—and, of course, the tradition of the Yankees. I believe it all started—which everybody does—with the '58 overtime game with the Colts. It carried over. The other thing is, that was the first time I saw a jammed stadium. Playing for the Redskins we got twenty-two, twenty-five thousand. All of a sudden I'm in Yankee stadium with these tremendous crowds. One thing my wife used to always mention was how everybody dressed for the game. Yankee Stadium on Sunday: That was the place to be. Everybody was all decked out. The men wore dress shirts and ties. It was a different atmosphere. It was a magical time.

Del Shofner: The Giants fans sure loved football. We used to say they were awful critical, but boy, when they said something you needed to take it home! They knew what they were talking about because they were big, big fans—and that was nice. They're gonna call it the way they see it—like it or not.

Midway through the first quarter, there was no indication that one of the greatest virtuoso quarterback performances of all time was underway. Tittle had just two completions in his first eight attempts and one of those was for an 8-yard loss. His other completion and a roughing-the-kicker penalty kept the Giants' first drive alive, though, and they found themselves on the Washington 26. Phil King dropped a pass, and Tittle and Walton failed to connect on third down. Don Chandler yanked a 35-yard field-goal attempt wide left. Later in the quarter, New York return man Johnny Counts botched a fair catch and Vince Promuto fell on the ball for Washington at the Giants' 44.

Snead wasted no time exploiting the turnover. On first down, he hit Bobby Mitchell for a touchdown for the ninth time that season. The next Giants series saw a holding call and two more incompletions, giving them a third and 19 on their own 10-yard line. And that's when things started to change.

Tittle completed his next pass to Gifford and was roughed in the process, moving the ball out to the 42. Things started to click. His next four passes were complete, three to Shofner and one to Walton. On third and 9 from the Washington 22, Tittle found Joe Morrison in the end zone, tying the score at 7. His first touchdown pass was on the books.

On the first play of the second quarter, Erich Barnes intercepted Snead and ran the ball from the New York 29 to the 44. On first down,

Tittle hit Shofner at the Washington 40, where he turned it upfield for another 18 yards. After another Shofner catch moved them closer, Tittle lit up the scoreboard for the second time when he found Walton in the end zone from 5 yards out.

Later in the quarter, Snead connected with Tittle's old 49ers mate Fred Dugan from 24 yards out for a score. Huff denied Washington the tie, however, when he broke through and blocked Bob Khayat's extra-point attempt. The Giants led 14–13.

Frank Gifford: We had a really good offensive line with Jack Stroud and Rosey Brown. Y. A. has talked about this many times. He had all the time in the world to throw the ball. That entire year, he had one of the great years in the history of the game.

Tittle was now in the midst of a run of 12 straight completions. His protection—excellent under normal circumstances—was even more so against the pass-prone Redskins. The *New York Times* reported that the Giants' offensive line, which also included Dess, Wietecha, and rookie Reed Bohovich, "gave Tittle plenty of time and room to study the field, and gave the receivers time to bamboozle or outrun their shadowers." On their last drive of the half, Alex Webster ground out the yards, moving New York from the 26 to the 43. From there, Tittle hit Shofner at the Washington 20, and he pressed on to the 4. Covering on the play was rookie cornerback Claude Crabb, whom the Giants would exploit throughout the day. The drive was completed when Tittle rolled out and hit Joe Morrison for the touchdown. The last play of the half was a failed 55-yard field-goal attempt by Khayat.

Heading into the break, Tittle had thrown for 236 yards and three touchdowns and things seemed to be getting easier for him. Was something special in progress? Could he keep defying the Redskins' defense the way he had in the second quarter?

Y. A. Tittle: It seemed like every time I threw the ball, somebody ran it for a touchdown. I had lots of yards. Seven touchdown passes was a record that had been there for some time.

Frank Gifford: Shofner had eleven catches that day. He had great speed and was a big target for that era. He didn't look like he was moving with the speed he was moving. Y. A. loved throwing to him. We were one of the first few teams to really work on the passing game. We spent a lot of time on it. When the defensive team was working in practice, Y. A. would get the receivers together. We would all work for several hours on pass patterns and precision cuts. That wasn't the big popular thing in the game at that time. Y. A. changed the game into more of a passing game than it had ever been.

Chandler's kickoff to start the second half sailed high and far, striking the goalpost, thus giving the ball to Washington at their own 20. On the first play from scrimmage, the Redskins pulled some trickery. At first it looked like an end sweep was developing. Instead, Snead faked the handoff and threw to Mitchell, who caught the ball at the New York 45. Barnes, who had intercepted Snead in the first half, was less fortunate this time. He was in position when Mitchell made the catch, but Mitchell made a move, eluded him, and blazed the rest of the way for the score, making it 21–20.

The Giants answered with a seven-play drive, five plays of which were Tittle completions. On the last one, he threw to the right side, threading the needle between safety Dale Hackbart and cornerback Jim Steffen to nail Shofner from 32 yards out, making it 28–20. Tittle had now thrown four touchdown passes.

It was Andy Robustelli who destroyed the next Redskin possession. He ran down Snead at the Washington 13, giving them a fourth and 17. Punting out of his own end zone, Doug Elmore got a roll just past midfield, but New York still had excellent field position. This time, Tittle shredded the Redskins on just three plays. After a short gainer to Webster, Tittle and Gifford connected for 24 yards to the 26. The touchdown-pass tally rose to five when Tittle connected with Walton again, making it 35–20.

On their next possession, New York started at the 12 and Alex Webster went to work. First he tore off 15 yards for a first down, then he caught a 10-yard toss for another first down. It was then that Tittle threw one to Gifford that eluded Steffen. Gifford broke loose and galloped

63 yards for the score, the longest play of the day for the Giants. With his sixth touchdown pass of the afternoon, Tittle was now within one of the pro record, then coheld by three men. (See "The Others," page 82.)

It was late in the third quarter; Washington, now trailing 42–20, was going to have to act fast if they were to have any hope of getting back in the game. Dick James set them up well with a 44-yard kickoff return to the New York 49, but the Redskins' drive terminated when Jimmy Patton intercepted a pass at the goal line.

On the Giants' second possession of the fourth quarter, Tittle collaborated with Shofner to the tune of 47 yards to the Redskins' 17 and hit him again for another first down. Tittle was now just 5 yards from tying the record.

Joe Walton: Y. A. is a very humble guy and he was not wanting to rub it in to the Redskins—that's the kind of guy he was. This is honest to God's truth. We were all in the huddle, down about the four- or five-yard line. We're all saying, "Y. A., go for the record, you got to go for the record." And he said, "Nah, we'll just run the ball, we have this game." We kept after him—me, too. And he said okay. So what did he do? He called a pass to me! And I'm coming out of the huddle and I'm saying, Oh, shit! I didn't expect him to throw it to me! I expected him to throw it to Frank or Del or somebody. I said to myself, What if I drop this son of a bitch? I wanted him to go for the score, but I didn't want him to throw it to me!

Dick Modzelewski: Y. A. threw the touchdown pass and said, "Way to go," and everybody went back to the bench. Nobody jumped around like they do now.

Tom Scott: Tittle took what he was given. He was very good at that. Walton could read the zone. He'd go down there and find an empty spot and Tittle would hit him.

Joe Walton: It was a bootleg and I caught it. We set the record. *He* set the record. I'll never forget: I carried the ball all the way to the bench and held onto it. And as soon as everybody calmed down a little bit,

I gave it to Y. A. It was a fun day. It was a memory that has very much stuck in my mind.

Chandler's seventh extra point made it 49–20 with just under nine minutes to play. Could Tittle break the league record for touchdown passes in a game? There was certainly enough time left to make it happen.

The Redskins would not go away. James took Chandler's kickoff on the 7 and went 66 yards to the New York 27. Snead eventually put it over himself to make it 49–27 and drove the Redskins across midfield on their next possession, aided by another interference call on Barnes. The drive appeared dead when Katcavage dumped him for a 10-yard loss on third down. Looking at fourth and 15 from the Giants' 35, Steve Junker got open and Snead hit him for a touchdown, pulling the Redskins to within 11 with under two minutes to play.

This was effectively an insurmountable deficit in the time allotted, especially in the days before the two-point conversion, but the Redskins were not throwing in the towel. Khayat bounced an onside kick and Washington recovered at the Giants' 49. Snead went for broke on first down, only to be picked off by Jimmy Patton at the goal line. Patton ran the ball out to the 23. There was enough time for Tittle to air a few out in an attempt to break the record.

Y. A. Tittle: I didn't realize I had thrown that many until Sam Huff said, "You have to go for number eight." He got mad at me and called me a chicken because I wouldn't throw. He wanted me to do it. We had the game won. It would have been total self-glorification. I don't mind glory, but not self-glorification. I could hear the Redskins saying, "That bald-headed SOB. Look at what he did to us! We should take it out on him the next time we see him."

With the ball on their own 23 and very little time on the clock, Tittle's teammates wanted more.

Y. A. Tittle: I had a chance to go for number eight with about a minute to go in the ballgame. My teammates were encouraging me to call a pass. They wanted me to get the record, but we were neck and neck with Washington for the division championship. We had to play them a few weeks later, and we had this game won. All we had to do was run the clock out, and the game was over. I had a feeling that maybe I better not rub it in and go for number eight for self-glory, because I didn't want to live to regret it when we played them again. It was probably not the right thing to do. That might have come back to haunt me. When I look back on it now, though—knowing no one has ever thrown that eighth touchdown pass—I wish I could do it again!

Taking a knee was not an option for a quarterback in 1962, so instead Tittle handed off four straight times to bring an end to the proceedings.

THE AFTERMATH

Y. A. Tittle: Being in New York was like a dream come true. We were down on Broadway after the game near where that big sign displays headlines that move around the corner in Times Square. It said, Y. A. TITTLE SCALPS SKINS, THROWING SEVEN TOUCHDOWN PASSES. My wife said, "Y. A. Tittle? That's you!" There's my name in the same place they are announcing all of the big things in the world!

It was a heady night for Tittle, the kind of which could only be experienced by a player with a New York team of that time. First, he appeared on the *Ed Sullivan Show*, which was a live broadcast. Sullivan was always one to single out local athletic stars in his audience or invite them onstage. As Tittle told *Football Digest*, they went to Toots Shor's for dinner after the Sullivan appearance and ended up sitting with Jackie Gleason for a while. Some kids asked Tittle for his autograph, then turned to Gleason and asked him who he was. "I'm a big, fat tackle, what does it look like?" *The Honeymooners* star replied.

For the Redskins, this game marked the beginning of the end. They held onto first place a bit longer, but won only one more game all year and finished 5–7–2. The Giants won out, including another 40-point game against them on November 25 in which Tittle threw three more touchdown passes. With the division title clinched, Tittle turned over the reins to backup Ralph Guglielmi for the next-to-last game of the year. New York kept it mostly on the ground, beating Cleveland 17–13. Tittle was back under center for the season closer against the Cowboys, though, and would nearly match his seven-touchdown-pass performance. His sixth and final scoring strike came on the Giants' last possession with barely a minute left in the game, so there was no question of tying the record. Tittle needed to be coerced to throw that one, too, but his teammates wanted him to break the single-season mark for most touchdown passes. His 8-yard toss to Joe Walton made it 33 on the year. It was a record that would stand for only one season, as Tittle would up the ante to 36 in 1963.

APPENDICES

The 500 Club
Quarterbacks who have thrown for 500 yards in a game

554 Norm Van Brocklin,
Los Angeles Rams vs. New York Yanks
September 28, 1951 (27 for 41, 5 TD, 3 INT): With Van Brocklin filling in for the injured Bob Waterfield, the Rams rolled up 722 total yards, winning 55–14 in the process. He eclipsed the league passing record, held by the Bears' Johnny Lujack, by 86 yards. Van Brocklin wasn't perfect, though. He was picked off three times and also had a lateral snared by Art Tait, who ran it the other way for a Yanks touchdown.

527 Warren Moon,
Houston Oilers vs. Kansas City Chiefs
December 16, 1990 (27 for 45, 3 TD, 0 INT): What a difference a year makes. On the Oilers' previous visit to Kansas City the year before, Moon was held to just 99 yards passing and the Chiefs dominated Houston, 34–0. This time, Haywood Jeffires had 245 receiving yards on nine catches as the Oilers prevailed, 27–10.

522 Boomer Esiason,
Arizona Cardinals vs. Washington Redskins
November 10, 1996 (39 for 53, 3 TD, 4 INT): Esiason rallied the Cardinals from a 14-point deficit late in the fourth quarter, but this game comes with an asterisk and a half. If not for the overtime period (in which it took Cardinals kicker Kevin Butler three tries to seal the 37–34 victory), Esiason would not be in the 500 Club. And then there are those four interceptions . . .

521 Dan Marino,
Miami Dolphins vs. New York Jets
October 23, 1988 (35 for 60, 3 TD, 5 INT): Not all 500-yard passing games are created equal. Marino was picked off five times, three of which were by Erik McMillan, who returned one of them for a touchdown in the Jets' 44–30 victory.

513 Phil Simms,
New York Giants vs. Cincinnati Bengals

October 13, 1985 (40 for 62, 1 TD, 2 INT): The good news was that Simms set the team record for passing yards. The bad news was the Bengals still won, 35–30. Despite being down 21–0 at one point, the Giants made a game of it, even holding Cincinnati to –3 yards in the second half. Unfortunately for them, George Adams fumbled away the ball at the Bengals' 2-yard line and also dropped a sure touchdown pass from Simms in the end zone. Despite his aerial onslaught, the day was less than perfect for Simms, too, as his interception and fumble led to two Bengal scores in a little over a minute.

510 Drew Brees,
New Orleans Saints vs. Cincinnati Bengals

November 19, 2006 (37 for 52, 2 TD, 3 INT): Further evidence that throwing for a ton of yards is simply not enough. The Bengals won going away, 31–16, as Brees counted a pick-six to Ethan Kilmer among his three interceptions.

509 Vince Ferragamo,
Los Angeles Rams vs. Chicago Bears

December 26, 1982 (30 for 46, 3 TD, 2 INT): At the time this was the second-most passing yards ever amassed in an NFL game, but the headlines belonged to the Bears' Walter Payton, not Ferragamo. Chicago won 34–26 and Payton passed 10,000 yards in career rushing, just the fourth man to do so at that point in history.

505 Y. A. Tittle,
New York Giants vs. Washington Redskins

October 28, 1962 (27 for 39, 7 TD, 0 INT): When Tittle threw for 500 yards, only fourteen men before him had thrown for even 400 yards in a game. His is easily the best performance of the 500 Club. The single-game passer ratings for each member of the club are: Tittle, 151.3; Moon, 123.1; Roethlisberger, 121.9; Van Brocklin, 118.1; Ferragamo, 106.1; Grbac, 99.9; Esiason, 91.9; Brees, 91.0; Simms, 82.3; and Marino, 68.9. Among the fifty-eight quarterbacks with perfect single-game ratings (158.3) through the 2008 season, only one threw for 400 yards or attempted more than 30 passes (Ken O'Brien of the Jets against Seattle in 1986). The system favors discipline and discretion, two things that are usually casualties in extreme big-yard games such as these.

504 Elvis Grbac,
Kansas City Chiefs vs. Oakland Raiders

November 5, 2000 (39 for 53, 2 TD, 2 INT): The Raiders killed the Chiefs 49–31 in this one, meaning the 500 Club won-loss record is just 5–5. The novelty in this game was rookie punter Shane Lechler coming off the bench for injured kicker Sebastian Janikowski and connecting on all seven of his extra-point attempts. This game remains his only NFL placekicking experience.

503 Ben Roethlisberger,
Pittsburgh Steelers vs. Green Bay Packers

December 19, 2009 (29 for 46, 3 TD, 0 INT): With the Steelers trailing 36–30 and just five seconds left on the clock, Big Ben took the snap on the Packers' 19 and threaded a perfect pass into the outstretched hands of Mike Wallace, who managed to get both feet into the end zone for the game-winning score. It is easily the most dramatic entry into the 500 Club. Just missing the milestone were the Broncos' Jake Plummer, who threw for 499 yards against Atlanta in 2004, and Joe Namath, who racked up 496 for the Jets in his famous shoot-out against Johnny Unitas and the Baltimore Colts in 1972.

The Others

Four other men have thrown for seven touchdowns in a single game. Of the five, Y. A. Tittle is the only one who did not throw an interception.

Sid Luckman
November 14, 1943

(CHICAGO BEARS 56, NEW YORK GIANTS 7) Two weeks prior to this game, Sammy Baugh of the Redskins passed for six touchdowns, setting the new record. It was to be a short-lived mark. En route to the first 400-yard passing performance in NFL history (443, to be precise),

Luckman threw two scoring strikes to Hampton Pool and Jim Benton and one each to Connie Mack Berry, Harry Clarke, and George Wilson. In all, the Bears had 488 passing yards to the Giants' 73. It was the worst Giants loss in team history to that point. Luckman had a chance at even more but was already in the shower when his understudy, Bob Snyder, was conducting a late fourth-quarter drive.

Adrian Burk
October 17, 1954

(PHILADELPHIA EAGLES 49, WASHINGTON REDSKINS 21) Aside from tossing three scores to future Hall of Famer Pete Pihos, Burk hit Bobby Walston (who also converted all seven extra points) three times and Toy Ledbetter once. Burk threw for "only" 232 yards, as four of the scoring passes were for less than 10 yards and none was more than 26. According to his teammate, the future Giant Tom Scott, Burk could have easily had eight: "A flair pass that would have gone for a touchdown was dropped by the halfback." Burk started only eight of the Eagles' twelve games in 1954 but managed to lead the league in touchdown passes with 23. This game made the difference, as runner-up Charlie Conerly of the Giants had 17.

George Blanda
November 19, 1961

(HOUSTON OILERS 49, NEW YORK TITANS 13) Blanda connected with Billy Cannon and Bill Groman three times each and Charley Hennigan once. He threw for 418 yards and converted all seven extra points himself. He broke his co-owned American Football League record of four touchdown passes, set the previous year against Oakland in the first game of the Oilers' existence. Against these same Titans a year later, Blanda threw for six scores in a 56–17 win. A seventh TD pass in that game came in the fourth quarter from backup quarterback Jacky Lee, so it is safe to assume that Blanda could have very well been on this list twice.

Joe Kapp
September 28, 1969

(MINNESOTA VIKINGS 52, BALTIMORE COLTS 14) The previous season, the Colts had allowed only 144 points. This installment of the team was not so stingy, but this was still an uncharacteristic blistering they received at the hands of Kapp. He threw, in order, for scores to Dave Osborn, Gene Washington, Bob Grim, Kent Kramer, Washington again, John Beasley, and Jim Lindsey. Kapp threw for 449 yards that day and could have had more, but backups Gary Cuozzo and Bob Lee shared the final 13 passes. (One of the referees that day was none other than previous seven-TD chucker Adrian Burk, who had entered officiating after his playing career ended.) The Vikings were terrors that season, finishing with the most points scored and least allowed. To illustrate how loaded they were, they later beat the Steelers by the same 52–14 score, only that time Kapp didn't throw a single touchdown pass.

Will anybody ever throw seven in a game again? In the opening game of the 2009 season, Drew Brees was sitting on six with plenty of time to go when it was decided that his New Orleans Saints would grind out the rest of the clock with their running game. Propriety suggests that teams not make an obvious showing of piling on points via the air game. Unless that stops being the prevailing attitude, another seven-TD performance seems unlikely, at least not in a blowout. It could occur in a shoot-out game, however. A 52–49 contest could produce such a showing for either winner or loser, but those games are few and far between.

Chicago Bears vs. New York Giants

NFL CHAMPIONSHIP
December 29, 1963

	1	2	3	4	F
New York Giants	7	3	0	0	10
Chicago Bears	7	0	7	0	14

Greatness denied is still greatness. For the third straight season and fifth out of six, the Giants would play for the league championship. While their losses to the Packers in 1961 and 1962 had been rather one-sided affairs, they were very much in the 1963 game in spite of conditions and major inconveniences that inhibited their strengths.

There are rarely clear demarcation lines in life: Eras usually melt from one into the next rather than abruptly end and begin. In hindsight, though, the Giants of this game can certainly be labeled as the last incarnation of a great team.

THE GIANTS

The 1963 New York Giants were like the 1962 Giants, only more so. They allowed the same number of points but took their offense up a notch, moving from 398 points to 448. While not a record for the most points ever or even for the most points per game, it was and would remain the most points ever scored in the era of the fourteen-game schedule.

What is even more stunning about the Giants' scoring prowess is that Y. A. Tittle missed the second game of the season and the Giants were blanked in Pittsburgh, 31–0. Had he been healthy and had the Giants responded with even a modest effort, they would have ended up with pointage in the 470 to 480 range—a figure achieved just once previously and not matched again until the schedule was expanded to sixteen games. The Giants gained over 5,000 total yards on offense, nearly 2,000 more than did the Bears.

Tittle was back for his third New York season and, at the age of thirty-seven, responded with arguably the greatest year of his career. He threw for slightly more yards in 1962 but was more accurate in '63, hitting on 60.3 percent of his passes. His interceptions dropped from 20 to 14 and he broke his own record for touchdown passes by three, hurling 36. Del Shofner remained his favorite target, catching 64 passes for 1,181 yards and 9 touchdowns. Frank Gifford excelled once more out of the flanker position, counting 7 TDs among his 42 catches, while Aaron Thomas and Joe Walton got their share as well. Out of the backfield, Joe Morrison grabbed 31 passes for 7 touchdowns and also averaged 4.8 yards per carry.

The Giants' season opened in Baltimore where Johnny Unitas and the Colts jumped all over them for a 21–3 lead. New York roared back behind three Tittle touchdown passes and eventually won going away, 37–28. After the Pittsburgh loss , they traveled to Philadelphia, where they built up a 30–0 lead on the Eagles before cruising to a 37–14 win. In Washington the following week, a 17–0 lead almost got away before Tittle iced it with a fourth-quarter strike to Walton. The 24–14 win put them at 3–1 heading to Yankee Stadium for the home opener, in which Cleveland's Jim Brown scored three times and the Browns blew past a 10-point deficit to prevail 35–24.

At that point in the season, the offense got completely right and reeled off scores of 37–21, 33–6, 38–21, 42–14, and 48–14, taking out the Cowboys, Browns, Cardinals, Eagles, and 49ers in the process. This was followed by the Giants' final loss of the season, a tough one at home against the Cardinals in which St. Louis went ahead 24–17 in the fourth quarter and then beat back two New York charges inside the 10-yard line to seal it.

Week twelve saw a valiant but sloppy effort in Dallas, where the 3–8 Cowboys ran up a 27–14 halftime lead. The New York defense shut them down in the second half while Tittle tried to make amends for his three first-half interceptions. With the score 27–24 in the fourth quarter, Don Chandler nailed a field goal from 53 yards out, then the third-longest in NFL history, to tie it. Tittle and Shofner connected for the game winner. It was also the pass that made Tittle the all-time leader in touchdown passes. The Redskins were easier fare the next week, committing ten turnovers as the Giants came away with a 44–14 win.

This set up the final-week showdown against 7–3–3 Pittsburgh. Because the NFL did not count tie games in the standings, if the 10–3 Giants lost and the Browns and Cardinals won their season finales, the Steelers would finish in first with an 8–3–3 record while New York, Cleveland, and St. Louis would finish behind them at 10–4. (Under the rules adopted in 1972 in which ties count as half wins and half losses, Pittsburgh would have finished fourth.) In any event, a Giant win would make them 11–3 and render everything else irrelevant. New York nearly sucked the drama out of the proceedings by building a 16–0 lead early in the second quarter, but Pittsburgh came back strong, narrowing the gap to 16–10 early in the third. Frank Gifford caught a key third-down pass and New York pulled away, winning 33–17. Joe Morrison scored three times.

That set up the meeting with the Bears, a team with formidable attributes.

Sam Huff: We were practicing at Yankee Stadium for the championship game and we were lined up against Tittle and the offense. Jim Katcavage weighed two hundred and sixty-five pounds, and he ran right over the top of Y. A. Tittle. Katcavage hit him straight on and knocked him four yards back on his head. Now I ran the defense on the field, so when I got in the huddle with Kat, I said, "Gee whiz, Kat, why'd you hit Y. A. like that?" He said, "He's got the ball, doesn't he?" He looked me dead in the eye and said, "What's wrong with you?" I said, "You can't hit Y. A. Tittle like that. He's our quarterback! We're playing the world-championship game in three days!" I said, "You're gonna knock out the quarterback?" He said, "He's got the ball, and that's what I do." He was yelling at me in the huddle! I said, "Okay, Kat—make sure we hit the Bears the same way!"

THE OPPONENT

The sobriquet "Monsters of the Midway" was coined when head coach George Halas was still a young man, but it fit the 1963 Bears like few others. You would have to go back to World War II to find a team that played defense like the '63 Bears did. When teams were averaging 22 points a game, the Bears held their opponents to just over 10. (It was the best mark since the '44 Giants had throttled wartime opponents to the tune of 7.5 per game.) The defensive unit was coordinated by the meticulous and talented George Allen, who would go on to coach the Rams and Redskins to a remarkable .712 regular-season winning percentage. He had taken over from Clark Shaughnessy, who was himself one of football's great innovative minds.

Joe Fortunato: Allen was really sharp. He left no stone unturned. He checked everything out. I learned a lot from him.

Stan Jones: George Allen was a very good coach. He was a great motivator. He kept a lot of statistics, so we were very conscious all the time of where we stood.

Joe Fortunato: We had a tendency chart based on first and ten, second and ten, and this, that, and everything else, and it really gave up what a team did in certain situations. We sure took advantage of that.

Ed O'Bradovich: We knew what a team was going to do on what down, on what side of the field, and on what yardage line. George Allen was a tactician. When Clark Shaughnessy was there, you'd get the tendencies of your next opponent going back a game or maybe two. When George Allen came in, those reports grew in size by maybe four times. They were the size of an encyclopedia. Every tendency by down and field location. If it was second and eight, what did they like to do? Run the ball? Pass it? He had it all broken down for us.

Doug Atkins: He didn't put a whole lot of pressure on you. He just gave you assignments that he knew you could handle and turned you loose.

The Bears' starting eleven totaled thirty-nine Pro Bowl appearances in their careers and were named to seventeen All-Pro teams. On average they played thirteen seasons in the NFL, with no man playing fewer than ten.

The linebacking corps was anchored by Bill George, an eight-time All-Pro who would be elected to the Hall of Fame in 1974. He was flanked to the left by Joe Fortunato, a five-time Pro Bowler and three-time All-Pro. Ironically, it would be the most unheralded of the trio, Larry Morris, who would play the biggest role in the title game. The defensive backfield featured Rosey Taylor, Dave Whitsell, Bennie McRae, and Richie Petitbon. All but McRae were Pro Bowlers at least once in their careers.

The defensive line was led by Doug Atkins, an agile behemoth. Even at six foot eight, Atkins was perfectly capable of high-jumping guards and tackles as they fell to the ground under the weight of the rush.

Joe Fortunato: Atkins was unbelievable. They'd put two or three guys on him and he'd push them aside like they weren't even there—or he'd jump over them. At that time he was one of the biggest guys who ever played.

He went to eight Pro Bowls and was voted into the Hall of Fame in 1982. The right tackle was Fred Williams, a four-time Pro Bowler who had been injured for much of the year and had played in just a handful of games but would be starting in the championship. At left defensive tackle was Stan Jones, who had been a seven-time Pro Bowler as an offensive guard but who had been successfully switched to defense by Allen in 1963. He was one of the first football players to bulk up by lifting weights. On the left end was Ed O'Bradovich. Like Morris among the linebackers, he would finish his career bereft of Pro Bowl honors, but, also like Morris, he would have the best day among the linemen in the championship.

The Bears had a plus-29 takeaway mark, best in the league. They intercepted 36 passes while allowing only 10 touchdown throws. They allowed 62 fewer points than the next-most stingy defense in the league, Green Bay.

The Chicago offense was quarterbacked by Bill Wade and was not known for its creativity. As Wade himself said on the television show *Once a Star* years later, "I didn't believe in the type of football we played, that is, the Lombardi type of football: Three yards and a cloud of dust. No excitement. I believe in the excitement of football."

Joe Fortunato: We used to raise hell with our offense! They were so bad! But they did just enough for us to win.

Doug Atkins: The offense didn't set the world on fire, but they didn't give the ball away like some offenses do.

Ed O'Bradovich: From the twenty to the twenty our offense could move the ball, convert on third, and eat up the clock. It used to drive Ray Nitschke of the Packers nuts. He hated that dink-and-dunk passing game we had. We would say to Bill Wade, "Don't screw this up. Don't go throwing interceptions."

The Bears were outscored by all but four of the fourteen teams in the NFL in 1963. The defense directly chipped in 28 of the 301 points they accumulated, which meant the offensive effort wasn't even as strong as it appeared. But, as should be asked of defensive powerhouses mated with lesser offenses, So what? It worked.

Wade's favorite target was tight end Mike Ditka, who caught 59 passes for 794 yards and eight touchdowns. The flanker was Johnny Morris, who had 47 catches for 705 yards. In the backfield, Joe Marconi, Ronnie Bull, and Willie Galimore averaged in the mid- to high threes per carry while Marconi had the most receptions among the trio with 28. On goal-to-go situations, Wade was as likely to keep it as not, as he led the team with 6 rushing touchdowns, while the running backs combined for 8. The special teams were notable for having, by far, the worst average return rate on kickoffs. Their season's longest return was also the worst in the league—only 29 yards. Of course, given their defense, the return team didn't get many chances.

Chicago won its first five games by a combined score of 137–48. They dispatched their main rival, the defending champion Packers, 10–3 in the opener. Their best offensive showing came in week five when they blasted the Rams in Los Angeles, 52–14. (Ditka caught four touchdown passes.) Week six saw their one true letdown of the season. They went on the road to play the winless San Francisco 49ers and let them build up a 17–0 lead before getting on the board, eventually losing 20–14. But the Bears stepped over that body lightly and won four straight, surrendering just three touchdowns in the process. In week ten they met the defending-champion Packers, with whom they were tied at 8–1. Intercepting five passes, the Bears very nearly pitched a shutout, but settled for a 26–7 win when Green Bay got a late touchdown. It was arguably the most convincing defeat of the Packers' golden era of 1960 to 1967.

This was followed by consecutive 17–17 ties against Pittsburgh and Minnesota, games in which they had to rally to avoid losing. The ties kept the Packers in the race, so Chicago couldn't clinch the division until they had dispatched Detroit and San Francisco to close out the season 11–1–2.

Sam Huff: [Bears running back] Joe Marconi was my old West Virginia roommate. We were great friends. Now we were against each other. I called him the night before the game. I said, "Joe, don't run the ball tomorrow." He said, "Why?" I said, "Cause I'll kill ya! You will not cross the fifty-yard line. I promise you, Joe. They may call your number, but don't run the ball because I gotta hit ya!" I warned him.

Ed O'Bradovich: Going into that football game, everybody was talking about the Giants! The Giants . . . the Giants . . . Y. A. Tittle . . . Gifford . . . Shofner . . . the running game . . . That really teed us off. Our reaction was, "Who the hell are these guys? A bald-headed freak playing quarterback? They're going to come into our living room and they're going to tell us what to do?" In Vegas we were seven-point underdogs. I was seething because we were the afterthought!

THE GAME

Game conditions were brutal at best. "The wind chill factor was seventeen degrees below zero," reported Bears quarterback Bill Wade.

"George Halas would not let me wear long underwear, but I put it on anyway and cut the sleeves off so he couldn't see it!"

Halas had tried to keep the field in playing condition by covering it with a tarp for a week and using blowers to force hot air under the tarp. It was hoped this would keep the turf soft. As Arthur Daley noted in the *New York Times*, however, "It was as delicious as sponge cake when the tarp was stripped off. Then the cold hit and instantly froze it solid all over again."

Greg Larson: We heard that the field had ice on it and that there was maybe a quarter inch of dirt on it. Cleats just wouldn't work, so they got everybody with tennis shoes. I went to Andy Robustelli's sporting-goods shop in Stamford and he had some—I don't know—I think they were lacrosse shoes, I'm not sure. I've never seen a configuration of rubber cleats like these were. They were about an inch in length and about three eighths of an inch in depth, or height. They were at different angles. These were black high-tops. So I bought a pair of those. We went out on the field and we tried doing the cleats and guys are sliding all over. With the tennis shoes, the top surface would break away, and I'm the only guy that had those things I was wearing. I thought that was, in my mind, the best game I ever played because nobody else had the traction that I did. I could push guys around, I could move—I could do everything. It was amazing what a difference just a pair of shoes could make.

Jerry Hillebrand: We weren't ready for that climate. Jesus Criminy, I grew up in it, but you don't get used to that six-degree weather out there. And we didn't have the gloves and all that kind of stuff. It took me about four or five hours to thaw out after the game was over. It was a nasty one.

Joe Fortunato: I almost lost my two big toes because of frostbite. The toenails fell off and they still aren't right to this day.

An indication of the playing conditions manifested itself on the very first play. Don Chandler kicked off to Billy Martin, who muffed the ball at his own 5. He retreated to the goal line and scooped it up, only to go sprawling facedown. He managed to get up again and advance the ball to the 10. The Bears had averted disaster, but disaster would find them soon enough. Chicago stayed on the ground on their first series. Wade got their first first down with an 8-yard keeper off right. Dick Modzelewski jumped offside, moving the ball out to the 29. Wade tried another keeper and broke through into the Giant secondary. There were no quarterback slides in those days, so signal callers had to take their lumps like everybody else. Dick Lynch came up and hit Wade, causing a fumble. Erich Barnes fell on it and New York was in business at the Bears' 41.

It was Joe Morrison who was mostly responsible for moving the ball downfield from there, getting to the 14 via numerous runs and an 11-yard screen pass. The drive was capped when Frank Gifford got separation in the end zone on cornerback Bennie McRae and Tittle hit him for the touchdown.

With a 7–0 lead the Giants' defense dug in, allowing the Bears one first down before forcing them to punt. New York got the ball back at their own 26. On third and 2, Tittle dropped back to pass and was nailed by Larry Morris for a 7-yard loss (it would not be the last time Morris would cause trouble for Y. A.). Chandler's ensuing punt was a 52-yard boomer with a short return and the Bears started at their 24. On first down, Willie Galimore took the handoff from Wade and went around the right end. What looked like a nice 7-yard gain for the Bears went awry when Galimore fumbled and defensive back Dick Pesonen fell on it for New York. On first down, Tittle went right for the throat.

Ed O'Bradovich: I beat Stroud and I was coming right at Tittle. I thought I was going to rip his head off. He ducked and I went flying right over him. He straightened right up and fired the ball to Shofner.

Del Shofner: I was alone in the end zone by myself—ball right into my hands, nobody around me—and I dropped the ball. I'm not saying that that was the reason why we didn't win, but my own personal thought about this is that as good a defense as we had that year, I don't think the Bears would have ever come back from being down

14–0. I didn't do it on purpose—it's one of those things I would like to have back. There are no mulligans, so we just have to take what we get. But I really do believe with the defense we had, that that ballgame was over if I came up with that ball.

The friendly confines of Wrigley were especially confining for a football field. It was an extremely tight fit. Its low brick wall and first-base dugout were flush with the end zone on one end of the field, while the left field wall loomed over the other end zone. The field was surrounded on all sides by hard, rough surfaces—a forbidding sight for anyone running full speed into the end zone.

Ed O'Bradovich: Dave Whitsell hollered out to Shofner, "The wall! The wall!" I don't know for a fact that it distracted him, but I guess it's possible.

Doug Atkins: If he would have gotten that one, we would have been in trouble.

Andy Robustelli would later write, "Blaming one player is too obvious . . . If he hadn't made some great catches in October and November, we wouldn't have played that game in late December."
On the next play, Tittle called for a screen pass to halfback Phil King. Tittle had not thrown an interception in a screen scenario all season and was highly regarded as a polished practitioner of that particular pass. Still, though, Sherman was wary of the Chicago defense.

Greg Larson: I can still hear Allie Sherman saying, "Y. A., you can't screen-pass against Morris and those linebackers. You just can't do it."

Del Shofner: Larry Morris—and God bless him, I played with him when I was with the Rams—intercepted the ball and ran it back all the way to the five.

Doug Atkins: He started off fast. Larry said later, "When I caught it, I thought they were going to catch me, and after a while I wished they would." He ran out of gas!

Greg Larson: Darrell Dess and I were able to catch the guys in pursuit because those linebackers were getting kind of old and couldn't move as well as we could!

It was a 61-yard return that was stopped by Dess with a touchdown-saving pursuit and tackle, but it only delayed the inevitable. On second and goal from the 2, Wade plunged in for the tying mark.

Del Shofner: It should have been fourteen to nothing and ended up being a seven-seven tie. Not to say it wouldn't have been something different had it happened the other way, but I would still like to have the fourteen points and see Chicago try to score more than that against that defense of ours.

Calamity nearly struck the Giants on the ensuing kickoff. Rookie return man Charlie Killett coughed up the ball and the Bears' Charlie Bivins recovered at the New York 13. Fortunately for New York, Steve Barnett had been offside on the play, necessitating a second kick. On that one, Eddie Dove made a nice 24-yard return, setting up the Giants at their own 38. An offside penalty and some Joe Morrison grinding brought the ball to the 50. Tittle then hit Aaron Thomas for 36 yards, putting the Giants in the red zone.

Aaron Thomas: That play still bothers me. Y. A. threw me a square out. I caught the ball and turned up the sideline, but I couldn't keep my feet in on that frozen field. I ran out of bounds—and I still wonder if there was something I could have done to stay in bounds. I know I could have scored.

Three King carries gave New York a first and goal at the 3. While the chorus in the huddle was for a hard charge up the middle, Tittle called time-out to check with the boss. Sherman ordered a sweep by Joe Morrison, which yielded no gain. Sherman called for a second sweep on second down, but Bill George came crashing through to dump Morrison for a 3-yard loss. On third down, King dropped a flare pass in the flat. New York settled for a 13-yard Chandler field goal and a 10–7 lead.

New York's next possession would prove fateful. As it progressed, it showed that the Giants were quite capable of moving the ball on the vaunted Bear defense. King picked up 19 yards on consecutive draw plays and New York was on the Chicago 32 with a first down. Tittle dropped back, stumbled, set, and began looking for Gifford. Linebacker Larry Morris was blitzing.

Alex Webster: That was my man. It was on a red dog—the linebacker blitz. I picked him, blocked him and down he went. I didn't hit him hard enough and he got back up and hit Tittle's knee.

Doug Atkins: Larry broke through, but they cut him down and he rolled in and caught Tittle's front leg. He hit it high enough to damage it. At about the time he caught him, I hit him from the other side.

Y. A. Tittle: I was tackled below the knee just as I was releasing the ball with my weight on the left knee. It tore cartilage.

Joe Fortunato: We knocked the hell out of Y. A. Tittle. We blitzed him quite a bit. All the other teams just let him sit back and throw the ball—we blitzed the hell out of him.

Jack Cavanaugh: The only backup they had was a twenty-three-year-old quarterback named Glynn Griffing, who rarely played and threw just forty passes during the regular season. And he came in and took Tittle's place while Tittle was hurt for a while, and he just looked lost out there. He looked absolutely lost.

Aaron Thomas: He had gotten married the week before the game. He missed two or three days of practice because he was snowed in down in Mississippi. He couldn't get back to practice.

Jerry Hillebrand: Tittle never came out of a game, so it was pretty tough for Glynn to get any experience at all during that year. That probably hurt the team because of the lack of experience, but we knew Tittle was going to play regardless of how he felt. He was a really tough nut playing quarterback. He had a linebacker mentality back there.

Griffing was not yet a year removed from starring in the Sugar Bowl with Ole Miss, where he had been a star (and is in their Hall of Fame). While many teams carried a veteran backup, the Giants had traded theirs—Ralph Guglielmi—to the 49ers earlier in the season after he performed poorly in the week-two loss to Pittsburgh. "Ralph also had a spotty preseason," Robustelli wrote, "but he had still proven himself more capable of handling the club than a rookie, and we were simply lucky that nothing happened to Tittle during the season or our title hopes would have been long gone."

Dick Modzelewski: [Griffing] looked like he was shaking all over the place, and we're thinking, "Oh, my God . . ."

Ed O'Bradovich: Doug Atkins hit him coming from the right side and I hit him coming from the left simultaneously. I heard a squeal.

His first and only pass on third and 7 was incomplete, leaving Chandler to try a field goal from 37 yards out. It fell short. The Bears' next drive was stopped just shy of midfield, but Bobby Joe Green's punt buried the Giants at their own 2. After two plunges into the line to create some space, Sherman sent in the punting unit on third down, indicating his confidence level in Griffing. The Bears took over on their own 47 but only moved the ball forward a yard before punting it away to the New York 19. The half ended with the Giants killing time on short runs, leading 10–7.

In the Giants' locker room, the team was contemplating thirty more minutes without its ace.

Dick Modzelewski: A few of us went to Y. A. at halftime and told him, "Hey, man, perk up a bit, we need you in this game."

Jack Cavanaugh: Allie Sherman said about Griffing, "I felt if I left him in he was going to get intercepted, so I asked Y. A. if he could come back in the second half and he said he could."

Sam Huff: They were taping up Y. A. I went in, and I probably shouldn't have, but I went to him and said, "We got 'em. Don't play the second half. Let Glynn Griffing play. Hell, he can just run three downs, and Chandler can punt the ball. That's all we need, Y. A. We'll win the world championship for you. We'll do it for you, Y. A." He said, "I gotta play, Sam. This is the only chance I have ever had to win the championship. I gotta do it." I said, "Y. A., stay out—you don't have to play. You're hurt. You can't do it." Now, I told him— one of the greatest quarterbacks of all time—don't play the second half. I said, "We got 'em. We got three points on 'em. That's all we need. Don't do it."

Dick Modzelewski: Years ago, guys were expected to play hurt—it was that way. I know when I was coaching, if one of my players got hurt, I was told, "Don't force him to play." So my job depended on him, and if he's hurt and he could play and he doesn't want to play because it might jeopardize his career, we were told to keep him out of the ballgame. Well, years ago, you didn't have any agents looking after your interests. You had to play. I got my back hurt against the Cardinals one year in Yankee Stadium and it put me in the hospital. I was in there for three days and all I got was a hot water bottle. Finally they taped me with analgesic balm from my shoulders down to my back and sent me home. Tom Landry told me what the game plan was and I played the next game. I played in a hundred and eighty consecutive games and broke Leo Nomellini's record for that. I'm paying for it now, but I'd do it all over again. I loved every minute of it.

Tittle answered the bell for the next round.

Jack Cavanaugh: Y. A. just had no mobility, couldn't get set; couldn't pass. The Bears knew he couldn't pass, knew he wasn't going to run.

Y. A. Tittle: I couldn't move and hobbled around. I wasn't as effective as I should have been. I was a sitting duck. I couldn't move around the pocket. I couldn't run. I just had to stand there and throw it. It handicapped me. It handicapped my team.

Greg Larson: And the footing was so bad—that didn't help him at all.

Jerry Hillebrand: That tough old bird came right back out there. Changed it up and came right out and played the rest of the game. I've got to give him credit for that.

Ed O'Bradovich: I was licking my chops thinking that poor kid was going to be back out there, but I'll be goddamned, who comes out for the third quarter? That little bald-headed guy. I tip my hat to Y. A. Tittle. He took a beating in that game—especially in the second half. I don't know how he did it, as injured as he was. What a man! What a football player he was. As a player and as an opponent, to this day I appreciate something like that because it was unbelievable.

Future Hall of Famer Hugh McElhenny, Tittle's old teammate from San Francisco where, along with Joe "the Jet" Perry and John Henry Johnson, he was a member of the Million-Dollar Backfield, was playing out the end of his career as a bit of an NFL vagabond. He had been with the expansion Vikings in 1961 and 1962 and spent 1963 with the Giants, returning kicks and spelling the starters in the backfield. Now thirty-five years old, he hauled in the opening kickoff of the second half at the 7-yard line and very nearly broke the game open right then. For the next several seconds, he looked like the King of old, wending his way upfield until he was finally hauled down at the Bears' 47 by Rosey Taylor. On third and 6, Tittle completed his first attempted pass since the injury, hitting Joe Morrison for a first down to the 35. On first and 10 he went for the gut, but missed Gifford in the end zone.

On the next play, the flip side of the Joe Walton trade came back to haunt the Giants. When they had swapped for Walton in 1961, they had given up defensive back Dave Whitsell, whom they had just gotten from the Lions in a trade. Whitsell refused to go to Washington, however, and a deal had to be worked out in which he eventually became a Bear. It was in this guise that he tangled with Shofner for the possession of Tittle's next pass and came out the winner at the 26-yard line.

For the first time that day, the Bears really began to move the ball. Wade dumped a screen to Joe Marconi, who took it 19 yards. On second down he hit Marconi again, this time down to the Giants' 21. His next three throws missed their marks, however, including an attempted scoring strike to Angelo Coia, broken up by Jimmy Patton in the end zone. That brought on Roger LeClerc to try the game-tying field goal, but he yanked it left from 28 yards out.

Later in the quarter it seemed as though the Giants might be able to survive the incapacitation of their quarterback by keeping things simple on offense and continuing to hold the Bears at bay. On first and 10 from their own 35, though, that hope evaporated. Tittle tried another screen pass but was pressured by Fred Williams.

Ed O'Bradovich: Joe Fortunato called the play. He said, "Watch for the screen." I was rushing and then I sensed this could be a screen, so I took a step or two out into the flat and I'll be damned: He threw the ball and I put my left paw out and brought it in.

He was hauled down at the Giants' 14.

Jerry Hillebrand denied Marconi on an end-zone pass on first down and Bull went nowhere on second. Facing a third and 9, it appeared as though the Bears might at least be held to a field-goal attempt. But Ditka cut over the middle and took in Wade's pass at the 9. Pesonen hit him and tried to wrestle him down, finally doing so at the 1-yard line. Wade attempted two sneaks, breaking through on the second to give Chicago the 14–10 lead.

Now, like it or not, the Giants were going to have to throw. The Bears knew this and responded by pulling a linebacker in favor of a fifth defensive back, J. C. Caroline. Joe Morrison put New York just across midfield with a 20-yard run on second down. Tittle threw on first down to Aaron Thomas and was very nearly picked off by Richie Petitbon. A bomb to Gifford fell incomplete and a toss to Shofner, with Whitsell covering, did the same, and the Giants had to punt.

The third quarter turned into the fourth and neither team was getting any traction. Joe Morrison lost a fumble at midfield, but the Bears stalled and LeClerc missed another field-goal attempt.

The Giants took over at their own 20 with 8:22 to go, trailing by 4. They knew they were running out of chances. Morrison gained 7 on first down, but was injured on the play. Although he would come back into the game, the Giants lost three other men to injury that day: Phil King, Tom Scott (who had his arm broken), and guard Bookie Bolin—not to mention the damage done to Tittle.

Alex Webster rushed in to replace Morrison and immediately ran for the first down. On second and 10, Tittle lost control of the ball but fell on it himself. Desperate now, he dumped a pass to Webster over the middle that was good for 18 yards. Ed O'Bradovich almost single-handedly terminated the drive on the next two plays when he forced Tittle to throw out of bounds on first down and then corralled Webster for a 2-yard loss on second.

Once more the possession hung in the balance, and once more Tittle found an open man to preserve the drive. This time it was to Gifford for 16. Tittle went long on first down but overthrew Thomas, who was open at the Bears' 10. Morrison, freshly returned to the game, caught a screen pass on second down, but for no gain. On third, Tittle went for broke. His target was Gifford, but two things happened to disrupt the connection. Larry Morris hit Tittle as he released, causing the ball to wobble, and Gifford slipped at the 5-yard line, allowing the pass to sail into the waiting arms of Chicago's Bennie McRae, who stayed in the end zone for a turnover and a touchback.

With 4:05 left, the Bears looked to Bull to wreck the clock. Wade gave him the ball four straight times, bringing the Bears to the two-minute warning. It was third and 3 a the Bears' 40. If Chicago could convert, the outcome would be academic. The give again was to Bull. He rammed into the line and, with the game in the balance, was swarmed by a desperate Giants defense. He made some headway but was forced down just one foot from the first-down marker and certain victory. With 1:52 showing on the clock, Halas sent out Bobby Joe Green for the punt, which rolled dead on the Giants' 16.

Tittle and the offense came out for a last try. There was 1:38 on the clock and they had one time-out left. Thomas caught the first pass for 10 yards and a first down. Tittle then hit McElhenny for 8 and New York used its last time-out. Another toss to McElhenny netted 12, putting the

Giants on their own 46 with 39 seconds to go. A failed sideline pass followed, and then Gifford hauled one in at the Bears' 40 but was ruled out of bounds. Tittle and Gifford reloaded and went the sideline route again, this time connecting for 15 to the Bears' 39 and stopping the clock. The next pass was out of bounds, leaving the Giants with one last shot.

With just ten seconds to go, Tittle looked for his favorite target, Del Shofner, who had somehow gone the entire game without a catch.

Jack Cavanaugh: Tittle faded back and as Shofner went flying down field as always, Y. A. threw a fifty-yard pass into the end zone, but he overshoots Shofner. Overshoots him! This is a guy with a bad leg, can hardly stand up on his good leg, and he threw a fifty-yard pass!

Doug Atkins: It was a flutter ball to nowhere.

Ed O'Bradovich: One play, anything can happen. I rushed and Y. A. released the ball. I turned around and saw it going up in the air, up in the air, and then it came down right into Richie Petitbon's hands.

Jack Cavanaugh: It was Y. A.'s fifth interception. Furious at himself, he yanked off his helmet, threw it to the ground, and left the field in tears. He was a great competitor and he came that close to pulling it off.

Y. A. Tittle: It was just one of those days.

Alex Webster: We missed so many opportunities. We couldn't get it together.

Doug Atkins: A game like this that's so close—it's just a matter of one play or one penalty. Ronnie Bull had a pretty good game that day and Bill Wade didn't do badly. The offense wasn't outstanding, but it didn't have too many mistakes. They didn't do a whole lot, but they did enough and they didn't put us in the hole, either.

Ed O'Bradovich: We were the best in the world and nobody could take that away from us. I threw my helmet up in the stands. About twenty-some years later, I got the helmet back from the guy who caught it.

Dick Modzelewski: If Y. A. didn't get banged up in that game, personally I think we would have won. I actually do, because Y. A. was having a good year and was a good quarterback.

THE AFTERMATH

Five hundred loyal fans were there to meet their fallen heroes when they deplaned at John F. Kennedy International Airport. Little did they know that it would be decades before they would again see another group of Giants so talented.

APPENDICES

The Best Three-Year Runs in Giants History

Regardless of what came later in Allie Sherman's Giants tenure, there is no mistaking that he was at the helm when the team had its best sustained regular-season run. While the type of dominance that was possible in the 1920s hasn't been achievable since World War II (the earliest Giants teams outscored their opponents by a ratio of more than three to one), the 1961 to 1963 entries won nearly four out of every five games. This is by far the best sustained showing in team history.

Years	W	L	T	Pct.	PF	PA
1961–1963	33	8	1	.798	1214	783
1937–1939	23	6	4	.758	490	273
1925–1927	27	9	1	.743	466	138
1938–1940	23	7	3	.742	493	297
1929–1931	33	11	2	.739	774	284
1960–1962	28	9	3	.738	1037	764
1950–1952	26	9	1	.736	756	542
1988–1990	35	13	0	.729	1042	767
1939–1941	23	8	2	.727	537	332
1959–1961	26	9	3	.724	923	651
1957–1959	26	10	0	.722	784	564
1958–1960	25	9	2	.722	801	614
1933–1935	28	11	0	.718	571	304
1949–1951	25	10	1	.708	809	609

For our purposes, ties count as a half win and a half loss.

The Best Defensive Efforts in Championship Losses (Since World War II)

There are no consolation prizes in football, unless one considers appearing on a list like this as some sort of reward. These are the teams that lost championship games and surrendered the fewest yards in the process. It is the great misfortune of the Sherman-era Giants to hold the first and third positions on this list. The first three games were all played in extreme weather conditions. It remains likely that they will hold their positions on this list unless the NFL breaks with protocol and schedules an outdoor Super Bowl in the northern regions.

Year	Game	Winner	Loser	Total Yards	Net Passing	Rushing
1963	NFL championship	Chicago Bears 14	New York Giants 10	222	129	93
1948	NFL championship	Philadelphia Eagles 7	Chicago Cardinals 0	232	7	225
1962	NFL championship	Green Bay Packers 16	New York Giants 7	244	96	148
1972	Super Bowl VII	Miami Dolphins 14	Washington Redskins 7	253	69	184
1961	AFL championship	Houston Oilers 10	San Diego Chargers 3	256	177	79

New York Giants vs. Washington Redskins

November 27, 1966

	1	2	3	4	F
New York Giants	0	14	14	13	41
Washington Redskins	13	21	14	24	72

Year in and year out, we watch football games from beginning to end. Why? Because there is always a chance to see something you've never seen before. Know this, though: You could watch every single NFL game for the rest of your born days and, while you may someday see a new record for most points scored, you will never see a game end quite like this one did.

THE GIANTS
Sports history is filled with teams that hang on to an aging core from their glory years for far too long and pay the price. Fewer examples exist, however, of clubs that all too aggressively dismantle their team before it ages and live to regret it. Such a team was the 1966 New York Giants, a club that experienced a series of defensive calamities the likes of which are matched only by franchises long since defunct. It can be argued whether or not the Giants began getting rid of their core defensive players too early. What can't be argued is that the older players' replacements were decidedly of a lower standard.

After their loss to the Bears in the 1963 championship game, the Giants nosedived to a 2–10–2 record in 1964. They bounced back in 1965 to 7–7, but that was illusory. They were outscored 338 to 270, which was an improvement on the previous year's 399 to 241 but still the kind of gap that usually doesn't lead to .500 seasons. What followed was one of the greatest disasters in league history: The Giants allowed 501 points in a fourteen-game season. At 36 points allowed per game, they do not hold the record: The 1950 Baltimore Colts allowed 462 in a twelve-game program, or 41 points per game. The difference between the two teams is that those Colts were a throw-in from a different league where they had been a doormat as well. The Giants were a long-standing franchise that had battled for a title only three years before.

There's an old saying in sports that it's better to trade a player away a year too soon than a year too late. It seems likely that Allie Sherman took that saw a little too much to heart, as the stalwart defense that throttled the Bears in the 1963 NFL championship was now a ghost of its former self. Rosey Grier was the first to go, shipped off to the Rams before the 1963 season for John LoVetere, a player ahead of his time in terms of physical conditioning and dedication to weight lifting. Unfortunately, LoVetere was himself now gone, the victim of a knee injury that ended his career in 1965. Elsewhere on the line, Lane Howell was now with the Eagles and Andy Robustelli was retired. Most infamous, of all the moves, though, was the one that sent Sam Huff to the Redskins.

Dick Modzelewski: My brother Ed and I had a restaurant in Cleveland. In the off-season after 1963, Sam Huff came to visit us, and while he was there Allie Sherman called him at our restaurant and told him that he got traded to the Washington Redskins. Sam came downstairs from the office looking angry, and I said, "What the hell's wrong with you?" And he said, "I just got traded to the Redskins." They were breaking up the defense. But the funny thing now is, two weeks later, I was working at the restaurant, and *I* got a phone call from Allie Sherman to tell me I got traded to Cleveland. Of course, I had a business there with my brother Ed, and I had a home there, but I was a Giant and I was really disappointed. So Sam Huff wound up telling all the rest of the Giants, "Stay the hell out of Modzelewski's restaurant, otherwise they'll trade your ass right out of there." The big thing is, though, it did me a favor, because in 1964 the Browns won the championship.

In the defensive backfield, Erich Barnes was also now with the Browns, and his compatriots Jimmy Patton and Dick Lynch were part-time and slowed by injury respectively (neither would play after 1966). Huff's linebacking colleague Tom Scott was retired and was now actually coaching the linebackers.

Jerry Hillebrand: To lose all those guys, and it was such a close-knit group, and everybody knew exactly what they were doing out there. When I was a rookie, they protected me all the time. I had Barnes on my outside and I had Jim Katcavage right next to me. I had pretty good help both ways there.

Tom Scott: He tried to rebuild the team and it didn't work.

Chuck Mercein: The team was derooted as far as veteran players. We were left with not much. That's why we didn't have too great a team. It was hard playing there then.

While nobody expected the Giants to contend in 1966, neither did anyone think they were headed for disaster. The preseason is usually an indicator of nothing, but no defensive catastrophes befell New York during its exhibition slate other than getting routed 37–10 by the defending-champion Packers. They held their own otherwise. Injury after injury reduced their ranks and destroyed any attempts at cohesion, however. For instance, linebacker Bill Swain was lost for the year before the bell rang.

The Giants broke camp with the veteran journeyman Earl Morrall, whose greatest moments lay ahead with the Colts and Dolphins, as their starting quarterback. By the time of the second Washington meeting, Morrall was sidelined for the season. His replacement, Gary Wood, was relegated to backup duty because of a severely bruised shoulder. This left quarterbacking chores to rookie Tom Kennedy, purchased from Brooklyn of the Continental Football League just the month before. (His coach there had been ex-Giants great Andy Robustelli.) Kennedy was celebrating his twenty-seventh birthday on the day of the Redskins game. He had been at the helm for most of the previous two contests

against Los Angeles and Atlanta and had some typical rookie problems. He fumbled four times, losing three of them. At the time he was
purchased from Brooklyn, he was leading the Continental League in
passing. He had been to preseason camps with the Rams and Steelers,
but his NFL experience prior to joining the Giants was eight minutes
of a 1964 exhibition game.

Mike Ciccolella: Kennedy played for some team in this other league
and the next thing you know he shows up because we had no quarterback and then he's thrown right into the fryer all of a sudden.

Ed Croke: That year—maybe the next year—Alan Alda was going
to play the part of George Plimpton in the movie version of *Paper Lion*,
and he never played quarterback or anything like that. He actually
called the Giant owners and asked if we could help out with a quarterback, maybe work with him, and show him a few pointers. So we told
him—and nobody hardly even knew who Alan Alda was in those
days—to come up to Yankee Stadium. So Alan Alda showed up and
Tom Kennedy took him down to the field and worked him out for
about a half hour, forty minutes. Kennedy told him how to take a
drop, how to hold the ball, and all that kind of shit. Fast-forward about
thirty years: I'm on a plane to Los Angeles and there I see Alan Alda
sitting up in first class. So I looked down at him and I said, "In a pinch,
can you still play quarterback?" And he looked up and I'm wearing a
Giants logo shirt and he kind of scratched his head and I said, "I'm
sure you don't remember me, but I'm the guy that set you up with Tom
Kennedy to take lessons at Yankee Stadium about thirty years ago." He
said, "Oh, that was you? Sit down, I want to talk to you about this." And
then he ended up asking, "Whatever happened to Tom Kennedy?" I
said, "Last I heard, he was a stuntman out of Hollywood."

Fullback Tucker Frederickson, the number-one overall pick in the
1965 draft, was injured and would not play a down all season. Running
back Chuck Mercein had been limited because of damaged kidneys.
Rookie defensive end Jim Garcia was out for the year and his place was
taken by second-year man Glen Condren. The Giants were having

some issues among the linebacking corps as well. At one point after the season-ending injury to linebacker Larry Vargo, they were starting an all-rookie trio of Freeman White, Mike Ciccolella, and Jeff Smith.

Mike Ciccolella: We had two actual linebackers. Larry Vargo was a defensive back and they threw him in at linebacker. The only line-backer that played that game that ever played linebacker was me. I think Freeman White, who was a great receiver from Nebraska, played one defensive linebacker and Larry Vargo, who was a defensive back, played the other linebacker because we had so many injuries. Bill Swain went down. I said to myself, "I'm the only linebacker that actually played in college and high school and in pros." And the other two guys, one was a receiver and the other one was a defensive back. Howard Cosell said, "The New York Giants' linebackers are the worst combined linebackers in NFL history. They gotta be the worst ever." I remember him saying something like that after one of our games, but you gotta remember none of us played line-backer except me. We had the four-three and everybody got hurt.

THE OPPONENT

The Redskins of the mid-sixties were often schedule fillers for the better teams in the league. They had not finished over .500 since 1955, nor would they until Vince Lombardi took over in 1969 and they went 7–5–2 in the gateway season to two decades of excellence. The most points they had scored before week twelve was 33, which they did twice, beating the Steelers 33–27 and the expansion Atlanta Falcons 33–20. Most interestingly, they were the victims of the '66 Giants' finest moment: In week six, New York had registered its sole win against them, a 13–10 triumph.

The Redskins were coached by the great former Browns quarterback Otto Graham, and they were not without talented players. They were led by the flamboyant Sonny Jurgensen at quarterback, a man of such arm strength that he could whip the ball behind his back harder and farther than most mortals could throw it the proper way. He was thirty-two in 1966 and had risen from his apprenticeship with the Eagles in the late fifties to become one of the game's elite field generals. He led the league in passing yards in 1966 and had one of the highest passer ratings (he would lead the NFL in '67). Jurgensen's targets included fellow Hall of Famer Charley Taylor, who was in his third year in the league and had only recently been converted from running back to running pass routes exclusively. He would lead the league in receptions in 1966. Bobby Mitchell was not quite the threat he'd been but was still solid in the flanker-back position. Jerry Smith was coming into his own and would develop into one of the best tight ends of all time.

No team relied less on its running game than the Redskins; they were third in pass attempts and last in rushes. A. D. Whitfield led the team with only 472 yards on the ground but had an impressive 5.1 yards per carry.

On defense, Washington was anchored by middle linebacker Huff. To his right was Chris Hanburger, who would make the first of his nine Pro Bowl appearances that season. In the defensive backfield lurked safety Paul Krause, who had announced his arrival in the NFL by leading the league in interceptions as a rookie in 1964. Naturally, teams were throwing away from him, so the talented cornerback Brig Owens led the team with seven picks and the other corner, Jim Shorter, had five. Krause would eventually break the career interception record of Giant great Emlen Tunnell and be inducted into the Hall of Fame.

The Redskins' home field was D.C. Stadium, later renamed Robert F. Kennedy Stadium. Although it was one of the newer parks in the league, it was not well-known for the quality of its groundskeeping.

Chuck Mercein: That field was the same field where the Washington Senators played. I remember they had the same infield as the Giants did in Yankee Stadium. The infield was all dirt, so if you're in there trying to run the ball you're scraping around and you're practically getting nowhere because it's chopped-up dirt. I remember that part about that stadium, that it was no fun to get scraped when you go down.

HUFF VS. SHERMAN

In Sherman's defense, he was dealing with a roster that was very much heading north on the age-o-meter. As Tex Maule and Morton Sharnik put it in their 1965 season preview for *Sports Illustrated*, "What remains for Sherman is a choice between losing with inexperience or losing with players headed over the hill." Sherman was, essentially, stuck. His identification of the aging problem was correct, but his strategy for solving it left something to be desired. It was simply not enough to denude the team of its oldsters; there had to be qualitative replacements, and there were not. It is not impossible to change talent on the fly and remain competitive. NFL history has its share of teams that managed the trick.

But Sherman had no such success, and nothing better exemplifies the feelings Sherman's purges generated than the effect it had on Sam Huff.

Greg Larson: He had been the subject of that TV show, *The Violent World of Sam Huff,* and I saw that, but I didn't really pay much attention to what he really looked like. So when I came to the Giants, I tried to figure out who he was, which guy was Sam Huff. I actually picked him out in the locker room, but the guy I picked turned out to be Jack Stroud because he was so big and well built and all that. I think Huff played consistently all the years that I ever played with him and against him. He was so smart and could do a talking job on the opponent that had such value to a team. But the press had him underrated and then they had him overrated, and it just went back and forth and I felt sorry for the guy because the press beat him up sometimes. And maybe Allie Sherman listened to all that crap and that's why he traded him, I don't know. Just a very smart player. He was one of the better blitzing guys. He would not just take a straight route, he would start one way and do a hand slap and slide the other way.

Huff thought he was going to be a Giant for all eternity. Instead, on April 10, 1964, he found himself packed off to Washington for twenty-four-year-old defensive lineman Andy Stynchula and defensive back Dick James (who was four months older than Huff). Five years later, Huff was still playing a full slate of games when both Stynchula and James were done with their NFL careers. Huff's age, twenty-nine, at the time of the trade was not the entire cause of his exit.

Sam Huff: Oh, my God, that was hard to take. I didn't do anything but play football for the Giants and work. I lived in New York and I worked for J. P. Stevens selling textiles in the garment district. I lived a clean life and I still do. Why I got traded, I do not know. Well, I do know. It was because Allie Sherman did not like his own defense, and that defense was built around me.

Greg Larson: Sherman just kind of wholesaled a bunch of people, and I don't know why he did it. We weren't the same cohesive team. We were like blood brothers before, and now you got new people in there and it just wasn't the same chemistry.

Huff, by his admission, chafed at the changes Sherman demanded to the defensive system left behind by Tom Landry.

Sam Huff: Well, Sherman won out. They traded me. After he traded Rosey Grier. After he traded Dick Modzelewski. Then me, the heart of the defense. Right out of the middle. Am I supposed to love him? No goddamn way! Print that! I will hate him until the day he dies.

He did have the satisfaction of watching the Giants fall to the nether regions of the Eastern Conference in 1964. On the field, however, New York actually took three of the first five post-trade contests with Huff's new team. By the second meeting of 1966, though, he could see that their defense was in a shambles.

Sam Huff: I said to Sonny Jurgensen, "I don't want you to show any mercy today." He said, "What are you talking about?" I said, "It's the worst defense. Allie Sherman's defense is the worst defense you have ever played against. We used to be the greatest, now they're the worst. They're friends of mine, but they're not friends when it's game time. Show no mercy, Sonny! Score at will!" I said, "I want to get Sherman fired, and we'll get him fired." That's the anger that came out in me. Just talking about it right now—it's still there.

A SEASON FOR THE (DARK) AGES

After rallying from a 14-point deficit to tie the Steelers on the road 34–34 to open the season, the Giants traveled to Dallas and were creamed, 52–7. Sizable but relatively pedestrian beatings at the hands of the Eagles, Browns, and Cardinals followed. In week six, the Giants held the Redskins to just nine first downs and 188 total yards and scored 10 points in the fourth quarter to grab their first victory of the year, 13–10. The following week they tallied an early touchdown on the Eagles, but it was nullified by a penalty and they had to settle for a Pete Gogolak field goal. It was their last good moment, as Philadelphia constantly pressured Morrall and his replacement, Gary Wood. Sherman kept switching them back and forth, but nothing worked regardless of who was calling the signals, and the Eagles triumphed 31–3. Week eight provided a close loss to the first-place Cardinals. The Giants rallied late and were driving for the go-ahead touchdown when Wood's foot slipped and he was picked off by Hall of Fame safety Larry Wilson. Considering the Cards were favored by two touchdowns, the 20–17 loss was unexpectedly close. Then came their lone interconference game.

Ed Croke: We went out to Los Angeles to play the Rams. We were practicing out there. Allie took me aside—you know he's such a paranoid guy, he's running around all worried because he thinks they've got people spying on us. He wants the security guys to keep people from watching the practice. Tom Kennedy goes, "What the hell are people gonna learn from our practices?" Jesus Christ, that's how bad we were.

Mike Ciccolella: We had had fifty-two points scored on us earlier. Then the Rams killed us. In that game Henry Carr intercepted a pass and went a hundred and six or a hundred and seven yards and set a record for an interception back for a touchdown. That was on defense. We scored one other touchdown and they beat us Fifty-five to fourteen. In fairness to that game, we went to Disneyland and stayed there for a whole week. It was unheard of that you do that. We went out there and practiced in Anaheim. The hotel we were staying at had these great rolls, and I think half the team gained seven pounds that one week and we all went into the game overweight and got fifty-five points scored on us. That was a massacre. That was terrible.

Jerry Hillebrand: We had a struggling team at the time, so Sherman decided to put a few defensive guys on the bench. I don't know what he was trying to prove—I guess trying to get younger guys in there, give them a shot and get some experience.

After the beating at the hands of the Rams, Sherman benched five starters and moved nine men either to starting roles or new positions. It didn't work. In fact, in a season of humiliations, the next game may have been the worst of all. The Giants were hosting the Atlanta Falcons, a brand-new team with an 0–9 record. They had surrendered 35 points per game, a bit more than the Giants. New York was favored to win, but Atlanta opened the game with a 69-yard scoring drive and never surrendered the lead. Another ex-Giant out for revenge was fullback Ernie Wheelwright, who contributed two touchdowns to the Falcons' 27–16 victory. Having been left open for the expansion draft by New York, he jubilantly tossed the balls into the stands after both scores.

THE GAME

That brought the 1–8–1 Giants to Washington to meet the Redskins, Though just 5–6, and having scored only three points against Cleveland the week before, Washington was installed as a 21-point favorite.

Tucker Frederickson: I was sitting there in a cast. Earl Morrall was sitting next to me. We had half the team in civilian clothes.

For a game that produced such a plethora of points, though, it took a while for someone to light up the scoreboard. The Redskins didn't dent the end zone until 7:28 of the first quarter. The score was set up when Kennedy was intercepted by Owens on his very first pass attempt. Washington converted when A. D. Whitfield caught a 5-yard pass from Jurgensen, but Charlie Gogolak's extra-point attempt was blocked by Jim Moran. What followed was a designed harassment of Kennedy that did much to shake him. Huff and the Redskins' defense were showing blitz on nearly every play—and following through often enough to make each threat look real.

Brig Owens: On the sideline, Sonny would say, "You guys have got to hold 'em." And Sam would say, "Just keep scoring!"

And score they did. Whitfield tore off a 63-yard run to make it 13–0 at the end of the first quarter. On the ensuing Giants possession, Hanburger got into the New York backfield and hit Kennedy from the blind side, forcing a fumble. Owens scooped up the errant ball at the Washington 38 and ran it the other way for a score.

Brig Owens: Things just seemed to fall in place. I was in the right place at the right time to pick up that fumble and also make a couple of interceptions. Things just worked out.

Down 20–0, the Giants didn't quit. Kennedy moved them downfield; the biggest play of the drive was a 35-yard completion to Aaron Thomas. Allen Jacobs cashed in from the 6 to make it 20–7. It would be the only touchdown of Jacobs's career.

The next two Redskin scores were set up by Kennedy interceptions. The first opportunity was converted on a carry by Whitfield and the second by the legendary Joe Don Looney, who ran the ball in from the 9-yard line.

Chuck Mercein: Sam Huff was screaming at Allie Sherman any time he got near the bench. Oh my God, he was just swearing at him and yelling at him. "How do you like me now?" He was absolutely beside himself with anger.

Tucker Frederickson: Every time they scored, he'd come by the bench and take his shots at Allie.

With the score 34–7 and Kennedy looking a tad shell-shocked, Sherman inserted Gary Wood at quarterback. The Redskins were the major contributor to the Giants' next drive, getting called for pass interference to the tune of 45 yards. Wood finished it off himself with a 1-yard plunge.

Brig Owens: The thing about the game was that things were happening so fast. We kept scoring and then they'd score. We'd get a turnover—an interception—and we would score, but then they'd answer. We were frustrated because we weren't able to do a better job on defense.

The third quarter was all about the long ball. New York and Washington exchanged scoring salvos: Wood hit Joe Morrison for a 41-yard score. Jurgensen connected with Charley Taylor for 32. Next, Wood and Homer Jones hooked up for 50. Then, having the last laugh, Jurgensen found Taylor again, this time for 74 yards. When the air stopped humming from all the action, Washington led 48–28.

GOGOLAK VS. GOGOLAK

Apart from everything else going on at D.C. Stadium that day, it was also the second professional meeting of the Gogolak brothers, Pete and Charlie, the placekickers for the Giants and Redskins, respectively. They had escaped from Hungary with their parents in the wake of the anti-Soviet revolution of 1956 and ended up starting a revolution of their own in their adopted country. Settling in upstate New York, they discovered that nobody was playing their brand of "football" at their schools. So they adapted their soccer style of kicking to the American game and pretty much changed the entire face of football. Pete, the elder by three years, headed off to Cornell while Charlie followed him to the Ivy League, going to Princeton. By the time they met in the Princeton-Cornell game in 1963, they were something of a national sensation because of their unique approach to that most basic of football procedures. It is probably hard today to understand just how jarring it was to see a kicker lining up to approach the ball from an angle. To most, it seemed like something between freakish and novel—like the occasional barefoot kicker. Not many were predicting that it would completely supplant the straight-on approach within a generation.

Pete was drafted by the Buffalo Bills of the AFL, becoming the first soccer-style kicker in the pro ranks. He caused a different sort of sensation when his contract was up.

Pete Gogolak: The pro leagues were drafting the same college players, so the players were getting offers to play for both the NFL and the AFL. I played two years for the Bills. I had a two-year contract that I signed with them in 1964. I had a one-year obligation and a one-year option. I played out my option, so I became a free agent. I signed with the Giants. This was the first time an active player jumped from one league to the other. That's when the war started. Al Davis started calling Giant players, and San Diego signed John Hadl and a couple of other players. In about five months, the two leagues merged and became the NFL. I guess I was a catalyst.

Pete's brother Charlie was drafted by both leagues. The Kansas City Chiefs took him in the seventh round, but the Redskins made history when they used their first-round pick to make him the sixth player chosen in the 1966 NFL draft. No pure kicker had ever been taken that high before. (Charlie and Garo Yepremian of the Lions became the second and third soccer-style kickers in pro football.) It wasn't long before the brothers met as opponents again, this time as pros.

Pete Gogolak: In the first game, when we won thirteen to ten, the novelty was for my parents. Mother sat on one side of the stadium and Father sat on the other side. To them it would have been a perfect game if it was ten-ten.

In the second meeting, Charlie tied Bob Waterfield's all-time record for most extra points in a game (see "The Highest Combined Scores in History," page 128), while the brothers combined for 14 PATs, also a record.

Charlie Gogolak: The game should have had two more points. You know, in college I kicked fifty straight extra points to beat the record of forty-four for an NCAA record back then. So for both of us to miss an extra point in that game was pretty darn unusual.

The Gogolaks met five times on the field: This was the one occasion in which Charlie outscored Pete, and the one time that Charlie's team beat Pete's. The elder brother had an 8–2 point advantage when Cornell crushed Princeton 51–14 in 1963. He outscored Charlie 7–4 in their first pro meeting in 1966, while Charlie bested Pete 12–5 in this game. They met twice in 1968 and Pete triumphed 12–3 and 7–4. A fifth pro meeting was possible in 1970 after Charlie had moved on to the Patriots, but Gino Cappelletti was kicking for Boston when the Giants traveled there. Cappelletti missed a 14-yard field-goal attempt that day while Pete was registering 10 of the Giants' 16 points in their shutout victory. Charlie took over the kicking for Boston the next week.

Charlie's most famous kick, though, was about to unfold in this game.

THE FOURTH QUARTER

The average combined score for an NFL game in 1966 was about 46 points. The Giants and Redskins had nearly doubled that in just three quarters. The fourth quarter, though, would be even more prolific.

Greg Larson: We were coming back in the huddle and I said, "You know, by the grace of God, you guys, we can still win this game!" Everybody looked at me funny and there were actually a couple chuckles. You have to be optimistic, right? I don't think anybody left the stadium for that game because every time somebody touched the ball there was a touchdown.

New York stalled deep in its own territory, setting up something the game had not yet had: a special-teams touchdown. Rickie Harris gathered in Ernie Koy's punt just past midfield and took it back all the way to make the score 55–28. The Redskins scored again immediately as Owens tallied his second touchdown of the day on a 62-yard pickoff of a Gary Wood pass. At that point Sherman reinserted Kennedy, who responded by leading the Giants downfield, culminating in an 18-yard scoring strike to Aaron Thomas. Pete Gogolak's kick was wide, so the score now stood at 62–34.

The Giants got the ball back quickly and Kennedy was really finding his rhythm. He hit Joe Morrison for 39 yards, setting up a 1-yard plunge by ex-Redskin Danny Lewis (the last touchdown of his career). By this time, the Redskins had lost three running backs to injury.

Whitfield, Joe Don Looney, and Steve Thurlow were all sidelined for good. Otto Graham looked to his flankerback, Bobby Mitchell, to fill the void.

"He doesn't even know the plays from that position," Graham admitted after the game. Mitchell hadn't carried the ball regularly since his Cleveland days in 1961, logging only six rushes since then. Naturally, because it was that kind of game, he responded with a 45-yard run off tackle that went for a touchdown, making the score 69–41.

THE FINAL THREE

The regular-season record for most points in a game was 70. (See "The Highest Combined Scores in History," page 128). As the Giants took possession in the waning moments of the game, it appeared as though the Redskins, playing defense while sitting on 69 points, were not going to be able to beat the mark. New York was deep in their own territory, not moving the ball, and staring at fourth down.

Chuck Mercein: I remember telling Tom to just give me the damn ball or run the thing. He kept throwing, which was a valiant thing because we weren't going to make up that many points.

Brig Owens: If we could have scored a hundred points, Sam would have wanted a hundred points.

Unfortunately, Kennedy thought it was *third* down. So with seven seconds left on the clock and the Giants 77 yards away from the Redskins' end zone, he intentionally threw one out of bounds to stop the clock—which it did, except Washington took over.

Sam Huff: I was a player-coach, and I yelled for a time-out, so they gave it to us. Seven seconds on the clock. Sonny came to the sidelines, and he said, "Who in the hell called time-out?" I said, "Me." He said, "What did you do that for?" I said, "Charlie Gogolak needs the practice."

Brig Owens: Sonny said, "Sam, enough is enough."

Huff was not the only ex-Giant on the Redskin sidelines spoiling for revenge and more points. After the first game of the regular season, Sherman looked to bolster his offensive line and made a trade with Washington to bring back fan favorite Darrell Dess. The former Pro Bowler had been with New York from 1959 to 1964 and was swapped back into the fold in exchange for linebacker Jim Carroll and running back Steve Thurlow.

Steve Thurlow: Jim had been drafted out of Notre Dame the previous year. I was in my third year with the Giants. I believe I started all nineteen games the previous year—five exhibition games and fourteen regular-season games with the Giants—and had a good year and really thought I'd be there for a long time. So, as would be the case with anyone in that kind of circumstance, it's natural to have a negative feeling toward people who made a decision to trade you. I would watch their scores as much as I would watch our scores. That sounds terrible. I was hoping they'd lose every game, even though most of my friends were with the Giants. I don't think it was that abnormal a reaction. I was very angry with Allie Sherman.

Chuck Mercein: Kennedy gave the Redskins a chance to rub it in—and did they ever!

Steve Thurlow: Otto Graham was a great guy, but kind of a pushover. He came off as a real tough, hard-nosed kind of guy, saying things like "I'd never have Jim Brown on my College All-Star team, because he doesn't block"—stuff like that—but the bottom line is that he was kind of a pussycat. Sam, Jim Carroll, and I went to him— I'm sure it was at Sam's instigation—and said, "Otto, you've got to kick a field goal against these guys."

Brig Owens: Sam wanted to do the kicking. I said, "Sam, when's the last time you kicked a field goal?" He said, "I can kick it."

Charlie Gogolak: Well, I didn't find out the complete story on this until years and years afterwards. In the late nineteen nineties I was watching ESPN Classic on a sleepy Saturday afternoon and they were doing this special on Sam Huff, so I kind of perked up and said to myself, I better watch that. They went through his high school career and his days at West Virginia and New York and then he says, "We were in D.C. Stadium and the Giants were playing the Redskins and we were winning sixty-nine to forty-one and we had this kicker Charlie Gogolak. We had only seven seconds left in the game. I put my hands around my mouth and kind of leaned down and shouted as loud as I could, 'Field goal team get in there.' So he said he actually called the play, and not Otto Graham.

Sam Huff: I don't like to dislike somebody. I don't like to do that. On a football field, I could take out my anger. I have no way of taking out my anger about that. But I did, when we scored seventy-two points against the Giants.

Charlie Gogolak: I still remember it was a low, line-drive knuckleball that just barely made it from twenty-nine or thirty yards.

Tucker Frederickson: Otto Graham was our coach in the College All-Star Game and he was a nice guy, but I guarantee this: I was watching Sam Huff go right up to him, saying, "Kick the field goal."

Mike Ciccolella: It just was rubbing it in to Allie Sherman. Huff hated him so much.

Charlie Gogolak: Of course, I never minded going in to kick a field goal. I relished every chance or every opportunity I had. I took a lot of heat and the Redskins took a lot of heat in the press the next day as to why they would run up the score. Allie Sherman wouldn't shake hands with Otto Graham. But over the years I had friends who were Giants fans who would say, "You shouldn't have gone in there to kick that." I said to myself, "My God—I'm a rookie kicker and it's not for me to tell the coach not to go and kick!"

Pete Gogolak: We couldn't believe it. It's kind of a gentlemen's agreement. When you are way ahead, basically, you sit on the ball, and that's it. It was just bad blood between the Giants and the Redskins, and it was not the right thing to do. It was pretty bad. Nobody could believe it, and everybody was upset in the locker room after the game. Not just the way we played, which was horrible, but rubbing it in like that was a very unpleasant experience.

Ed Croke: When the game was over and they asked Otto Graham, "Why'd you put that guy in?" Otto said, "Well, we just wanted to make sure he got enough work during the day." As if nine extra points isn't enough. Then you find out later on that the guy that really made Otto Graham take the time-out was Sam Huff.

Steve Thurlow: Of course Otto caught a lot of heat for the rest of his life for having done that. Obviously we shouldn't have kicked a field goal. It was a stupid thing to do, but in the heat of the deal, that's what happened.

Mike Ciccolella: When it was over, everybody seemed to be shocked. There wasn't any arguing going on or fights or anything like that. It was like shock, but they all knew how bad the defense was, but like I say it wasn't just the defense. It was just a terrible year. To be honest with you, I was a rookie and I couldn't completely grasp the fact. But there were guys that didn't show up and guys that were angry. And I'm talking about the old pros like Dick Lynch and so on. They did not like Allie Sherman. And I loved him, of course. He liked the way I played football. I was happy with him, but a lot of guys just weren't happy. A lot of the old vets weren't happy and I think that was just part of the entire year. And of course when you're losing, things like that happen. People get upset and they gotta get upset at somebody, so they're gonna get upset with the coaching staff.

THINGS THAT CONTINUE TO FASCINATE

This game can generate pages of factoids. Some of the highlights:

- Somehow, in between the sixteen touchdowns and one field goal, there were a total of ten punts in the game. The Giants gained more first downs than Washington (twenty-five to sixteen) and ran twenty-nine more plays.

- While it is quite routine for a team to outgain its opponent and still lose, one would not expect it in a game decided by 31 points. New York had 389 yards to Washington's 341. (Washington had –2 net passing yards at halftime.)

- This being the pre-net era, the Redskins complained that they lost $315 worth of footballs (a little over two thousand dollars at the modern rate of exchange). Thirteen balls were kicked into the stands on extra points and a fourteenth was tossed to the crowd by a jubilant Brig Owens after one of his touchdown returns.

- Throughout history, the thirty-two current NFL franchises have produced forty-four teams that had either zero or one victory. Of these forty-four teams, only one managed to score at least 40 points in a game. That was, of course, the '66 Giants, who did it in consecutive weeks and lost both games.

- Prior to the 1966 season, Washington sent veteran defensive back Jim Steffen and a fifth-round draft choice to the Dallas Cowboys for Brig Owens, tackle Mitch Johnson, and guard Jake Kupp. They also purchased running back A. D. Whitfield from Dallas around the same time. A series of injuries prevented Steffen from playing another down in the NFL, but the Redskins got their money's worth from those two deals in this game alone: Whitfield and Owens combined for five touchdowns.

- With 48, the Redskins and Giants fell far short of the NFL record for most points in a first half. It had been set four seasons prior on December 16, 1962, by St. Louis (31) and Philadelphia (28). Unlike the Redskins and Giants, however, those two clubs slacked off to a 45–35 final in favor of St. Louis. That record has been eclipsed since, and is currently held by Philadelphia (42) and Detroit (21), registered on September 23, 2007. (They also had a quiet second half, though, as the final was 56–21.) The Houston Oilers and Oakland Raiders set the AFL record for first-half points, going to the intermission tied at 35 on December 22, 1963.

- The Giants and Redskins' record of 65 points in the second half held for thirty-eight years and a day. It was finally broken by the

Cleveland Browns (35) and Cincinnati Bengals (31) on November 28, 2004. (See "The Highest Combined Scores in History," page 128.)

THE LEGACY

The losing continued. The Giants built a 20-point lead over Cleveland the following week and were still holding on with 1:20 to go in the fourth quarter before finally succumbing 49–40. (It's no mean feat to score 81 points in two weeks and lose twice. The Redskins allowed 31 points the following week and won, another nifty trick: allowing 72 points in consecutive weeks and coming away 2–0.) The Giants allowed another 47 points to Pittsburgh in week thirteen in a game that saw Kennedy throw four touchdown passes without an interception. For all of Kennedy's lapses in poise, he did have the sixth-highest passer rating among NFL quarterbacks who had a minimum of 100 attempts in 1966. It would be his only year in the big leagues, though.

New York's season died with a whisper, as the Cowboys came to town already having clinched the conference title and looking to rest their regulars. Jerry Rhome started in place of Don Meredith and Dallas came away with a modest 17–7 victory.

It would be another two years before New York would get a 1966-style clobbering. That time it was a 45–10 loss to Cleveland during the Giants' disastrous four-game losing streak to close out the 1968 season, a run that evened the team's record after a 7–3 start. It is an illustration of the Maras' loyalty that Sherman managed to hang on to his job after that debacle, following as it did the collapse of 1964 and the disaster of 1966—but he did. It wasn't until the preseason of 1969 that the family-run team finally ran out of patience with Sherman's leadership. When the Giants lost all five of their exhibition games, Mara had heard enough of Giant fans singing "Goodbye, Allie"—their theme song of the past five years—and made the switch to a very surprised Alex Webster.

Mike Ciccolella: My claim to fame is that I called the defensive signals as a middle linebacker for the Giants in the highest-scoring game in NFL history. And it's still the record. I used to say, "Hey, defensive coordinator Pop Ivy sent the signals into me, so it wasn't all my fault."

Sam Huff: It's not that I disliked the Giants. I loved the Giants. I am still great friends with the Mara family. I still think about them all the time. They still treat me great. One guy calls it all, and you turn everything over to the head coach. You're turning over a multimillion-dollar thing over to a head coach, and that's what they did. He hated his own people. He had to. Why would you get rid of your own defense? The record stands for itself. They built it back eventually after they fired him. It took a long time, it really did. It's hard to overcome. Once you go down in sports, once you lose that thing, it's very difficult to get the momentum back and get that camaraderie back. It's a balanced league. You got the draft choices. You got agents now. It's pretty difficult nowadays. It wasn't so difficult then.

Mike Ciccolella: I was named the Rookie of the Year for the Giants. No big deal, it was a bad year, but nonetheless I was named Rookie of the Year for the New York Giants in 1966. And I sent a letter out. I wish I would've grabbed that letter, but out it went to Wellington T. Mara. It said how I had a good year and was named Rookie of the Year and how I wanted a raise from—I think I signed for nine thousand dollars that year, plus a thousand-dollar bonus. In fact, my teammates used to make fun of me, saying, "When we get our checks, we'd all go to the bank to cash ours, but he'd go to the delicatessen to cash his." When you're a starter and a rookie, they'll make fun of you.

I wrote this letter asking for a raise to eighteen thousand and he wrote back—and I can remember the words verbatim: "With a record of one, twelve, and one in 1966, the worst record in New York Giants history, a person should not ask whether he deserves a raise, but whether he has a job when he comes back." Honest to God, that's basically what it said. And I signed the letter for twelve thousand and sent it back.

Frank Gifford: Jack Whitaker and I did that game together on CBS television. It was bizarre and embarrassing because I was still a

Giants fan. Wellington Mara was my presenter when I went into the Hall of Fame. When he went into the Hall of Fame, I was his presenter. We had a wonderful relationship, and I hated to see that happen. I remember that Allie Sherman was trying to change his team too quickly. There were too many moves in one year. He started trading players around the league, and they were great players. He affected these players emotionally, and it affected them on the field.

Brig Owens: I really only look at the fact that we won. I am a very poor loser. I don't even let my grandkids beat me at anything.

Charlie Gogolak: Nothing stands forever. But it's just fun to have a record. I remember a few years back. Cleveland and Cincinnati were playing and the game turned out to be something like fifty-eight to forty-eight or some such number. It was just below a hundred and ten points. I said to my wife, "Oh, boy, I know in the papers tomorrow they are going to be mentioning the seventy-two-to-forty-one game. That this came pretty close to tying the highest-scoring game." I would clearly rather have the longest field goal or the best field-goal percentage, but you can't have what you want. So I am happy to land with this one, and it's pretty historic that two brothers were playing in the same game.

Mike Ciccolella: I was listening to a local radio sports show one time and they asked this trivia question: "What is the highest-scoring game of all time?" I called in and got it exactly right. They said, "How do you know that?" I told them, "Hell, I played in the game—I ought to know what the final score was."

APPENDICES

The Highest Combined Scores in History

The Redskins and Giants broke an eighteen-year-old NFL record (and three-year-old professional record) with their scorefest. Their combined mark, though, has stood the test of time, lasting nearly five decades.

113: Washington Redskins 72, New York Giants 41
November 27, 1966

106: Cincinnati Bengals 58, Cleveland Browns 48
November 28, 2004
With 1:43 left and trailing 51–48, the Browns were trying to get down the field to create the first 50-plus-point tie in league history. Instead, Deltha O'Neal picked off a Kelly Holcomb pass and took it 31 yards in the opposite direction to break the century mark and seal the game for the Bengals. Before that, Holcomb had thrown five touchdown passes and Cincinnati's Carson Palmer had tossed four of his own.

101: Oakland Raiders 52, Houston Oilers 49
December 22, 1963
This game broke the American Football League mark, previously set by the Los Angeles Chargers (50) and New York Titans (43) in 1960. It could well have been the highest-scoring tie ever, but Mike Mercer's 39-yard field goal with 4:37 left iced it for the Raiders in the presence of 17,401 (announced) fans. (On November 21, 1948, the San Francisco 49ers beat the Brooklyn Dodgers 63–40. At 103 points, this was the highest-scoring game in the four-year history of the All-America Football Conference.)

99: Seattle Seahawks 51, Kansas City Chiefs 48
November 27, 1983; overtime
Curt Warner rushed for 207 yards for the Seahawks as they were the last team standing in this battle of lead changes. Norm Johnson tied it with a field goal in the fourth quarter and then, following a 47-yard

kickoff return by Zachary Dixon to start overtime, he won it with his third 42-yard field goal.

98: Chicago Cardinals 63, New York Giants 35
October 17, 1948

The defending-champion Cardinals came into New York and combined with the Giants to obliterate the league record for total points, which had been set the year before when Philadelphia beat Washington 45–42. Charlie Conerly threw for four touchdowns and scored one himself in the losing cause.

98: San Diego Chargers 54, Pittsburgh Steelers 44
December 8, 1985

The Steelers overcame a 17-point deficit and held a 44–41 lead in the fourth quarter when the Chargers scored the go-ahead touchdown. They left a ray of hope for Pittsburgh, however, when the extra point was missed, keeping the score at 47–44. On the first play from scrimmage after the ensuing kickoff, rookie safety Jeffery Dale grabbed David Woodley's pass and ran it 47 yards the other way for the final score.

97: Los Angeles Rams 70, Baltimore Colts 27
November 22, 1950

The Rams lost 162 yards on penalties, had three passes picked off, and coughed up one fumble. Still, they managed to set the all-time record for touchdowns in a regular season game with ten (a record tied by the Redskins in 1966). Had Bob Waterfield attempted the last point after touchdown (instead of Elroy Hirsch), he would own the single-game record for PATs with 10.

96: Arizona Cardinals 51, Green Bay Packers 45
January 10, 2010; wild-card playoff; overtime

In what is the highest-scoring game in playoff history, the two teams combined for 1,024 yards as Green Bay fought back from a 31–10 deficit to eventually send the game into overtime. After mostly allowing the Packers to move at will, the Arizona defense came up with a strip and score at 13:42 of overtime to win it. Arizona's Kurt Warner and Green

Bay's Aaron Rodgers combined to throw for 800 yards and nine touchdowns.

96: Cleveland Browns 51, Cincinnati Bengals 45
September 16, 2007

The two Ohio teams put up their second top-ten scoring effort in four years. Carson Palmer had a chance to throw seven touchdown passes and lead the Bengals to a one-point victory in the process, but he was picked off with twenty-seven seconds left, 21 yards from the Cleveland end zone. Derek Anderson tossed five touchdown passes for the winners.

96: New York Jets 51, Miami Dolphins 45
September 21, 1986; overtime

Fellow 1983 first-round draftees Ken O'Brien and Dan Marino combined for 884 passing yards. With under two minutes to play and trailing by seven, O'Brien—who had just been hit in the groin—drove the Jets downfield. A hook and lateral brought the ball to the Miami 21 with five seconds left. Despite a secondary full of eight Dolphins, Wesley Walker dove to catch a pass at the 1 and rolled in for the tying score (with PAT) as regulation time expired. He also caught the game winner—his fourth TD catch on the day—2:35 into overtime.

95: Green Bay Packers 48, Washington Redskins 47
October 17, 1983

This was the highest-scoring game in Monday Night Football history, as well as the highest-scoring one-point game ever. The Packers owned and lost six different leads before finally overcoming the Redskins for good with fifty-four seconds left in the game on Jan Stenerud's 20-yard field goal. Washington went right back down the field and had a chance to win, except Mark Moseley missed a 39-yard field-goal attempt with three ticks left on the clock.

95: Philadelphia Eagles 58, Detroit Lions 37
December 30, 1995; wild-card playoff

The Eagles were cruising with a 51–7 lead midway through the third quarter when the Lions poured in 30 points. The high tally was boosted by Detroit going for two-point conversions after each of their last two touchdowns, converting both times. It was the highest-scoring playoff game of all time until the Cardinals and Packers broke the record.

The Giants' Worst Beatdowns

What is the Giants' worst loss ever? We're not talking about the last-second heartbreakers, or the messy performances like their 1984 loss to the Rams in which they set the league record by allowing three safeties, rushed for only eight yards, and missed both extra points. We're talking about the soul crushers, the losses so convincing and terrible they left the beaten team thankful that it was finally over. While New York allowed ten touchdowns in this game, scoring 41 points of their own suggests that *something* was going right—which might be enough to disqualify it from consideration, except that it does symbolize one of the most promiscuous defensive seasons ever. What follows are the worst beatings ever administered to the Giants, either in terms of total points surrendered, point differential, or one-sidedness. The good news for Giants fans? Most of the games are in the distant past.

Detroit Wolverines 28, Giants 0
October 21, 1928
28-zip doesn't sound so bad, right? It does when you put it in context, though. In the Giants' first ten years, they surrendered 28 points just twice. The previous season—in which they had won the league championship—they gave up just 20 points *all year.* The good news from this game was that the Wolverines' star player, Benny Friedman, became a Giant when Detroit closed up shop after one year of operation and the Maras bought the team. In this game, he scored on a 58-yard run and set up another touchdown with a 40-yard pass while kicking all four extra points. He was a huge factor in getting the Giants to 13–1–1 in 1929.

Chicago Bears 56, Giants 7
November 14, 1943
This was Sid Luckman's seven-touchdown game. (See "The Others," page 82.)

Philadelphia Eagles 45, Giants 0
October 10, 1948

Over six decades later, it remains the highest-scoring shutout loss New York has ever suffered. The Giants crossed midfield only twice and never penetrated the Philadelphia 40. Meanwhile, Eagles tailback Tommy Thompson threw two touchdown passes and ran for another himself. The Eagles blocked several New York kicks and would have won 52–0, except an offside penalty cost them another touchdown. (Coincidentally, the champion Eagles won three games by this same score in 1948.)

Chicago Cardinals 63, Giants 35
October 17, 1948

One week later, the harried New York defense got rolled again. The Eagles and Cardinals were both in the midst of back-to-back division titles while the Giants were rebuilding, and the qualitative differences were on full display in these two games. The Giants remain the only team in history to score five touchdowns in one game while also losing by four touchdowns—and they've done it twice!

Pittsburgh Steelers 63, Giants 7
November 30, 1952

In his book, *The Whole Ten Yards*, Frank Gifford recounted how frustrated he was when the team left him home for its trip to Pittsburgh on account of a pulled groin muscle. Because both Charlie Conerly and backup Fred Benners got injured, Gifford was chafing because he was missing his chance to fill in at quarterback. Then he watched the game on television and saw what the Steelers did to poor Tom Landry, a defensive back pressed into emergency service over center, and his frustration turned into relief. In a light snowstorm, Lynn Chandnois took the opening kickoff 97 yards for a score and Pittsburgh never looked back. They intercepted seven New York passes, blocked a quick kick for a touchdown, and held the Giants to 15 yards rushing. The Giants' lone score was something, though: From his own 30, Landry passed to Bill Stribling, who shuttled the ball to Joe Scott. He then tossed it back to Stribling, who raced for the score. Unfortunately, the Steelers had already scored five touchdowns.

Cleveland Browns 62, Giants 14
December 6, 1953

A 31–7 loss is a pretty sound beating, right? *Two* losses by that score—the exact totals for each half—is downright humiliating. With the division title wrapped up, the Browns started George Ratterman at quarterback in place of Otto Graham. Ratterman threw three touchdown passes before Graham, in a brief tune-up appearance in the fourth quarter, tossed a TD pass of his own. (The Giants had held the Browns to just seven points in their first meeting that season.).

Green Bay Packers 37, Giants 0
December 31, 1961

New York has had some rough losses in championship games—26–7 to the Lions in 1935, 27–0 to the Packers in 1939, 28–0 to the Redskins in 1943, and 34–7 to the Ravens in Super Bowl XXXV—but this was the worst. New York drove early, but Kyle Rote dropped a pass at the Packers' 10 and it was all Green Bay after that. They converted two Y. A. Tittle interceptions and a Joe Morris fumbled punt return into short scoring drives. Paul Hornung scored 19 points for the winners and received a Corvette as the game's MVP. Immediately after the game, ex-Giants offensive coordinator Vince Lombardi called his Packers the "greatest team in NFL history."

Dallas Cowboys 52, Giants 7 *and* Los Angeles Rams 55, Giants 14
September 18, *and* November 13, 1966

The Giants have allowed 50 or more points only ten times in their history, and three of those occasions came in 1966. In the Dallas game, future Giants coach Dan Reeves got the start at halfback for the injured Mel Renfro and caught three touchdown passes from Don Meredith. Dandy Don got to five before getting pulled by coach Tom Landry in the third quarter. Two months later the Rams were struggling when the Giants came to town, but got right in a hurry and set a league record with thirty-eight first downs (a record that's been topped just twice since).

San Francisco 49ers 44, Giants 3
January 15, 1994; divisional playoff

It was just a bad day all around. The Giants failed to pressure Steve Young, allowing him to pass at will, and Ricky Watters found the end zone five times. New York's vaunted rushing attack was held to 41 yards and the Giants didn't pick up a first down until late in the first half. Then, to put the rotten cherry on the poison sundae, Lawrence Taylor announced his retirement just after the game.

The Worst Giants Teams of All Time

For sustained losing, the 1973–1974 Giants have no match in team history. Their combined run of 4–23–1 is the low ebb of the franchise over a two-year period. For one season, though, it's hard to argue with the '66 entry. Even removing the infamous 72–41 game from their points differential, they still have the lowest expected won-loss percentage of any Giants team. Here are the ten worst Giants entries of all time, based on expected won-loss percentage.* Any New York team with a bad won-loss record that you don't see on this list (such as the 3–12–1 team of 1983) was better than the actual record indicated, at least in terms of points scored and allowed.

Season	Record	Points For	Points Against	Expected Wins	Expected Losses	Expected Pct.*
1966	1–12–1	263	501	2.5	11.5	.179
1928	4–7–2	79	136	2.8	10.2	.215
1980	4–12–0	249	425	3.5	12.5	.219
1964	2–10–2	241	399	3.3	10.7	.236
1947	2–8–2	190	309	2.9	9.1	.242
2003	4–12	243	387	4.0	12.0	.250
1973	2–11–1	226	362	3.5	10.5	.250
1971	4–10–0	228	362	3.5	10.5	.250

Season	Record	Points For	Points Against	Expected Wins	Expected Losses	Expected Pct.*
1953	3–9–0	179	277	3.1	8.9	.258
1974	2–12–0	195	299	3.7	10.3	.264

*The record they could expect to have based on the number of points scored and allowed. Based on the baseball work of Bill James, the formula is PF × PF/ (PF × PF)+(PA × PA). This is adjusted with an exponent of 2.37, which, it has been determined, is the most accurate predictor of NFL success.

Washington Redskins vs. New York Giants

November 15, 1970

	1	2	3	4	F
Washington Redskins	0	12	21	0	33
New York Giants	7	7	0	21	35

In the history of every sports franchise, there a few landmark moments—times when a team changes its destiny. For fans of the New York Giants, that moment appeared to come in week nine of the 1970 season. It was then, after several years of futility, that the Giants proved beyond all doubt that they had arrived among the league's elite teams. With a winning streak the likes of which had not been seen since the club's glory days of the previous decade, it certainly appeared that this was a team upon which providence was smiling. The harsh reality of sports, though, is that what one senses to be true is often exposed as otherwise in the proving ground of subsequent events. Anyone who watched them mount the greatest Giants comeback ever against the Redskins on November 15, 1970, would have sworn that the team had battled fate and wrested from it that most elusive and mythological of all sports beasts: momentum. That the long-term ramifications of the game proved otherwise does nothing to detract from its status as one of the most memorable in team history.

THE GIANTS
The Wilderness Years, as they are known, were well underway by the time Wellington Mara finally ditched the much-maligned Allie Sherman in favor of Alex Webster just prior to the 1969 season.

Alex Webster: I was on my way to play golf when I got the call [from Wellington Mara]. I didn't want to go, but he insisted I come in. I walked into that office and he looked like hell. He'd been up all night. He told me that he had to let Allie go. I was wondering to myself, "What the hell is he telling me for?" That's when he said he wanted me to be head coach. I didn't think I was qualified for that yet. Sure, I got along with the players and they got along with me, but I'd only had a year and a half as an assistant. In my mind, it took eight or nine years to become a head coach. The reason I took it was the money.

Greg Larson: I respect Allie Sherman more now than when I played for him. He expected so much of you and he expected you to do certain things and he told you what he expected you to do. When Alex Webster came in, he was a players' coach and he knew that you knew how to do your job and he was going to just let you do it—which, from a player's point of view, is pretty good. Their philosophies were a lot different. I don't think Webster had quite the discipline that we needed, but he was good. From my understanding of Jim Lee Howell, Alex was kind of like him—just a figurehead up there. Alex let everybody run the thing and he was just the figurehead.

Fred Dryer: Alex smoked cigarettes and walked along the sidelines encouraging people. He let his coaches coach and the players play. That was the environment he created. It was much different from the way it had been in previous years. Everyone was kind of freed up.

Tucker Frederickson: Webster was like one of the guys. Up to a point, a coach can get away with that, and Alex was able to do it, especially that year. We had great camaraderie and Alex was part of that.

The 1967 season had seen the arrival of Fran Tarkenton, the quarterback from the Minnesota Vikings who was, at that point in his career, more famous for his ability to scramble than anything else. (As Tarkenton has said, he didn't choose to be a scrambler, he had scrambling thrust upon him.) With Tarkenton in the fold and Ernie Koy, Aaron Thomas, and Homer Jones enjoying fine seasons, the offense tacked an extra 100 points on the board, and the defense, while not great, was no longer the worst in the league. The result was a 7–7 season, a vast improvement from 1966 and, perhaps, something to build on. After ten games of 1968, it seemed as though the Giants were doing just that and that their trip into the wilderness would be ending after just a handful of seasons. Instead, a 7–3 record turned into another 7–7 season when they dropped their final four contests. With Webster at the helm, 1969 began promisingly with a dramatic come-from-behind victory over one of the best teams of the era.

Fred Dryer: Our first game in '69 was against the Minnesota Vikings at the Stadium. We upset them. The hilarious thing was that we carried Alex off the field! He was such a great guy, but you could see that the organization was just staying alive game by game. There wasn't an infrastructure there. We wound up six and eight.

Doug Van Horn: When I first came to the Giants, I flew into LaGuardia. This disheveled-looking guy picked me up at the airport in a station wagon. It had football equipment in the back of it—a total mess. He started driving me to Kings Point, where the Giants trained. We went across a couple of bridges and he'd say, "This is the Fifty-ninth Street Bridge." He was pointing out the sights, right? I got into camp, they equip me, and I see that this guy was still hanging around. I also noticed that he's always got the reporters around him and the staff was always over there talking to him. I thought the guy was just an equipment man or something. I was making comments to one of the other players during practice about how the equipment guy got all the attention and he said, "That's Wellington Mara!"

The Giants had higher hopes for 1970. Rather than treat Tarkenton's scrambling as unpredictable improvisation, Webster and offensive coordinator Joe Walton built the offense around it.

Greg Larson: Tarkenton was fun to play with. I could see he was going to be a politician. On Tuesday each week, after they put in the game plan, he'd come up to me and the other guys and say, "What do you think of that play?" And I'd say, "I don't like it. I don't think we should block it this way." About Thursday, the line coach would come over and say, "We're gonna change that play—we're gonna block it this way." And I said, "I'll be damned. Tarkenton went and did it!" I just knew that the man should have been in politics. He just knows how to rub people's backs and get people to do things the way he wants them to do it. And so I realized after a while that he was asking me because he knew he didn't want it that way, he wanted it the other way.

Tucker Frederickson: Fran was very involved in the offense and Alex would listen.

Prior to the 1970 season, New York acquired a number of key players such as defensive tackle Jerry Shay from Atlanta, who was a high first-round draft choice in both leagues in 1966.

Tucker Frederickson: Things came together. We picked up line-backer Matt Hazeltine from San Francisco.

Fred Dryer: We got the linebacker Jim Files out of Oklahoma in the first round of the draft and there was optimism coming into the season.

Ed Croke: We now had Ron Johnson and veteran tackle Jim Kanicki because we had traded Homer Jones to Cleveland for them during the off-season.

Fred Dryer: With Ron, we now had a rushing presence where we re-ally didn't have it before. We had a legitimate runner and that made all the difference in the world. We were able to control the ball of-fensively and, therefore, give our defense a chance to be effective. So all of those things that make up a good team were beginning to show themselves after kind of a hectic first season in '69.

Greg Larson: Ron had all the talent that you could ever expect in a running back. He was elusive, he had speed, he had power, and he had strength. He and Bob Tucker had this backgammon game that they played, and they deny it, but I know they did it at their lockers at halftime when they had a free moment.

Taking the place of Homer Jones as the team's long threat was Clifton McNeil, late of the San Francisco 49ers.

Clifton McNeil: In 1969, I was starting for the 49ers and Gene Washington was behind me, on the bench. I was getting off to a very good season. Then, all of a sudden, I had a mysterious shoulder problem. I was benched after the fifth game all the way to the last game of the season. The media was told I was hurt. Every player and everyone that was there knew I was *not* hurt. Nothing was wrong except some words had come down from powerful sources. That's what led to my being traded. Y. A. Tittle, who was one of the coaches with the 49ers, left them and went back to the New York Giants. He was the one who recommended me very highly to come play with the New York Giants. Some people wanted it to seem like I was a bad guy—like I was difficult to get along with, which was the farthest from the truth. I always had great relationships with coaches and players. I don't know exactly how things were operating, why the powers that be chose to do whatever they had to do. But I'm thankful that Y. A. Tittle was a person who could say, "No, this guy is not like that at all. He's basically a coach's dream. He would be a tremendous asset." When I heard I was going to the Giants with Fran Tarkenton there, I thought, "This is going to be great."

Bob Lurtsema: With Tucker Frederickson being healthy, he felt confident. He was such a tremendous athlete. He generated such a positive attitude for winning. He made things look so easy. He was contagious with that. Tarkenton back there for his fourth year and enough of the veterans, our defensive line—Kanicki and the crew—we had a lot of experience there. We had been together for quite a while. There was no quit in us.

The Giants had modest leads in their first three games, but they all slipped away. In all three contests they did the majority of the early scoring and were then blanked the rest of the way. A 13–7 lead against Chicago turned into a 24–16 loss. A 10–0 halftime lead in Dallas devolved into a 28–10 beating, and a 10–0 second-quarter lead in New

Orleans wound up as a 14–10 defeat. The New Orleans game was an especially tough one, though, as it was marred by a very pivotal and very obvious officiating mistake on what would have been the go-ahead touchdown in the third quarter.

Greg Larson: They had the thick white sideline, where the players were supposed to stand so they wouldn't go on the field. Between the goals, it was out of bounds, but in the end zone the white line went three feet *into* the end zone. And Aaron Thomas's knees hit in the white part of the thing in the end zone, and the official got confused, and it was a touchdown he threw away. It was so frustrating.

Aaron Thomas: I've thought about that play through the years. I was inbounds by at least five yards. The official got mixed up. In 1970, I was kind of on my way out with the Giants. They had brought in Bob Tucker, who was having a fabulous year, and he became a great tight end. I was thirty-two, thirty-three then and at the end of my career. That was a big catch for me and for the Giants. For me, if they had counted it, I probably would have been able to play more. I don't know. That did cost the ballgame. If there had been instant replay, it would have been a touchdown.

Doug Van Horn: When you look at the film, he is a good two to three yards inbounds. At that time, there was a competition between NFL cities as to who could paint up the end zone the best. That thing looked like mardi gras. One year in Yankee Stadium they had the Empire State Building in the end zone—the whole thing. This is the way it was around the league. That all changed after that play.

Bob Tucker: Now Alex Webster did a very shrewd thing. He got the whole team together and we all watched the films of the New Orleans game. That never happened—we would always break up into groups by position. He took every play every player made and got on them. He went through the whole team. Then he said, "Yeah, that sorry son of a bitch blew that call in the end zone, but who *really* lost this game?" That was the last that I heard about officiating, and he was absolutely right. There were so many opportunities we had to make plays, and we didn't make them. It was a very shrewd lesson.

Greg Larson: We kept telling ourselves that we couldn't let that game hold us back because an official made an error.

Alex Webster: I just told them they were as good as the other teams. We had lost three games, but we really beat ourselves with mistakes. I was trying to get them to believe in themselves. The hardest thing is getting players to believe how good they can be and what they can do.

Indeed, there were certainly other ingredients to that loss, including one of Webster's own making: his decision in the second quarter to go for a field goal on fourth down when the Giants were just inches from the goal line. Thinking the team was a full yard out, he sent in Pete Gogolak for the 8-yard attempt. There was also a breakdown on special teams when the Saints got their go-ahead touchdown on a blocked punt. Three Tarkenton interceptions didn't help the cause any, either.

The Giants came back strong the following week, racing to a 17–0 lead on the winless Eagles by way of a 68-yard Ron Johnson touchdown run and a touchdown punt return by Bobby Duhon. Their first win seemed assured. They nearly let the season slip through their fingers right then and there, however, as Philadelphia chipped away and tied the game at 23 in the fourth quarter. New York got the ball at their own 36 with less than two minutes to play. Tarkenton later stated he was just trying to set up Gogolak for the winning kick, but Johnson found a hole on a trap play and raced 34 yards up the right sideline for the winning score.

From there, it was a happy trip to a winning record. New York recorded its first shutout since week eight of 1961, blanking the Boston Patriots at Harvard Stadium. They brushed aside the Cardinals 35–17 and beat the Jets 22–10 in the first-ever regular-season showdown between the two New York teams.

Fred Dryer: We had a patchwork type of a defense. We had a lot of players from different teams. There weren't a lot of original draft choices, maybe three or four that the Giants made over the years. We were kind of discovering ourselves each week.

Next up was their rematch with Dallas. It did not go well in the first half, and, when the Cowboys converted Tucker Frederickson's fumble into a field goal to go up 20–9 early in the third quarter, it looked as though the winning streak might come to an end. New York answered with a Ron Johnson touchdown, however, to make it 20–16 heading into the last quarter.

Doug Van Horn: We would practice in Yankee Stadium and we'd wear out the grass. The middle of the field was bare. You wouldn't know it from a distance because they would pour paint in the middle of the field. So we got a time out, I don't remember the exact yardage. At the time, Tarkenton was calling three quarters of the plays himself. He said, "Here's what we're going to do," and he drew it up in the dirt like kids do on a sandlot! He told the receivers where to go, and he said, "Now, you guys on the line—you figure out how you want to block it." We broke the huddle and we looked back and Tark was rubbing out the play on the ground with his foot! He threw the touchdown to Ron Johnson and we won.

THE OPPONENT

After their ascent to respectability in 1969, the following year was a brief step backward for the Redskins. It was the lone season between the death of Vince Lombardi and the coming of George Allen. While the Redskins would thrive once Allen arrived, 1970 was a mixed bag under coach Bill Austin. By the time they met the Giants in week nine, they were 4–4 and had beaten an excellent Lions team while humbling the Bengals 20–0 and the Broncos 19–3. They had also stayed close to an outstanding Vikings team. Three of their losses were against teams that would make the playoffs that year.

Washington would accumulate the second-most yards in the NFL in 1970. Still running the show on the field was Sonny Jurgensen. While it would prove to be his last year as the Redskins' number-one quarterback, the thirty-six-year-old was in the midst of a fine season, leading the league in completion percentage and throwing just 10 interceptions while connecting on 23 touchdown passes. Charley Taylor and Jerry Smith were still on hand, scoring 8 and 9 touchdowns respectively.

The Redskins were not as dependent on the pass as they had been now that Larry Brown was in the backfield. The second-year man from Kansas State led the league in rushing with 1,125 yards on just 237 carries. He was also third on the team in receptions with 37. His backfield partner was fullback Charlie Harraway, who had caught 55 passes the year before after coming over from Cleveland. The star of the offensive line was center Len Hauss, a five-time Pro Bowler.

The defense was vulnerable. Only five teams allowed more points in 1970, although this first meeting with the Giants was a demarcation line for Washington. Before it, they allowed 18 points a game. From week nine forward, that ballooned to 29 per game.

THE GAME

It was rainy and 49 degrees when Pete Gogolak's foot met the ball at 1:08 eastern time to start week nine of the Giants' season. The New York defense immediately had a major test on the first series of the game. On third and 4 from their own 26, Jurgensen dumped a short pass to Brown and he was soon in the open field. Brown made a move, getting the first down and then some. Only a last-ditch tackle by cornerback Scott Eaton prevented him from going all the way. Eaton knocked him out of bounds at the 8 after a 66-yard gain, but was himself knocked out of the game in the process. One could argue that, given the final result, this early play was a game saver because, on third and goal from the 3, rookie Jim Files intercepted Jurgensen on the goal line and brought it out 8 yards. The Giants responded with a ten-play, 92-yard drive, culminating in Tucker Frederickson crashing over from the 1.

After Bob Lurtsema batted down a third-down pass, forcing the Redskins to punt, the Giants took over again at their own 35. Pat Fischer stepped in front of Tarkenton's third-down offering, however, and ran it from his own 40 to midfield. Once again the Giants' defense was able to dig in deep. Washington got to the 2 but had to settle for a Curt Knight field goal. On the Giants' next possession, Frederickson was slammed just as he was hauling in a pass at the New York 45. The ball went up in the air and Brig Owens came down with it, returning it 15 yards. Washington failed to get a first down, though, and Knight's

27-yarder made it 7–6. The Redskins had banged on the door three times and New York still had the lead. Could the Giants hope to win while continually tempting fate like this?

The next series started from the New York 20 and saw the Giants get first downs on four consecutive plays, the second of which was a run by Tarkenton—an improvisation necessitated when the Redskins had all his receivers blanketed.

Brig Owens: Fran was a great quarterback and a great leader. One thing about a scrambler is that you have to stay with your receiver, not get pulled up to think you're going to make a big play on him. He was in play for you as a passer until he crossed the line. Fran made a lot of big plays and threw a lot of completions because people came up, thinking that they were going to kill him. You had to have the discipline to stay with your man. Scrambling quarterbacks are tough even in today's game. You get a quarterback that can run and it creates a lot of problems.

Greg Larson: He was a gifted guy. Hard to block for, though! I'd be there blocking, and then, all of a sudden, I could feel the guy I was locked up with slipping in another direction, and I'd just assume that Fran was off on one of his scrambles. Of course, then he'd change direction two or three times. He was elusive. He wore those big boys down. On those hot days when he'd start scrambling, boy, I'll tell ya, those guys wore down fast.

Aaron Thomas: With Fran, you had to be in much better shape than with other quarterbacks. You would run a pass route and look for the ball and Fran would be scrambling around. The classic drop-back passers like John Brodie and Y. A. Tittle, you ran your pass route and looked for the ball. If it's not there, it's never coming. But with Fran you never knew. It was exciting with him. He made the most of anyone's ability I've ever seen.

Bob Tucker: Fran was a great quarterback. He was not going to overwhelm you with size, but he would overwhelm you with his brain.

He was a general. His purpose was to outsmart, outconnive, out-scheme, outmaneuver, and out-anything the defense.

Tarkenton drove the Giants to the Redskins' 17. On second down, he handed off to Johnson, who rumbled to the 3 where a crunching tackle jarred the ball loose. It skittered into the end zone and was fortuitously smothered by wide receiver Clifton McNeil.

Clifton McNeil: That was a fun play. I was amazed at how fast Ronnie was running. It was nothing but pure luck that I was there. He and I laughed about it because, in an earlier game, I ran an end around and they went and tackled me at the one-foot line. They wouldn't give me the touchdown. On the next play, he ran it in. We were laughing about how I got even. I told him, "You did all the work and I got all the glory." We were in that kind of mind-set. We would take any negative and turn it into a positive.

Now trailing 14–6, it was Jurgensen's turn to move his team down the field. He deftly passed the Redskins from their own 26 all the way to the New York 14 before an incompletion and a Jim Kanicki sack forced Washington to settle for a field goal yet again. It was Knight's third of the day. The Giants then handed Washington another scoring opportunity. After the team stalled on three plays, rookie punter Bill Johnson mishandled a high snap. When he finally corralled the ball and tried to kick, it slid off the side of his foot and was downed on the New York 33, only 4 yards from scrimmage. With just 0:05 showing on the clock, Knight was immediately brought in and kicked a 40-yard field goal to make it 14–12 at the half.

Johnson had more bad fortune on his first punt of the second half. His kick from the Giants' 36 landed on the Redskins' 30 but bounced backward all the way out to the 43. It was the prelude to an onslaught.

Doug Van Horn: The play that started it was this trap [running play] that hadn't gone anywhere all day long. This time, though, they broke this trap for sixty yards. They popped this run to start the third quarter. That's the play that broke our defense's back because they finally popped one. I said, Uh-oh.

On that play, Charlie Harraway did what the Redskins couldn't manage in the entire first half: get into the end zone. They now led 19–14. When Washington next got the ball back, Jurgensen found Charley Taylor in one-on-one coverage with Eaton's replacement, rookie Kenny Parker, and hit him for 41 yards down to the New York 28. The Giants got resolute on the first two downs, but on third and 10 Jurgensen found Taylor isolated with Parker once more and connected for a score. (1970 would be both Parker's and Bill Johnson's only years in the NFL.)

Trailing now 26–14, the next Giants series was truncated when Tarkenton was sacked again, this time by John Hoffman. Johnson's punt traveled only 24 yards and the Redskins were in business at their own 45. Harraway capped a nine-play drive with a run around the right end for another touchdown.

Bob Lurtsema: When that happened, there was a big letdown. Having that awkward score at halftime, and then they bomb that one right away. It took the wind out of our sails. It was deflating as almost any play I'd ever been involved in. We lost it. We lost the edge that we had at halftime.

Doug Van Horn: I will never forget the feeling on our bench. I just felt the air go out of the entire team.

Bob Lurtsema: When we were down thirty-three to fourteen in the third quarter, Tarkenton said to me, "Lurts, keep your boys going— we're still going to win this bitch." Fran being a preacher's son, I couldn't believe he said that. He got my attention.

The fourth quarter began with the Giants starting from their own 29-yard line. The drive appeared to die aborting when Tucker was called for offensive pass interference, giving the team a first and 25. Tarkenton overcame two sacks, though, and connected with wide receiver Don Herrmann as well as Frederickson coming out of the backfield to bring New York to the Washington 30. From there he hit Aaron Thomas down to the 5 and finally, on the thirteenth play of the drive, Ron Johnson bulled over to make it 33–21. The possession had taken over five minutes off the clock. Sure, it was good news, but could New

York afford any more sustained drives like that if they were to have any hope of erasing the deficit?

The defense obliged by holding the Redskins to a three and out, and the Giants got the ball back in quick order. Tarkenton hit Frederickson for 8 yards and then, on second and 2, found him open 27 yards downfield. Frederickson gathered it in at the Washington 30 and went the rest of the way for the touchdown, avoiding would-be tacklers the entire way and making the score 33–28 after Gogolak's extra point. It was proving to be one of the better days for Frederickson, a player whose talents were so often denied by injury. He would catch 10 passes for 165 yards in this game.

Greg Larson: Tucker Frederickson, had he not had knee injuries, would have been All-Pro every year. He was just a powerful, smooth runner. Man, he had deceptive speed! He had everything. He really did. I think he might have been the best fullback that the Giants ever had. He had such good hands and he was extremely smart and strong and he would block.

Doug Van Horn: He wasn't the most graceful receiver. He would turn around, get all contorted, then turn back around to try and catch the ball and somehow snare it.

Alex Webster: He could still do it all, but he wasn't as quick as he had been before the injury.

Tucker Frederickson: In 1970 I stayed healthy and contributed. Obviously, Ron Johnson helped a lot and so did Tarkenton, who was a great quarterback and leader. It was nice to contribute, it really was. I was always part of the team, but at some point you want to contribute and sometimes, physically, you can't.

Bob Tucker: Contributing to the comeback was the fact that the Redskins had such a lead that—just like teams do today—they went into the protective mode, so to speak. They went into that mind-set where it's like they're saying, "Let's not do this, that, or the other thing. We'll just run the time out because this team can come back." And we ended up starting to pour it on. Once they turned it off, they couldn't turn it back on.

Initiating play from their own 22, the Redskins gave the ball to Larry Brown to chew up the remaining time. He tore one off for 10 yards, fumbling, but out of bounds. After an incompletion, Brown delivered another first down, this time with a 15-yard run. Then the New York defense stiffened. Dryer and Shay chased Brown and nailed him for a 7-yard loss back to the 41. Jurgensen tried a screen pass, but Hazeltine jammed it up for only a 2-yard gain, forcing a punt. Mike Bragg boomed a 51-yarder, but Duhon brought it out to the 27. On third and 2, Tarkenton hit Tucker for 20 yards and then found Frederickson for 13 more at the two-minute warning. On third and 6 from the Redskins' 28, Hoffman slapped Tarkenton's pass away, bringing up fourth down.

Bob Tucker: We had this particular pass play that was a part of our passing series that we called our Teen because they were numbered thirteen, fourteen, fifteen, sixteen, seventeen, eighteen, and nineteen pass. And that's what we'd call it in the huddle. This particular play was thirteen pass, an option. Just calling that thirteen pass, it's not a very lengthy or descriptive term, but everybody knew what was going on and it was descriptive in our own system. So this play worked about eighty percent of the time when we ran it, no matter what team we were playing, and it was designed to go to the half-back or the fullback. The only thing that would make it a problem is if the team had a weak-side blitz or if they went into a nickel plug, because they'd plug up the middle with the safety so it made it difficult to run the play. But on this occasion the Redskins didn't put that defense in. They were running regular man coverage, regular zone coverage. These pass plays were designed to go to the halfback or the fullback over the middle. And we would just kill teams. It wasn't just the Redskins. In these situations it was eight yards, fifteen yards—it was just hard to stop the play, we ran it so well. We were so disciplined in our passing routes, all attributable to coach Joe Walton, who was in charge of the passing game. So we would go down the field many times with a single play. And we did this exten-sively with the Redskins. I mean we didn't call it every play, but I bet you we ran it sixty percent of the time. So Fran called it and Ron Johnson caught a pass on fourth and six for seven or eight yards. He got blasted when he caught it, but he held on to the ball.

Brig Owens: Back then, your running backs coming out of the backfield had options—as opposed to today, where they run the pattern. Then they had options and you had linebackers that could really cover those guys. Today they play a lot of zone. Back then you played a lot of man-to-man, so the linebackers could be very vulner-able if you had a quick back that could also catch. It creates a lot of problems.

Fred Dryer: Tarkenton was a big believer in throwing to those half-backs out of the back slot—throwing underneath, getting a lot of yards underneath, and keeping the momentum moving.

Bob Tucker: Johnson and Fredrickson knew how to run pass patterns. We were very deliberate in what we were going to do, the moves we were making, and you popped open in a hurry and there was the ball and it was pretty much unstoppable. It holds true today: If you don't have running backs that can get involved in the passing game, you're really putting the handcuffs on yourself. They don't use the running backs like we did. We used running backs like pass receivers. Now they make a living out of this I formation, which, in my opinion, is a di-saster because you see where the linebackers line up—they're five yards off the ball. These linebackers are very close to their coverage before they even start. This thirteen pass and a bunch of these plays—this was West Coast offense stuff, they just didn't call it that at the time.

Tarkenton followed that first down with a pass to McNeil, good for 10 yards down to the 9, giving New York a first and goal to go.

Doug Van Horn: Fran said, "Boys, we don't want to score too soon. What we're going to do is run a couple of these sweeps and then we're going to score." That was Tark—making stuff up on the go. "Whatever you do, don't go out of bounds," he said. So what do we do? First play, we run it in! Tarkenton handed the ball to Johnson, who ran around left end for the score. Now we've gotta give the ball back to Jurgensen with a minute left and now we gotta sweat it out. When Johnson scored, that place went nuts. It was pandemonium. The only thought on our minds was, Oh shit . . ."

Because even with just a minute left to play, having Jurgensen at the helm with time-outs to work with meant it was not unreasonable to believe that Washington could get into Knight's range. Ted Vactor took Pete Gogolak's kick at the 2 and returned it 30 yards. The first pass was to wide receiver Walter Roberts, but it fell incomplete.

Bob Lurtsema: The one thing about Sonny and Joe Namath is that they could read so fast—like Brett Favre. As soon as the ball was snapped, they knew where the other twenty-one people were. They read your progression so fast. That's what made Sonny Jurgensen so great. He was a smart quarterback, and what a gunslinger. Even when you had a good, clean pass rush and you were saying to yourself, "Wow, I got him," and you'd be getting ready to nail him—and he'd be sitting back there yawning because he'd already let the pass go. After a while, you'd rush with your hand in the air and hope you'd knock one down. That's what I did.

For the second time in the game, Lurtsema got in Jurgensen's face and batted away a throw. On third down, Jurgensen tried to hit Larry Brown coming out of the backfield, but it, too, was incomplete.

Now there were just thirty seconds on the clock and Washington was looking at fourth and 10 from their own 32. Jurgensen dropped back and was forced from the pocket. On the move, he hit tight end Jerry Smith, who was hauled down at the New York 44 for a 24-yard gain. Now all Washington needed was one more successful pass and Knight would have a good chance to make it 36–35.

There was, however, the small matter of the flag back upfield. The officials had called Jurgensen for throwing the pass beyond the line of scrimmage, a penalty that brought with it a loss of down, giving the ball to New York.

After two short keepers, Tarkenton killed third down by doing what he did best: dancing around in the backfield. When he was finally tackled, the Redskins called their last time-out with just six seconds to go. On fourth and 9 from the 26, a hole opened up in the Washington line and Tarkenton exploited it, heading for the end zone. He was brought down at the 6-yard line as time expired.

Fred Dryer: I remember Tarkenton saying, "Can you believe this? Winning six games as a team!" Everybody was kind of like self-aware— not self-conscious, but self-aware, asking, "Jesus, how in hell are we doing this?" That was as good as that team that year could play. Winning six games in a row in that league was a feat in itself.

"What makes you feel proud is the way they wouldn't give up," said Alex Webster after the game. "When the last quarter was starting, I just kept telling them that Washington had scored three quick ones and we could turn around and do exactly the same, if the defense would get us the ball."

Tucker Frederickson: I was awarded the game ball. The only memorabilia in my house from my time with the Giants is that ball.

The next night, Dallas was stunned at home 38–0 by the upstart Cardinals on Monday Night Football, then in its premiere season. It appeared that they were dead at the side of the road with a 5–4 record. At 6–3, New York trailed 7–2 St. Louis by one game but could do much to control their own destiny by beating the Cardinals in their upcoming game in week thirteen and winning at least three of their other four remaining contests.

THE AFTERMATH

Clifton McNeil: That was one of the most exciting games of the year. What that did was help to fortify the belief in each other. After we came back from a deficit like that, we felt we could beat everybody now. It was a reward within itself because everybody contributed.

Fred Dryer: I remember how much fun it was to go practice every day, to be in a winning environment. What was very pleasurable for me was how I could see that the surrounding support system of the Giants was very, very happy. The press, the fans, the organization—how excited they were about all of this stuff! It was a lot of fun to be around, not only just winning, but to be a part of contributing to turning the franchise around.

Bob Lurtsema: We were the toast of New York. Everywhere I went on the street, people would stop and talk to me.

And in the storybooks, the Giants would have gone 5–0 the rest of the way, taking the division from the Cowboys and Cardinals. Instead they went into Philadelphia on a freezing-cold Monday night the next week and things got away from them. Playing the 1–7–1 Eagles at blustery Franklin Field, the Giants were undone by a fumble that set up Philadelphia's first touchdown, the effects of the weather on their receivers, and two long kickoff returns by the Eagles. The rematch with the Redskins followed, and it was nearly a reverse of their first meeting. This time it was the Giants coughing up a big lead in the fourth quarter. Down 24–10, Sonny Jurgensen's two touchdown passes in the first five minutes of the fourth evened it up, and he was driving Washington to the go-ahead score when he was picked off by Willie Williams. New York drove to the 13, where Gogolak put one through the uprights at 1:53 for the lead. The last play of the game was a fake field goal that the Giants sussed out successfully. This was followed by wins over Buffalo and the fading Cardinals, who fell from first to third by losing their final three games.

In the final week of the season, New York hosted the Los Angeles Rams. A win would have given the Giants the Eastern Division title. Instead they came out flat and were humbled, 31–3.

And so the Wilderness Years would continue until the Giants reached a point so low that there was nowhere to go but up . . .

APPENDICES

The Largest Comebacks in Giants History

While this game does not represent the biggest deficit the Giants have ever overcome, it is certainly the largest they have ever bridged in the fourth quarter. What follows are the greatest deficits New York has ever overcome to achieve victory. (This does not include games in which the Giants came back big only to lose eventually, such as their 26–24 loss to the Packers in 1981 in which they led after trailing 20–0.)

21 points vs. Philadelphia Eagles: 28–21, December 2, 1945

It was the Steve Van Buren Show for most of the game as the Eagles' halfback ran for two scores and returned the opening kickoff of the second half 98 yards to put the Giants down 21–0. Then, in a quick turn that caused the *New York Times* to suggest Giants fans would need smelling salts, Arnie Herber came off the bench and hit Frank Liebel on three sizable touchdown passes to tie it in a span of less than five minutes on the game clock. The second score was set up when Sam Fox recovered a Van Buren fumble at the Giants' 49. Herber's final strike was a spot pass to Fox late in the fourth quarter for the 28–21 lead. The Eagles drove for the evener but were stopped on downs at the Giants' four.

21 points vs. Chicago Cardinals: 41–38, October 30, 1949

The Comiskey Park crowd enjoyed halftime with their team leading 28–7, but Jack Salscheider commenced the third quarter by retuning Pat Harder's kickoff 95 yards for a score. A minute later, Frank LoVuolo scooped up a Charlie Trippi fumble for another touchdown and, soon enough, the Giants had a 34–31 lead after two Gene Roberts plunges. The Cards fought back and held a late four-point lead until Charlie Conerly connected on a 68-yard bomb to Roberts with four minutes left, setting up Joe Scott's 1-yard end-zone breach for the winner.

20 points vs. Baltimore Colts: 55–20,
November 19, 1950

A Colts beatdown was a weekly NFL feature in 1950—the year they came over from the AAFC—as they lost by such scores as 55–13, 51–14, and 70–27. In fact, had the 1950 Colts not been mentioned in the famous prewedding quiz in Barry Levinson's *Diner*, they would be completely unknown to latter-day fans. In this game, they got ahead 20–0 in the second quarter on the efforts of a young passer named Y. A. Tittle. It was their largest lead of the season to that point. The Giants had run the A formation the week before and crushed the Cardinals 51–21, but were getting nowhere with it against Baltimore. Instead they scrapped the A, sat Charlie Conerly, brought in rookie Travis Tidwell, and went with the T formation. They revived, responding with eight touchdowns and one of the great unanswered runs in league history. It would prove to be the only year in the league for this version of the Colts.

19 points vs. Washington Redskins: 35–33,
November 15, 1970

See main article.

17 points vs. Philadelphia Eagles: 30–24 (overtime),
September 17, 2006

The Eagles entered the fourth quarter with a 24–7 lead when things bounced the Giants' way—literally. Plaxico Burress coughed up the ball at the Philadelphia 16 and it made its way to the end zone. At one point, safety Michael Lewis seemingly had it corralled. Instead, tight end Visanthe Shiancoe fell on Lewis, and Tim Carter fell on the ball for the score. The comeback was underway. A key Brian Westbrook fumble put the Giants in position to pull within three. Eli Manning (20 for 26, 233 yards in the fourth quarter) drove the Giants from their own 20 into Jay Feely field-goal range with less than a minute to play, aided by a 15-yard unsportsmanlike-conduct penalty on the Eagles' Trent Cole. More than twelve minutes into overtime, Manning defeated an Eagles blitz and hit Burress for the 31-yard game winner.

17 points vs. Philadelphia Eagles: 26–24, October 21, 1951

When the 2–0–1 Giants went into the locker room at halftime trailing Philadelphia 17–0, they were treated to an earful of vitriol from coach Steve Owen. They responded with 26 unanswered points via five diverse scores (TD pass, safety, a TD return of the ensuing free kick by Emlen Tunnell, rushing TD, and field goal) and won going away. Key fourth-quarter interceptions by Otto Schnellbacher and Harmon Rowe closed out Philadelphia.

17 points vs. San Francisco 49ers: 21–17, December 1, 1986

This comeback win had the added bonus of clinching them a playoff spot. The Niners rolled to a 17–0 halftime lead on the quick passes of Joe Montana, one of which was a TD score to Jerry Rice, who also scored on an end around. The most famous play of the game came on the second snap of the second half. Phil Simms connected with tight end Mark Bavaro over the middle. He managed to elude the tackle of Hall of Famer Ronnie Lott but quickly attracted other 49er defenders. No fewer than four of them were affixed to him as he struggled downfield for an extra 18 yards (31 total). Two plays later, Simms hit Joe Morris for a touchdown and New York scored three times on fifteen plays in the span of ten minutes. Stacy Robinson caught a touchdown pass and Ottis Anderson bulled over from the 1 for what proved to be the winner. New York had to snub a late charge by the comeback-friendly Montana. He drove the 49ers to the Giants '17, at which point the New York defense stiffened. On fourth down at the 20, he was pressured by linebacker Andy Headen and threw poorly, ending the drive and San Francisco's chances.

17 points vs. New Orleans Saints: 20-17 September 28, 1986

The Giants were missing many of their key offensive weapons. Mark Bavaro, Joe Morris, and Lionel Manuel were all sidelined. New Orleans built a 17–0 lead only to have the Giants defense dig in and hold them for over half the game while Simms and the offense chipped away.

Return man Mark Collins lost his helmet while fielding a punt, but gamely continued on, only to be knocked silly on the ensuing tackle. The Giants thought it excessive; Harry Carson called it a turning point in the game. With the score 17–13 early in the last quarter, Kenny Hill hit Saints running back Rueben Mayes, causing a fumble which was covered by Leonard Marshall. Seven plays later, Phil Simms hit Zeke Mowatt from the 4 and New York had the lead it would never relinquish.

17 points vs. Dallas Cowboys: 27–24 (overtime),
November 4, 2001

When Dexter Coakley intercepted a Kerry Collins pass and ran it back 29 yards to put the Cowboys up 17–0 in the second quarter, it looked as though New York was headed to its fourth straight defeat. There was some hope when the Giants answered with a score, but Mario Edwards responded with another pick-six on Collins, this one for 71 yards, and they trailed 24–7 at the half. After the break, New York switched up its game plan, throwing more to the backs. The Giants' defense also came up big, intercepting three passes, including two in the end zone. The game-tying Collins-to-Ike Hilliard touchdown was set up when Thabiti Davis blocked a Micah Knorr punt at the Dallas 23. In overtime, Collins was 3-for-3 including a key 33-yard toss to Hilliard. This set up the closer: a 42-yard field goal by Morten Andersen.

Philadelphia Eagles vs. New York Giants

November 19, 1978

	1	2	3	4	F
Philadelphia Eagles	0	6	0	13	19
New York Giants	14	0	3	0	17

When people discuss memorable or great games, more often than not what they are really referring to are games that contained a single, memorable, game-turning play. Most fans would be hard-pressed to name another incident in such classic sports events as the Shot Heard 'Round the World, the Immaculate Reception, game six of the 1975 World Series, and the Catch. Such is also the case with the Miracle at the Meadowlands. In fact, the game's signature play overshadows all that came before it to such an extent that the Giants' participants remember little else about it. And, like the battles of the American Civil War, this game is known by different names to the combatants and supporters of the opposing sides. The Miracle at the Meadowlands is its Philadelphia/South Jersey sobriquet. In New York and North Jersey, the game is known in Giants circles as the Fumble.

It marks the absolute nadir of the franchise. In fact, a case could be made that it marks the absolute nadir of *any* franchise in any team sport. This was no mere loss, but a defeat that seemed to symbolize the decline and confusion at the top of one of the NFL's flagship organizations. The burden of proof would be on the party claiming to have found its equal in sports annals.

THE GIANTS

New York had finished 8–6 in 1972 and then endured the two worst back-to-back seasons in its history. (See "The Worst Giants Teams of All Time," page 134.)

Brian Kelley: We finished two eleven and one in '73, but a lot of people don't realize our three top guys got injured. Ron Johnson, Bob Tucker, and Norm Snead—all three went down in '73 before the season started. We had a guy Randy Johnson come in and play quarterback and we were trying to run a running back, Rocky Thompson, and you never knew what he was going to do. We really got hurt. That put us behind the eight ball in the '73 season. And then Bill Arnsparger came in as head coach. Bill was a great defensive coordinator, but I think Bill's biggest problem was—don't get me wrong, I like him a lot—but he tried to do it all. He didn't let his defensive coordinator run the D, he tried to do it all, and he brought in younger coaches—he brought in college coaches because he wanted complete control. I think that was his downfall, that and not bringing in a good offensive coordinator.

Doug Van Horn: We always had a little bit of tension between the offense and the defense. Ever since Arnsparger came, that was part of the Giants' psyche. Arnsparger was a defensive guy and we had no offense. Prior to that, we'd been an offensive team. Under Alex Webster we could score thirty-five points a game, but we had no defense. Arnsparger came in and it was the opposite. Throughout the seventies that was the situation. Whenever you have an imbalance it's going to be the same. I remember when we were scoring points, we would bitch and moan at the defense. When you don't win, that stuff gets magnified. If you're winning it's not even an issue. Winning covers a multitude of sins.

Brian Kelley: And it was tough playing in those days. Here's a New York team that is used to winning, and all of a sudden here we are, we can't even buy a win. It was a struggle. The biggest part was, week to week, we didn't even know who the quarterback was going to be. I can name quarterbacks you don't even remember that played for us. That's what we were on offense. The defense, we stuck together and we were respectable for what we could be. We were on the field a lot back then. I could tell it in Wellington Mara's face—he loved to win and he would do everything to win, and when I would read in the paper that they said Wellington Mara was too cheap to buy players—that guy, he would do anything to win.

Ed Croke: The year that ended it for Arnsparger was our first one at Giants Stadium in '76. We started that year off 0–6 and we were going to play the Steelers at home. Terry Bradshaw was out, so they had the backup quarterback playing. I remember Andy Robustelli saying that we could stay close to the Steelers. But what do we do if they blow us out with the second-string quarterback? That may be the end of Arnsparger. And they did blow us out with the second-string quarterback, twenty-seven to nothing, and Arnsparger got fired the next day.

Brian Kelley: Then we went from Arnsparger to John McVay, which really set us back even farther because his coaching staff was probably the weakest I've ever seen in my life. Marty Schottenheimer was with him for about a year and then he realized he didn't have anyone around him as far as assistants go, so he was smart enough to get out of there. John was a great guy, but just didn't have the right people around him at all.

Andy Robustelli, the Giants' director of football operations in this period, wrote in his autobiography how he tried to convince McVay to hire veteran NFL coach Norm Van Brocklin to run his offense. He also agitated for former Giant Joe Morrison, who had been coaching in college. Robustelli even went so far as to bring in the innovative Bill Walsh of Stanford to put on an offensive clinic, with the ulterior motive that he might jump at the chance to be the Giants' offensive coordinator. McVay turned aside all requests, sticking with Bob Gibson, an old colleague from his days in the World Football League.

J. T. Turner: If it hadn't been for Bob Gibson, I wouldn't have been a Giant. He was my head coach with the Charlotte Hornets of the World Football League, my first year in professional football. After that I went and played ball in Canada for a year, where I fractured my sternum for the second time, so I decided to retire. I returned to Greensboro, North Carolina, and got a job with Container Corporation of America, and was in management. In the interim I got engaged. Bob Gibson came to see me and asked if I wanted to play for the Giants. I told him I didn't want to play anymore. He left three years' worth of contracts with me. I took them and stuffed them in a drawer. After I got married and my wife moved in, she found them. She asked me what they were and what I planned to do with them. I told her I didn't want to play anymore. She told me to think about it. I did. I took a vacation from my job and went to training camp. I ended up making the team.

Losing had become routine by now: Seasons of 5–9, 3–11, and 5–9 preceded 1978. The '78 season was a little different, though. For the first time in six years, New York was over .500 at the halfway point. Promising though that seemed, there were also signs that they weren't out of the woods yet. Although 5–3, the Giants' wins were against teams that would post a combined 19–45 record in 1978. They had been outgained in six of these eight contests. After that, the cracks began to show up in the final results. By the time they reached the game against the Eagles, things weren't quite as rosy. They were developing a habit of surrendering late leads (see "The 1978 Giants: Wild-card Team?" page 181) and, having lost three in a row to the Saints, Cardinals, and Redskins, were now 5–6. Furthermore, there was trouble at the top. Owner Wellington Mara was feuding with his co-owner, nephew Tim, son of Wellington's late brother, Jack. Their discord was doing the franchise no favors.

THE OPPONENT
Like the Giants in 1978, the Eagles were attempting to end their own sojourn into the wilderness. After beating the Packers for the championship in 1960, the Eagles went 10–4 in 1961 and narrowly lost out on the

Eastern Division title to the Giants. For the next sixteen seasons, they managed to finish over .500 just once, sporting a 9–5 showing in 1966. The Eagles amassed a record of 73–142–9 in that time, just slightly worse than the Giants' 84–156–4 ledger since their last championship-game appearance in 1963. After holding the Packers and Jets to a combined 12 points in weeks ten and eleven, Philadelphia was 6–5 heading into their matchup with the Giants, giving them a shot at finishing over .500 for the first time in a dozen years and perhaps even a wild-card bid.

Philadelphia was coached by Dick Vermeil, now in his third year with the club. He had inherited a 4–10 team and was slowly bringing it to respectability. His quarterback was Ron Jaworski, acquired in a trade with the Rams. He was not yet at his peak, but he was improving steadily every year. His favorite target was Harold Carmichael, the four-time Pro Bowler. Wilbert Montgomery, a second-year man, was coming into his own. He would finish fifth in the league in rushing with 1,220 yards and was also a receiving threat out of the backfield. The defense was anchored by perennial Pro Bowler Bill Bergey at left inside linebacker. The left tackle, Stan Walters, was also selected to the Pro Bowl in 1978. The team leader in interceptions was a young cornerback named Herman Edwards.

Vince Papale: We used to call Herman "the Cobra" because he was as quick as one. We used to like watching him in his transition from a backpedal to a forward pedal.

Joe Pisarcik: Here's a bit of trivia: My first NFL touchdown pass in 1977 was an eighty-yarder to Jimmy Robinson against the Eagles. You know who was covering him? Herman Edwards.

Bill Bergey: We had beaten the Giants six times in a row. We were beating them twice every year. We would get our clocks cleaned by everybody else, but we could always beat the Giants twice and we looked forward to it.

Vince Papale: The Meadowlands was always a special place for me. Any time we played there, we'd all go up the Turnpike from South Jersey in our conversion vans.

Joe Galat: A number of coaches from either team were chatting before the game. Some of the managers were coming out with these carts loaded with buckets of Gatorade. As they turned the corner, the Gatorade spilled everywhere. [Eagles assistant coach] John Ralston said, "I hope that was an omen." I said, "I hope it's not." About a year later, somebody brought it up. I guess the Gatorade being fumbled was a preview of what happened later.

THE GAME

The Eagles lost no time in establishing the kind of day they were going to have. After forcing the Giants to punt from their own 8, John Sciarra fielded the kick at the 45 and brought it across midfield to the New York 41, giving Philadelphia excellent field position. They didn't get very far, though, and when Nick Mike-Mayer came on to try a 45-yard field goal, he missed wide to the left.

New York was in a period of quarterback crisis. In 1976, they had gone 3–11 using veterans Craig Morton and Norm Snead. They had taken Jerry Golsteyn in the twelfth round of the '76 draft and Randy Dean in the fifth round a year later and drafted no quarterbacks in 1978. Neither Golsteyn nor Dean ever developed. In the meantime, they had also looked beyond the draft to Canada, where they found Joe Pisarcik, an undrafted twenty-five-year-old out of New Mexico State, playing for the Calgary Stampeders. He was given the reins in week four of the '77 season and had been starting ever since.

On his first possession against Philadelphia he crafted a masterful drive starting from the Giants' 28, going 5-for-5 in the air and running 8 yards for one of the four first downs achieved en route downfield. On the ninth play of the drive, he found Bobby Hammond on the left side of the end zone for a touchdown. Joe Danelo's extra point made it 7–0 Giants.

New York got the ball right back on a Brad Van Pelt interception, which he returned 12 yards to the Philadelphia 38. On first down, Pisarcik deftly eluded a hard-charging Reggie Wilkes and hit Johnny Perkins for 18 yards. After a hold pushed the ball back to the 30, Pisarcik found Perkins biding his time alone in the end zone, left unattended by Herman Edwards, who had forgotten his coverage on the play. It was just ten minutes into the game and the Giants were leading 14–0.

The Eagles very nearly buried themselves for good on their next series. When their drive stalled on the Giants' 42, Mike Michel came in to punt, only to have the snap sail over his head. Under pursuit, he scooped it up all the way back at his own 24 and managed to get the kick away on the run. It went to the New York 35; though credited with just a 7-yard punt, Michel had dug his team out of a very deep potential hole.

The Eagles had two more scoring opportunities. On the first, Harry Carson blocked Mike-Mayer's second field-goal attempt of the day. On the next one, a Jaworski-to-Carmichael collaboration went for 47 yards, setting up Wilbert Montgomery's touchdown run, making the score 14–6. Kicking-game problems continued to plague the Eagles, however, as the snap on the extra point was high. Improvising, Mike-Mayer tried to pass it into the end zone but failed.

He then kicked off short and New York took over at their own 41. With just 1:21 left in the half, Pisarcik hustled the Giants downfield, immediately finding Jim Robinson for 44 yards and then getting 8 yards himself with a quarterback draw. On third and 2 from the 7, he tried to hit Emery Moorehead in the middle of the end zone but found veteran cornerback Bob Howard for the interception instead. A chance to put some distance between themselves and a struggling Eagles team had been missed. Still, new York went in at halftime with an 8-point lead, more than enough to feel good about after six straight losses to the Eagles.

The Giants' first drive of the second half took more than seven minutes off the clock. It was perpetuated by a Larry Csonka line crash on fourth and 1 from the Eagles' 41, a good call on the part of John McVay in a position where a punt would have been the safer choice. Eight plays later, the Giants were facing another fourth and 1, this time at the 20. If they converted, it would give them an opportunity to make it a three-score game. Instead McVay sent in Danelo, who kicked the 27-yarder to make it 17–6.

The Eagles' woes continued on the next series when Ernie Jones ballhawked a pass intended for Harold Carmichael at the Giants' 42 and brought it back to the Philadelphia 35. Pisarcik loaded up on first down, trying to connect with tight end Gary Shirk at the goal line. This time, Herman Edwards was not asleep at the switch. He knocked the ball away, saving a touchdown. When Wilkes came up big on the next two plays, the Giants were forced to punt, negating the advantage of the turnover. Neither team generated any movement on their next possessions, but the Eagles' special teams nearly undid themselves once again. Return man John Sciarra tipped Jennings's punt as it went over his head. The Giants' Odis McKinney got a hand on it, but it was eventually covered up by Papale, the Eagles' special-teams specialist, at the 9.

There then followed a coast-to-coast drive, to which the Giants contributed their fair share of the gas money. Terry Jackson was called for pass interference twice, setting up a first and goal at the 4. The Eagles were denied on their first two tries. When tight end Richard Osborne dropped Jaworski's pass in the end zone, it looked as though the Giants had held. Unfortunately for New York, John Mendenhall was called for roughing the passer, giving the Eagles four more tries from the 2. On third down, Mike Hogan went in, making it 17–12. There it would stay as, once again, the Eagles failed to convert the extra-point attempt. Sciarra, the holder, couldn't control the snap and Mike-Mayer tried to pass again, only to be rolled under by the Giants—this time getting knocked out of the game for his trouble.

The Giants were not going to go to the winner's circle without a struggle, though. On second down at their own 35, running back Doug Kotar headed into the line and was plastered by rookie defensive end Dennis Harrison. Kotar lost the ball and Reggie Wilkes came up with it at the 33. The Eagles had had the kind of afternoon that teams have nightmares about: dropped passes, fumbles, interceptions, a punt muff, a key blown coverage, and a failure not once but twice on that most automatic of plays, the point after touchdown. And yet here they were, just 5 points behind with field position, time-outs, and enough time on the clock to find the end zone and victory.

After dropping Jaworski's flare attempt, Hogan caught a pass over the middle for 7 yards. On third down, Billy Campfield broke through for a 5-yard gain and the first down but lost the ball en route. It was his teammate, tackle Jerry Sisemore, who gathered it up at the 19, keeping Philadelphia's hopes alive. Their joy was not long-lived, however. On second down, Jaworski's pass to Hogan tipped off his fingers into the grateful embrace of Odis McKinney at the Giants' 10. He ran it back to the 21. With 1:23 left, there was nothing for the Giants to do but handle the business of time.

Joe Pisarcik: You couldn't just kneel down. The defense had to touch you for the play to be whistled over. It was a lot different then.

On first down, Pisarcik retreated 3 yards and hit the deck. There being no victory formations yet (the episode that caused their invention still being thirty seconds in the future), he was hit by the Eagles.

Bill Bergey: Joe Pisarcik went back to kneel down. Frank LeMaster was the cavity—inside—linebacker with me and we were both trying to jam the line and hit a crack to make something happen. Frank got through and fell into Pisarcik. Today it absolutely would have been a fifteen-yard penalty.

There was a lot of pushing and shoving at the end of the play, with flags being thrown on both teams.

Joe Pisarcik: [Wide receiver] Jimmy Robinson came waltzing on the field and I said to myself, "What does he want?" He had come into the huddle with a play: a handoff to Csonka. We ran the play and he went off tackle to the right side and he went eleven yards.

Joe Galat: When you get a near penalty like the Eagles did, defenses have a tendency to back off a bit. And when they backed off, Csonka made a great run. Frank LeMaster has said the Eagles were very upset at having given up eleven yards on the previous play. They thought it was going to be a "show the union card and take the knee" situation.

It was now third and 2. The Eagles called their last time-out, stopping the clock at thirty-one seconds. With one play left and no need to do anything but be tackled, the game was effectively over and the Giants were victorious.

THE PLAY

Experience told those watching and playing exactly how the next thirty seconds would play out. Everyone had seen its like transpire Sunday after Sunday, year after year. On CBS television, the credits were being flashed on the screen during the Eagles' time-out. Announcer Don Criqui was reading them off—a sure sign that the end was near.

Joe Galat: As at every game, Wellington Mara had one of the team chaplains with him. They were sitting next to the coaches' booth with a light glass partition between us. There was a heated discussion after each down between Bob Gibson and Lindy Infante [the receivers coach, who was on the sidelines]. Probably not very pleasing to hear for Wellington and the priest.

Down below, tight end Al Dixon trotted onto the field, replacing wide receiver Johnny Perkins. They passed going in opposite directions. Dixon joined the huddle, where he found quarterback Pisarcik, halfback Kotar, fullback Csonka, left tackle Gordon Gravelle, left guard Doug Van Horn, center Jim Clack, right guard J. T. Turner, right tackle Brad Benson, tight end Gary Shirk, and wide receiver Jimmy Robinson.

Brad Benson: He brought the play in and Pisarcik said, "What?" It was supposed to be a dive—just a very simple dive play for the fullback, Csonka. And Dixon said, "Bob Gibson said make sure you hand the ball off." And Pisarcik said, "What do you mean, 'Hand the ball off'?" And Dixon said, "Hand the ball off." Pisarcik said, "I'm not handing the fucking ball off." Dixon said, "He said you better hand it off."

Joe Pisarcik: I was going to call the sneak again, but they called the same running play to Csonka. If you do that play, ninety-eight out of a hundred times, it's going to be okay.

J. T. Turner: Jim Clack was telling Joe Pisarcik to fall on the ball. All the offensive line agreed and told him to fall on the ball. He refused to do it. I think even Csonka told him to fall on the ball.

Allan Webb: Joe Pisarcik wasn't your ordinary do-what-I-tell-you quarterback. That's not a knock. In other words, he wasn't as disciplined as a quarterback should be. Not that he didn't have talent. He had talent.

J. T. Turner: Joe had a bad habit of calling his own plays. Coach was sort of mad at him. He told him if he ever changed another play, that would be it.

Joe Pisarcik: In weeks before this, I would have changed a play and I would get reprimanded for it. I was scratching my head over the call, but I knew who is going to get it if I didn't run what was called. The guard and the tackle can disagree and tell me to run something else, but I'm the guy they're [the coaches] going to say to, "Why the heck did you do something else? Why don't you run the plays that I call?" This happened in weeks prior.

Ed Croke: During the time-out, McVay took his headset off because he was figuring the game's over. Gibson was having a feud with Pisarcik at the time.

Gordon Gravelle: We learned it in Pop Warner football, and everyone in America knows that when you're third and two, you've got thirty seconds left on the clock, and the other team doesn't have any time-outs—what do you do? You snap the ball and drop on one knee. Game over—you win.

Vince Papale: I was sitting on the sideline and Coach Vermeil was pissed off because we couldn't stop the clock. It was a game we thought we should win and would win. I asked Coach Vermeil if he wanted me to start a fight if he thought it might help.

J. T. Turner: It was a hard-fought game. We were feeling good about it. We all thought that we had won it.

On the CBS telecast, Criqui's voice had taken on a tone of finality that is only natural to adopt at moments like this. He was quickly recapping what brought the teams to this point and what it meant for them going forward.

Bill Bergey: The guys on the Giants were coming to the line of scrimmage yelling, "Joe, just kneel down," and Joe was saying, "No, I gotta do what the coach says."

Joe Galat: Frank LeMaster told me years later that he and Bergey were yelling across the line: "What the hell are you guys gonna do?" LeMaster says that when Jim Clack came up to the line he said to the Eagles, "We're running it." Knowing Jim Clack and what a competitor he was, it was not to tip them off, but to let them know they were going to play football, not sit on the ball like they did on first down. Button up your chin strap.

Vince Papale: Never-say-die Herman, as intense as he was, was playing up on the line of scrimmage, waiting for something to happen.

Bill Bergey: Where the cornerbacks should have been back quite a few yards, Herman Edwards was on the line of scrimmage.

Joe Pisarcik: [Eagles nose tackle] Charlie Johnson really got into Clack, and I didn't get a clean snap. It was a little bit short. My fingers grabbed the middle of the ball, which meant I didn't have the whole ball in my hand.

Gordon Gravelle: The offensive line all fired out to knock our guys down.

Bill Bergey: He made the stupidest play I've ever seen. Not just a handoff, but a handoff on a reverse pivot.

Vince Papale: Csonka didn't even get his hands up to take the handoff. It was like he didn't want the ball!

Joe Pisarcik: In a split second, I tried to get the ball and give it to Larry and I hit him right on the hip with the ball.

Allan Webb: Well, there was a miscommunication between the OC and quarterback as to whether we were going to give the ball to Larry Csonka or take the knee and run the clock out. By the time we got all that straightened out, we had fumbled.

Joe Pisarcik: It's the end of the game—you want a straight handoff. Larry took too direct a route to the hole. He needed to go wider and then cut in, but he didn't—he ran straight. And Larry would cheat up a bit. He got there too quickly and I got there too late because I was having problems handling it. On film it looks like he's not even taking the ball.

Don Criqui: It was a room-service fumble recovery for Herman Edwards. The ball bounced straight up in the air. You couldn't have rehearsed something like this as a prank. Edwards was just shooting a gap and there was nobody there to stop him.

Gordon Gravelle: I tried to jump up to go get the ball, but my guy was lying on my legs. It was one of the most helpless feelings I've ever had in football. I couldn't respond and get the ball. I was two to three yards away from it and I saw Edwards come up and grab it.

Ed Croke: It was a perfect bounce. It couldn't be any easier. If the ball went any other way, somebody could have fallen on it and the game would have been over.

Gordon Gravelle: I've been cut, I've been hurt, I've been operated on, I've been traded—none of that stuff could even come close to the frustration of that one play, just for the simple stupidity of the call.

Joe Danelo: I don't remember any of my kicks from that game, but I do remember seeing that ball bounce in the air. All I could say was, "Edwards . . ." as I watched him scoop it up. Talk about opportunistic . . .

Bill Bergey: I met Herman in the end zone and we were all going crazy. I was looking around, saying to myself, "Is there a flag? I've played too many years of pro football—it can't be this easy. Nothing is this easy in football!"

Don Criqui: Sonny Jurgensen was my color man that day. The two of us were wondering if anybody did anything unusual that would negate the play, but there were no flags. You'd think a simple hand-off to a future Hall of Fame running back would be carried off without any problems.

Brian Kelley: I never watched that fumble because it irritated me so much—I never watched it on film or anything, and then about two months ago they were showing it on TV, on something like ESPN Classic, and the play before, Joe Pisarcik took a knee and I'm thinking, Why, if he took a knee before, would he hand off? I never remembered that part, that he took a knee the play before, so that even irritated me more. Why would you run the frickin' ball if you took a knee before? It just didn't make sense. It was sort of funny.

Ed Croke: It was the worst play in history.

Vince Papale: My father, like most Eagles fans, left the game early. Then they heard this cheer followed by booing. A lot of them ran back into the stadium.

Brian Kelley: I was on the sideline, and back then in those years, when a game was pretty much over and you lined up like that, every once in a while you'd get a nose tackle that would slap the ball away from the center before he snapped it and it would be offside. Well, that is what I thought had happened! I was looking the other way. We had just stopped the Eagles, so I was taking my pads off because the game was over. When I heard the crowd start yelling, I turned around and looked and saw Herman Edwards taking the ball and running it in for a touchdown. I turned back around and thought the center slapped the ball away or something like that. I thought it would be called back. I was looking at the fans the whole time and I saw the fans' faces and I thought, Oh my. I turned around and I saw the referee signal a touchdown and I thought, "You've got to be kidding me!" It was devastating.

Don Criqui: My spotter at the time was John Mara, the son of Wellington Mara. He was the best spotter I ever had. He was so disappointed, he got up and left the booth. After that game he never spotted again. He was just too disappointed. He ended up becoming president of the New York Giants, a position he still holds.

Ed Croke: I was in the Giants' end zone right near the locker-room entrance talking with Timmy Mara. Timmy said, "That was a squeaker, right?" Next thing you know, we hear this fucking howl. We turn around and Herman Edwards is running right towards us with the ball up in the air. Timmy said, "What the hell was that?"

Vince Papale: Vermeil jumped in my arms for a moment and then I sprinted to the end zone and jumped on the pile.

Bill Bergey: It was the craziest ending to a game I was ever involved in, including my thirteen years in pro football, my four years of college football, and my four years of high school football.

Joe Danelo: I was saying to myself, "Did I just see what I think I saw?" Next thing, this thing passed us—and it was an empty bottle of booze that came whipping out of the stands. The fans were just emptying stuff from the stands. The coaches said, "Put your bonnets on, boys." So we put our helmets on. We exited shoulder to shoulder. That was one time it was really nice to be short. Anything flying was going to hit the big boys first. There was just stuff everywhere.

Brad Benson: I just remember Wellington Mara's face. Never saw him like that before—never saw him like that again. I don't know whether he wanted to cry or shoot somebody. He was a very honorable man and it was very upsetting for him.

Joe Pisarcik: After the game, I was hiding in the training room. Wellington Mara came to me and said, "You have nothing to be ashamed of. Just keep your head high and you'll get through it. Just walk out there and tell those reporters what happened."

Joe Danelo: We went into the locker room and we were all in disbelief. It was dead silence. We had this doorman named Tony Siano, an older gentleman who had played in the early NFL for the Boston Redskins and Brooklyn Dodgers—a really nice man. He came walking into the locker room and, in the loudest voice he could muster, said, "Does anyone own a baby-blue Lincoln Continental with license plate NYG 9?" Joe Pisarcik looked up and said, "That's my car." We looked out and they had flipped his car over. We stayed there for quite a while. In fact, they eventually escorted us out of the visitors' side of the stadium.

George Martin: Without question, that was the lowest point in my career and, dare I say, in Giants history. We literally snatched defeat from the jaws of victory. It was a horrible experience and it was self-inflicted. It wasn't anything that the Philadelphia Eagles had done to us, and Herm Edwards became immortalized as a result of that and we were sort of demonized.

THE IMMEDIATE AFTERMATH

Vince Papale: The celebration went on and on and on. We celebrated all night, ending up at my house in Voorhees, New Jersey. The entire team was there. Mike Schmidt was my neighbor. He came over and so did another neighbor, Dougie Collins from the 76ers.

Joe Danelo: The very next morning, Coach Gibby [Bob Gibson] walked into his office and, about five minutes later, was carrying a briefcase going back out. He was very unceremoniously let go.

Doug Van Horn: We found out the next day, but we knew he had to go. This is not something that just happened—he'd been doing that all year long. That didn't just happen on that play. Those plays had been coming in all year that made no sense for the situation we had on the field. Then we had to listen to Pisarcik get reamed. We know what type of play fits the situation at hand. I don't know why McVay didn't see it. He brought Gibson in, so he was McVay's man. They weren't stupid football people, they had a sense, but why he didn't address that situation and get the offense together and talk about it—we weren't trying to upstage him. He could have at least had him ream Pisarcik in private. During a football season you want to try and get rid of that nonsense. That's the kind of stuff the good head coaches take care of. Good coaches get that stuff aired out and get everybody on the same page.

Allan Webb: I'm not putting the blame on anyone. It was just one of those things.

J. T. Turner: The next day I saw Bob walking out and he didn't look happy. I didn't get a chance to talk with him at length. I just said, "How you doing?" He said, "Fine." And he kept walking. I haven't spoken to him since that day. What I understood at the time—before that play happened—was that Andy Robustelli was supposed to retire, McVay was supposed to become general manager, and Gibson was supposed to be head coach. That play put an end to all that.

Brian Kelley: That was a big game for both Philly and us. I think that game sort of spurred Philadelphia on as far as them becoming competitive throughout the league. Two years later they went to the Super Bowl. It sort of changed their whole attitude around and everything. We were expecting to make the playoffs. We ended up losing three more after that, and they ended up making the playoffs for the first time in a long time.

George Martin: I realistically refer to that period of time as the era in which the New York Giants became the doormat of the industry because we literally lost our pride. It was embarrassing to say you played for the Giants at that time. I know none of us took a great deal of pride wearing a Giant cap or T-shirt or anything of that nature. It was almost like we were in the witness-protection program for athletes. We had very little confidence in ourselves and it sort of was permeating throughout the entire organization. So when the changes took place, they were not only timely, they were absolutely necessary to do an entire housecleaning to the organization.

Brad Benson: Fans were burning tickets. It was really bad. When I would stop for gas I would try to hide the fact of who I played for. Thank God they pumped the gas in New Jersey for you so nobody could see me out in public.

George Martin: One of the things you try to guard against as a team is to not let those things divide you and separate you—because at the end of the day you're all still wearing the same uniform—but it was tough to do during that period of time.

Brian Kelley: That was probably the most embarrassing moment ever for the New York Giants.

THE LONG-TERM AFTERMATH

Harry Carson: Losing a game when it was in the bag—just like that—teams around the league learned from that one experience.

Dave Anderson: It provoked a meeting of the fans, a rally, at a hotel near Giants Stadium. And later on that season, that plane went over towing a banner that read, FIFTEEN YEARS OF LOUSY FOOTBALL, WE'VE HAD ENOUGH.

Gordon Gravelle: This whole thing permeated down through the ranks all the way to the players, the equipment managers, trainers . . . we were a totally dysfunctional organization and we were better than that. If they would have just allowed us to play and allowed the coaches to coach and have a winning atmosphere in that locker room, we would have been a lot better. We had better talent than what our record shows. You've heard the saying, "I'd rather be lucky than good." You've also heard the saying, "Good teams seem to make their own luck." The reverse was true with the Giants. We made our own bad luck because we were so dysfunctional. That atmosphere and environment we were in the whole season led directly to our coach making that call and us running that play and us fumbling the thing and losing the ballgame.

Brad Benson: Coming from a program like Penn State, when I got to the Giants I could not believe what I saw going on there. It was horrendous—it was terrible. The lack of professionalism of the players they had there in those years. And I wouldn't get into names or anything, but it was really helter-skelter. I mean the deal with the fumble was just a culmination of all those events. It was a fitting end.

Gordon Gravelle: That call was the epitome of the dysfunctional environment that the team was in the whole season. When I say dysfunctional, it started at the top with Mr. Mara and the ownership. What I remember about those two years with the Giants was that was at the time when Wellington was trying to run the team as he always had, but then he had his nephew Tim. I'd come from the Steelers, who ran a wonderful, first-class organization where everyone was called by their first names except for two people: There was Mr. Rooney and Coach Noll. They had open-door policies—go see whomever you needed to see, from Dan Rooney on down. It was a pleasure to play in an organization and be an employee of an organization that was so well run. When I got to the Giants, they had a brand-new, state-of-the-art stadium, beautiful facilities, the huge New York market, great fans, et cetera, et cetera—but up at the top, they had two fighting owners. It was to the point that we would get conflicting directives sent down to us. We got directives from Wellington, who would come down and say one thing, and then five minutes later Timmy would send down a directive that was counter to the first directive. I mean sent down literally, because their offices were on the third floor of the stadium and we players couldn't go up to the offices. We had to call up to a secretary, explain who we needed to see and why we needed to see them, and then the secretary would send down a hall pass. Believe it or not, the security guards would come and give us the hall pass to use to get up the elevator into the front office. Absolutely absurd.

Many believe that the Fumble brought an end to this age of absurdity in the Giants' hierarchy.

Brad Benson: It was probably the best thing that ever happened to the Giants.

Dave Anderson: The Pisarcik game is what changed everything.

Harry Carson: There was tremendous fallout as a result of a play that never should have taken place. With that one play, so many things changed within the organization. So in some ways it was very, very bad, but it led to some pretty good things happening from a talent standpoint and a coaching standpoint as we moved forward.

Don Criqui: It changed the entire complexion of the Giants team after that. In the long run it was more value to the Giants losing the game than it was to the Eagles for winning it.

Dave Anderson: And that was what got everything going for Andy Robustelli to resign as director of operations, and then that brought in George Young, and Young brought in Ray Perkins to coach, and Young drafted Phil Simms.

Understanding that a perennially weakened Giants franchise was doing the NFL no good, Commissioner Pete Rozelle stepped in to moderate the Mara feud.

Ed Croke: It's an amazing thing both Wellington and Timmy agreed on Young. Before that, they each had their own candidates. Pete Rozelle said to the two of them, "Let's end this stuff. Why don't you put down a list of ten names and give them to me." They did, and Young was the only one who was on both lists. Everybody who knew football knew about George Young. All these press guys, like Paul Zimmerman, said this guy's a heck of a freaking value. He had coached with the Colts when they won the Super Bowl, then Don Shula brought him to Miami and he was a freakin' genius down there. While it was really surprising to a lot of fans that he was the choice, a lot of insiders said, "If you want to turn a team around, you got the right guy. He knows what he's doing." We ran a big press conference at Gallagher's in New York where we announced him.

Joe Danelo: I was drafted by Miami when George Young was a special-teams coach there, so I had a firsthand knowledge of who he was since he worked with the kickers. He was the person responsible for me playing in the NFL, because when Green Bay's kicker went down, he called me up and said, "You're going to play in this league. I made a call to Green Bay—they're going to call you within the hour." Sure enough, Green Bay called within ten minutes. When the Giants hired George Young, I said, "This guy is going to do some great things"—and he sure did. He was probably one of the best football minds out there. He knew personnel better than anybody at that time.

It is interesting to speculate what would have happened if Bob Gibson had called for Pisarcik to sit on the ball as he had on first down. New York would have won 17–12 and, all else being equal, finished 7–9 instead of 6–10, out of the playoffs—unless one believes that they were demoralized by the loss and that caused their subsequent fourth-quarter collapses. (See "The 1978 Giants: Wild-card Team?" page 181.) It is very possible that a shake-up was still inevitable, given the ongoing battle between Wellington and Tim Mara, as well as the fact that director of operations Robustelli has said he was planning on leaving football and returning to his private business long before Gibson helped deliver a miracle to the Eagles. The Giants had been muddling through for so long, though, that a 7–9 season might have been seen as something of an improvement, and everything would have remained status quo.

Harry Carson: It's just one of those things that was very difficult to come to grips with, but you go through it and just move forward and learn from it.

George Martin: Sometimes it takes that bitter pill you have to swallow before you can realize and appreciate the greatness of the good times.

Gordon Gravelle: I was with the Steelers and played in the Immaculate Reception game, and, living out here in the suburbs of the Bay Area close to Oakland for many years, I've had to deal with explaining the Immaculate Reception. So I played in both the Immaculate Reception and the Miracle at the Meadowlands, and, between the two, the one that really stands out more so is the fumble with the Giants.

Pisarcik played well the following week against Buffalo but had a bad game against the Rams in week fourteen and was benched. He returned for the finale against the Eagles and also faced them in the 1979 opener.

Joe Pisarcik: Playing the Eagles twice a year like we did, they got to know what I'm made of.

After being replaced by Phil Simms in week six of the '79 season, Pisarcik was relegated to backup duty with the Giants. He had won some fans in an unlikely place, however: the Eagles' coaching staff.

Joe Pisarcik: I've asked Dick Vermeil why they traded for me, and he said, "We played against you three or four different times and we hit you with everything we had and you just kept getting up and throwing that ball. I watched you throw the ball on film, and when it went through the air I couldn't see it that well. I knew you had a pretty strong arm. In the first game of the 1979 season you were coming back in the fourth quarter after we sacked you seven times! You wouldn't quit."

Bill Bergey: Herman Edwards's locker was always exactly across from mine at Veterans Stadium. I always had a football in my locker. I'd wait for Joe to come in and I'd throw the ball right in the middle of the floor and I'd say, "Herman, just do it one more time!" And he'd scoop up the ball and he'd run down the locker room, putting moves on everybody. At the end of the locker room he would spike the ball. And he'd yell, "We got 'em again!" Joe would respond with some unprintable stuff. It was all in the name of fun and games.

Vince Papale: He was a tremendous backup for Jaworski for five years. When Jaws went down a couple of times, he came in and was a capable quarterback. He had a strong arm. He was just a victim of some bad play calling.

Joe Pisarcik: At Wellington Mara's eightieth birthday party he said to me, "I'm really sorry about what happened with the fumble—that you have to carry that little anchor around with you." The guy was a saint. If we had gotten a clear exchange from center, Csonka probably would have gotten the ball. People fumble in life in every avenue of pursuit, whether it's in the stock market, fixing a car, or making a sales presentation. Maybe this fumble is the same kind of thing—although it was in front of seventy thousand people and everyone who is still talking about it three decades later probably sees that a little differently. I think in life what counts is not the fumble or failing on a sales call, it's how you react when it happens. Do you get up and dust yourself off? Do you live and learn from that experience and get strong from it, or do you say, "Woe is me. It's bad luck. Everything happens to me . . ."? I wanted to turn the other cheek and say that it helped me. I say that it's something that shouldn't have happened and say it's not totally Bob Gibson's fault, either.

APPENDICES

The 1978 Giants: Wild-card Team?

From the What If? History Department: Just about every team blows a lead or two in the fourth quarter during the course of a season. Sadly, unlike all the hundreds of other teams that have done so, the '78 Giants are known for it due to the spectacular fashion in which they let their game against the Eagles get away from them. Aside from that loss, however, New York let four other games slip through fingers with fourth-quarter collapses.

- *October 1 at Atlanta:* With the Giants trailing 16–14 at the end of three quarters, Joe Danelo hit on field goals from 23 and 45 yards to give them a 20–16 edge on the Falcons, but it was not a lead long for the world. Atlanta's Haskel Stanback ran in from the 9 to put New York away, 23–20.
- *October 29 at New Orleans:* The Giants were 5–3 and holding their own, one game behind the 6–2 Redskins (who would fade to 8–8) and Cowboys. On this Sunday, they built a 17–7 halftime lead against the Saints and still led 17–14 heading into the last quarter, but New Orleans tallied two more times to close them out, 28–17.
- *November 12 at Washington:* The Redskins and Giants were locked in a kicking duel, with Danelo and Mark Moseley hitting two each. Six minutes into the fourth quarter, George Martin sacked Joe Theismann for the fourth time—only on this occasion the ball came loose. Troy Archer scooped it up at the Washington 20 and ran in for the score, putting New York ahead 13–6. The Giants couldn't hold the lead, however, as Theismann drove the Redskins to the tying touchdown with a little over a minute to go in regulation. Moseley kicked the tiebreaker with 6:28 left in overtime, and the Giants lost, 16–13.
- *November 26 at Buffalo:* The Bills had lost four straight and were 3–9 when the Giants came to town. It appeared to be business as usual for downtrodden Buffalo as New York went up 17–7 in the

third quarter when Joe Pisarcik hit Doug Kotar on a 19-yard scoring pass. The Bills answered with a touchdown, but the Giants still led heading into the final period. It was then that the roof fell in: Buffalo scored 27 unanswered points in the fourth quarter, more than they scored in fourteen of their other fifteen games entire. The Bills were ranked last in their conference in rushing but managed a staggering 366 ground yards against the Giants.

Doug Van Horn: The Eagles game was a devastating loss, but the way we lost to the Bills was terrible, too. We wanted a little revenge, and it was a great opportunity for it because it was a team we should beat. The Bills were awful that year and that loss to them was the nail in the coffin.

If New York had been able to hold four of the five fourth-quarter leads they lost, they would have been the home wild-card team with a 10–6 record. They could have even gotten away with three wins in these games, provided two of them were against Philadelphia and Atlanta—the eventual wild-card teams. Had they done that, they would have been 9–7, with the Eagles and Falcons at 8–8, instead of 9–7. This would have sent the 8–7–1 Packers to the Meadowlands for the wild-card game.

Dallas Cowboys vs. New York Giants

December 19, 1981

	1	2	3	4	OT	F
Dallas Cowboys	0	0	0	10	0	10
New York Giants	0	0	7	3	3	13

In comparison to some of the longest-suffering teams in NFL history—
the Lions, the Cardinals, the Browns—the Giants' years in the wilderness are but a brief excursion. But that didn't make them any easier to
endure for the generations of fans used to something better, nor for
those who came of rooting age in their midst. And to those fans, deliv-
erance came in 1981.

When new general manager George Young looked for John Mc-
Vay's replacement, his eyes fell on San Diego. The Chargers had gotten off to a rough start in 1978, leading to the dismissal of coach
Tommy Prothro. His offensive coordinator was Ray Perkins, a former
wide receiver with the Baltimore Colts who had played under Bear
Bryant at Alabama. Perkins, who was in his first year with San Diego
after five years on the staff of the Patriots, was not replaced by the new
head coach.

Ray Perkins: Don Coryell was living right there, so they hired him.
He came into my office and said: "Hey, I like what you're doing. Let's
just keep doing it. I might just have a suggestion here and there. Are
we a go?" I said, "Let's go." That was really a great last three-quarters
of the year, know what I'm saying? The first five games really weren't
too good for us. None of us really did a very good job.

After a 1–3 start under Prothro and a few more bumps in transition, the Chargers began to click, winning six of their last seven. They closed out the season with wins of 40–7, 37–10, and 45–24, averaging 460 yards per game in that three-game span. Perkins's stock was very high. The Giants weren't the first team to talk to him about a head-coaching spot.

Ray Perkins: We had a bunch of fun doing it and then, at end of the year, I interviewed with Al Davis of the Raiders twice. Then George Young got the job in New York. George was an offensive-line coach when I was playing with the Colts. I pretty much knew before I went that I could win that interview. He offered me the job and I accepted. I don't think he got as much of the credit as he deserved for getting that whole team back after a lot of years being dormant around there.

PHIL SIMMS ARRIVES

Young and Perkins did not have to start from scratch. There was talent on hand. Many of the players from the 1978 disaster would still be around when the team improved in the ensuing years, but there were some key holes that needed filling.

Ray Perkins: We had three minicamps. I think the number-one thing we had to find out in the camps was if we had a quarterback that could take us to the Super Bowl. After we concluded that we did not, we went to the scouts and asked them for the top four quarterbacks.

Even knowing the outcome decades later, the Giants' choice still seems surprising: a quarterback from a small, obscure college—a school that wasn't even any great shakes on the field. Only one player who made it to the NFL had been drafted out of Morehead State before, and only one other Morehead player had lasted more than a single season in the league: the Giants' own tight end Gary Shirk.

Ray Perkins: I went and worked all of them out. The scoring came back, and I think George already knew that I was going to take Phil Simms. He had, at least, already seen him on film. I told him: "You're not going to believe the one I like best." He said: "Yeah, I think I would. It's Phil Simms, isn't it?" I said: "Yeah, how'd you know?" So he kind of knew beforehand. George was a great football man.

George Martin: When it was announced that Phil Simms would be our number-one draft choice, it was almost a mutiny. A crescendo of boos went over the audience. People were upset by that choice and, as a result, Phil was not embraced with open arms initially.

Ed Croke: Well, that shows you how much those boobirds at the draft know about anything. When we picked Simms, me and Pete Rozelle were standing there and we laughed that people were yelling out stuff like, "The Giants must think it's *Billy* Sims!" Phil Simms was from Morehead State—he wasn't even a Division I player. So anyway, he showed up, he went to camp, and he was working out pretty good. We were playing the Steelers in the first preseason game that year in Pittsburgh. As usual, I went down there three or four days before the game. I went into the Steelers' training camp to see the Pittsburgh writers and do all the shit you used to do in the old days. Bring film clips and talk to the press about your team. As I got finished, the Steelers' PR guy, Joe Gordon, said to me, "Chuck Noll wants to see you for a minute. You want to go see him?" I said sure. Joe took me to his dormitory room at their camp, and Noll was in there reading a magazine, and he said, "Come on in. How's that Simms doing in your training camp?" I said, "Doing pretty good, why?" He said, "Let me tell you something, if you didn't take him in the first round, I'd have taken him in a New York minute. That kid is gonna be some player, take my word for it." When I got back to camp, I said to Simms, "You know, Phil, you look a little nervous. Chuck Noll was talking about you and he said he would have taken you in the first round if we hadn't. He thinks you have a great future." Phil was beaming.

Much as the Giants had been the cradle of coaches some twenty-odd years earlier, they were about to become so again. Perkins would have on his staff two of the most influential coaches of the next twenty-five years. First there was the aborted stint of Bill Parcells, who was named defensive coordinator by Perkins only to quit after two months because his family didn't want to leave Colorado, where he had been the head coach at Air Force. Perkins would hire him again in 1981, however. He also brought in a twenty-seven-year-old position and special-teams coach who already had four years of NFL experience with four different teams.

Ray Perkins: There was a film guy that we had in New England, a quality-control guy named Ernie Adams. Ernie and I got kind of close. When I left New England and went to San Diego, I told him: "Ernie, I'm going to be a head coach one day, and you're going to be the first guy I come and hire." He said: "All right." I didn't know it was going to be so quick, but a year later, I called him and he was the first guy I hired. He had a suggestion for me to meet someone for my staff. He said: "He's out in Denver. He's been breaking down films for Baltimore for a few years, Detroit for a year. Then Denver kind of had him coach the tight ends or something like that." I said: "What's his name?" He said: "Bill Belichick." So when I went home to San Diego to clean up some personal business, I called him and asked him to fly down to San Diego. We met in a hotel there at the airport for about four hours, and I wound up hiring him as my special-teams coach. The next year, Parcells is in there as the defensive coordinator. We kind of let Belichick ease in over there on the defensive side and break himself in as coach of the special teams and linebacker coach.

Though key pieces were assembled, the transformation was not immediate. In 1979, the Giants again finished 6–10, with an even worse point differential than in 1978. They were 6–5 in games started by the rookie Simms, however. Furthermore, there was a completely new attitude under Ray Perkins and the retooled front office.

Harry Carson: We were accustomed to, I guess you could say, coaches who were pretty laid-back; not quite as intense. Bill Arnsparger was like that and then John McVay, who was pretty cool. Once Ray Perkins came in, he pretty much popped the whip and things were different. If you weren't able to adhere to more discipline as part of the entire team structure, then you were going to be gone. I was able to adjust to it. He came in being a hard-ass. He came in basically laying down the law. After a while, Ray even learned how to chill out in some way and adjust to the players. You can't be a hard-ass all the time. I think both sides got to understand one another and respect one another, so it was a good experience.

George Martin: We came from a rather lackadaisical environment where there wasn't a lot of discipline. We didn't have a great work ethic. And then Ray Perkins and George Young came in and it was like day and night. We did three-a-days during training camp, which is absolutely unheard of! Guys were getting hurt, there was a lot of competitiveness, there was an awful lot of discipline. And I think initially your natural tendency is to fight it because you're not accustomed to it. It divides the team, but eventually it makes you better because you realize that from a self-preservation standpoint, you've got to put out in order to remain a part of that team.

Brian Kelley: I could tell the change when Ray Perkins came in. We played the Steelers in his first preseason game and we lost like 13–10. This is 1979 and the Steelers were a good team. I knew things had changed when I came in the next day—this is on a Sunday after a Saturday game—and Ray Perkins is having us go hard. We were doing goal-line stands against the first-team offense, like twenty-five plays on goal line, full speed. It was unheard of. We came into the meeting that night and a lot of veterans were saying, "This is bullshit, we're not going to put up with this shit, you're beating the shit out of us." Ray Perkins got up and said, "I'll cut every one of you motherfuckers. I'll play with twenty-one or twenty-two rookies, I don't care!" You knew things had changed. And we needed that.

The 1980 season seemed like an even greater step backward as injuries decimated the roster and the Giants fell to 4–12, getting outscored by 176 points. From this giant glitch of a season came opportunity, though, in the form of the draft. The Giants were in a position to draft the single biggest impact player in their history.

THE COMING OF LT

Dave Anderson: George Young was holding his breath. Really. He held his breath for about a month. But George never tipped his hand. He never came out publicly and said, "Well, we hope Lawrence Taylor is there." Nothing. He just said, "Well, we'll see who's there when we pick."

Harry Carson: Initially, when we realized that the Giants were considering him, we made it known that we really didn't feel that we needed another linebacker because we were pretty good. He was a little offended by that. He actually sent a message that if he was going to be upsetting the apple cart, so to speak, then it was a good idea if the Giants didn't draft him, but the Giants went ahead and drafted him anyway.

Ed Croke: In that particular draft, I was in New York at our table. I was on the phone back to Giants Stadium with George Young and he said, "Listen, New Orleans has the first pick, we have the second. Get two cards. You're gonna write down two names. George Rogers, running back, and Lawrence Taylor, linebacker. Just keep 'em in your lap. Whichever one Bum Phillips takes, get that second card in as fast as you can." I had seen LT on film and I was just praying that Bum would take the running back. Please! Then Pete Rozelle made the announcement, "The New Orleans Saints, with the first pick of the draft, pick running back George Rogers." They made the announcement: "The Giants are next, they have fifteen minutes on the clock."

Dave Anderson: It took a second to send up that card saying, "The New York Giants draft Lawrence Taylor, linebacker, North Carolina."

Ed Croke: Let's get going, get it over with! I had that card out of my hand, yelling, "Here!" All those Giants fans were yelling, "LT! LT!" They weren't stupid—they knew what was coming. And then we announced that we had taken LT and the place was bedlam. He's the greatest player I ever saw in my life.

Harry Carson: When he came in, it didn't take us long to understand why the Giants drafted him, and that he was something special and unique. So I think the first day of practice we saw him from a physical standpoint, he was a nice-size physical specimen. We had seen quite a few guys who were physical specimens, but once he got on the field and he started going through drills, we could understand wholeheartedly why the Giants used a second pick in the draft to choose him. He was head and shoulders above everybody else. It didn't take him long to go from third team to first team.

Brian Kelley: When Harry Carson came, they moved me from the middle linebacker to the right outside and put Harry in the middle. Then in '81, when we went from the four-three to the three-four— we were sort of playing the three-four at the time, it started in '79 when Perkins came in—and LT came in, they moved me from outside back to inside back. So I always say, "I think I'm the only person to move to two different positions to make room for two different Hall of Famers." So I can't gripe about having to switch—they were good moves.

Harry Carson: I was very comfortable playing the four-three middle linebacker position. They offered the challenge of learning a new position as an inside linebacker. It was up to me to take on that challenge and make the adjustment. You find that in sports in general, everything is not going to go as you want it to be. I had been pretty successful as a four-three linebacker, then I had to change to three-four. So I was able to make the adjustment. It took a little while to get there, but I made the adjustment. We were able to play that defense pretty well and we got some success with it. Brian Kelley and Brad Van Pelt and I were a pretty good trio of linebackers for a couple of years until Lawrence Taylor came in. Then we became not just a trio, but a quartet of pretty good linebackers.

George Martin: I think, typically, a veteran's response to the arrival of the next big thing is always be skeptical to the nth degree because, until a guy gets there and can show you something definitive, you're not going to believe that he's worth that investment. And that had been the way for a long succession of top draft choices for the Giants. So this was certainly not going to be any exception.

Joe Danelo: You never saw a guy like LT before! Not physically imposing, but that changed when you got him on the football field. Now remember, the kicker has the best seat in the house, so for all those years I got to see some of the best, and then here LT came along. Not the biggest, most imposing linebacker you ever saw, but that quickness! For a guy that size to do the things he did was just mind-boggling—he shouldn't be moving that fast!

Ray Perkins: He was Mr. Football. He's the best football player that I've ever been around. I'm not saying that just because we picked him then, but from a raw-talent standpoint, from an intelligence standpoint, from a want-to standpoint, from a want-to-be-the-very-best-that-he-could-possibly-be standpoint, I've never been around anybody that possessed all those qualities more than Lawrence Taylor.

George Martin: I saw Lawrence put on that uniform and, on that very first day of practice, he left every skeptic in the nation aghast because this guy was the absolute real deal. He looked phenomenal from day one.

Ed Croke: His first team scrimmage in training camp, I think he had three sacks. It was unbelievable how fast he was coming off the ball. In college he played mostly as a down lineman. We turned him into a linebacker. Bill Parcells was the guy that worked with him. It was Parcells's first year as defensive coordinator and that's who he gets to work with.

J. T. Turner: Before him, they used to talk about defensive ends and the sack. Then there were outside linebackers and the sack, because he took it to a different level.

George Martin: He was an impact player, and now we're thinking, "How could anybody have passed this talent up?" He was legitimate from the first snap, and he was that way until he retired. One of the greatest privileges in my life is to say that I had the honor of playing with the great Lawrence Taylor.

THE 1981 SEASON

The difference that Taylor made was immediate and astounding. In 1980, the Giants allowed 429 points, the second most in the league. The offense wasn't much better, managing to score just 249 points, better than only two other teams. In 1981, the offense was about the same, but the defense made a great leap forward, scoring four touchdowns of its own and allowing just 259 points. This was the third-lowest total in the league and helped the Giants experience a 214-point swing in their point differential.

New York was suddenly in games that would have gotten out of hand the year before. At the midway point they were 5–3, having won three in a row, including a 32–0 road shellacking of the Seahawks and an overtime win in Atlanta in which a 40-yard Joe Danelo field goal provided the margin of victory. Slippage followed. The Jets came out of the gate slowly in '81 but were hitting stride when they shut out the Giants' offense: The Giants' only score in the 26–7 loss came on a Beasley Reece fumble recovery. What is more, Simms strained his groin in the contest and would be replaced by Scott Brunner. He would return in week eleven, only to miss the rest of the season with a shoulder injury.

The Giants then went to Green Bay and fell behind 20–0. They rallied and actually took a 24–23 lead, eventually losing to the Packers 26–24 on a Jan Stenerud field goal with 2:36 remaining. It was the second loss to the Packers that season. It was rare, but not unheard of (it happened twenty-five times between 1978 and 1994), for nondivisional clubs from the five-team divisions to meet twice in the same year during this period. In this case, the two meetings would end up having ramifications in the wild-card determination.

The Cowboys and defending-conference-champion Eagles were both 8–2, so, at 5–5, New York needed a win to stay relevant in the wild-card race. They appeared to have one in hand in Washington in week eleven. Trailing 24–20 with just 1:48 on the clock, Brunner drove the Giants from their own 32 to the Washington 27. Facing a fourth and 10, Brunner hit a wide-open John Mistler for the go-ahead score. There were only forty-five seconds on the clock.

Joe Danelo: Our game plan was to keep it away from their return man, Mike Nelms. We had an unbelievable tailwind, though, and one of the caveats was, if it is windy and you feel confident enough, we'll go ahead and kick it deep. It wasn't the swirly winds like they used to have at Shea Stadium or in Buffalo. I had already kicked one eight yards deep, and then ten yards deep from this direction, so I've got all this adrenaline going. I went back to the sideline thinking I can kick this one to the third row. The word came down from Coach Belichick up in the booth that I was to squib it. I said, "I can kick it deep—I know it." Coach Perkins came over with those steely blue eyes and said, "Is there a problem here?" I said, "Well, Coach Belichick wants to squib it." To which Perkins replied, "Then squib it." I said, "Yes, sir."

Now I had to look the other ten guys on the kickoff team in the eyes and tell them we're going to squib it. Terry Jackson looked at me and said, "Don't you dare. I'll take the heat." I said, "I'm sorry. I can't!" A squib kick, even if it is executed perfectly, is not a ground ball, it's a crap shoot at best. But somebody somewhere developed this thing and I never really quite understood it, but you're told to do certain things as a player and do what you're told. It wasn't a very good squib kick, I'll admit that. The up guy, Darryl Grant, picked it up after a couple of bounces. It was poor execution, but I thought it was a bad decision.

Moseley came in, kicked a field goal to send it into overtime. They won the toss. I kicked off from the same direction as in the fourth quarter and I kicked it about three to four yards out of the end zone—it took two bounces and went in the third row. It was frustrating. They won the game in overtime.

After the 30–27 loss, Belichick was asked about the play call. "I made a bad decision on the squib kick," he admitted. "We had talked like they were going to get something good on the return. We just gave them too good field position."

Joe Danelo: I went into the locker room and I couldn't keep my big mouth shut, but those are the life lessons you learn: You have to learn to walk away when you're emotional. I didn't do it, I was disappointed in the decision and voiced that opinion to one particular reporter and it was all over the papers. I went in the locker room the next day and Coach Perkins called me into his office. I won't tell you what he said, but I called my wife and told her she might want to start packing. It was my own fault. Couldn't keep my mouth shut when I should have.

It was the kind of play that could have been just as costly as the Fumble in 1978. Instead, all parties survived and the Giants rebounded. New York took out the first-place Eagles the next week, 20–10. Then, after a road loss to the eventual Super Bowl champion 49ers, they cleaned out the Rams and Cardinals to move to 8–7.

THE OPPONENT

In 1965, both the Cowboys and Giants went 7–7. Beginning the next year, the Cowboys began making the playoffs with predictable regularity while the Giants gave up the practice altogether. Heading into their second 1981 contest with New York, Dallas had spent only five weeks under .500 since the beginning of the 1966 season—that's five weeks out of 224. (In 1974, they got off to a 1–4 start and finished 8–6, failing to make the playoffs for the only time until 1984.)

The '81 Cowboys entry was a running team. Nobody handed off more that year: Their 630 rushing attempts were the most in the NFL. They amassed 2,711 yards on the ground, second only to the Billy

Sims–centric Detroit Lions. Tony Dorsett had the second-most rushing yards in the league with 1,646 (behind number-one draft choice George Rogers, who had 1,674) on a healthy 4.8 yards per carry. When they did pass, quarterback Danny White's favorite targets were Ron Springs out of the backfield and wide receivers Drew Pearson and Tony Hill. On the other side of the ball, Dallas was known for its talented front four of Harvey Martin, John Dutton, Randy White, and Too Tall Jones. None was selected for the Pro Bowl less than three times in his career; Randy White was eventually designated for enshrinement in Canton. Rookie left cornerback Everson Walls led the league in interceptions and would do so again the following year. Later on in his career, he would end up on the Giants and retire tied for eleventh all-time with 57 picks. The other cornerback, Dennis Thurman, had a career-high 9 picks in '81, and rookie safety Michael Downs had 7. In all, the Cowboys swiped 37 passes (while throwing only 15 picks) and held opposing quarterbacks to a 46 percent completion rate, an outstanding figure.

Cowboy seasons of this vintage are remarkably the same: week after week of high-level competence with the occasional letdown and thriller thrown in. Their worst showing was a 45–14 loss in San Francisco, a game with tiebreaker consequences. Their most exciting win was a late two-touchdown rally to nip the Dolphins, 28–27. Their other two losses were close ones to the Cardinals and Lions, both of which were decided by fourth-quarter field goals. The rest of their games were part of the relentless parade of victories that was the trademark of the Cowboys of this era, including an 18–10 win over the Giants in week four, the thirteenth downing of the Giants in fourteen meetings.

George Martin: I liked to call Dallas the Giant Killer because we had a lot of battles with them and we always seemed to manage to come out on the short end of the stick. One of the things that assistant coach Ralph Hawkins said when he first came on board as defensive coordinator, which I was so impressed with, was, "Gentlemen, from now on we're going to start to beat the Dallas Cowboys. And if you don't beat them you can leave. But we're going to beat those son of a guns." And when he just made that prophetic statement I said,

"Wow, what a great attitude, to walk in and say we're going to beat our perennial foes in the division."

By week sixteen Dallas had already clinched the division, but the game was not without meaning for them. A win over the Giants coupled with a 49ers loss later in the day would afford them home-field advantage throughout the playoffs. Tom Landry's take on the game is an interesting one, given the annual arguments about what a team that has clinched "owes" other teams who need them at their best—because of who they're playing down the stretch. "We have a problem in motivation," he said. "They're playing to get in the playoffs, and we're relieved to have won the division. But we can't rest our regulars when our opponents are going for the playoffs. That would not be fair to other teams trying to get in the playoffs."

THE GAME

Jim Burt: I don't think the Cowboys wanted to be there.

Brian Kelley: My initial thought was that I knew we could beat Dallas. You know what I was worried about? The Jets beating Green Bay. I didn't trust those guys. I thought they would lay down or something. I knew we could beat the Cowboys. We'd come together as a pretty good team. Defensively we were tough. Our defense was awesome that year. We lost to San Francisco seventeen to ten—it was a great game. We should have beaten them, but defensively we did our job. Our offense just didn't do much that day. I knew we were a good team, I knew we were good enough to beat the Cowboys.

Billy Ard: That game was a game within a game for me. The Dallas Cowboys had their great defensive lineman Randy White. He was in the prime of his career and I always had great respect for him—he played with an unbelievably high level of intensity. He'd have a tough time playing now with all the rules changes. He couldn't do half the stuff he did back then. So here was this guy, a multiple All-Pro, Super

Bowl co-MVP, and he's going to come to town wanting to wreak havoc. So I made up my mind I was not going to be denied in that game—I really wanted to block this guy. I was so mentally juiced for that game. I remember the first play. I came at the ball the very first run. Randy White had bubble wrap that he would put on his forearms and hands and tape it up. He would use it like a cast. So he came up and I hit him as hard as I could and he hit me probably as hard as he could. He hit me in the head, and I definitely got my bell rung. I'm like, "Okay, if that's the best you can do, I can handle that." That was me: talking myself into it. I played him as hard as I possibly could. I'm not sure how many tackles he had that day, but I know he didn't have any sacks.

The battle in the trenches notwithstanding in the cold and wind at the Meadowlands, the Giants' day got off to an inauspicious start. Their two first possessions began with great field position made better by Rob Carpenter's running and two sizable passes to Dave Young and Earnest Gray. Both drives stalled in the red zone, however, and New York opted for field-goal attempts.

Joe Danelo: Some of the worst games I had were at the end of the season, because that time of year the wind didn't really come at you or away from you, it came around. Not making a big deal about it, just kick the ball and fire it right in there. But I had a horrible, horrible day that day, nobody to blame but myself. I was getting more frustrated, I didn't have a very good pregame warm-up—by that point you're used to the weather, so you can't blame the weather, and I just wasn't kicking well that particular day. What I do remember is having missed one field goal, it was really two, because one of those field goals there was a penalty and I got another opportunity and botched that.

The first opportunity was missed wide left from 21 yards out. The second was a 32-yarder that hit the upright. Then, on the mulligan thanks to the offside penalty on Too Tall Jones, Danelo missed to the right from 27 yards away. The first quarter ended with Danny White's third punt of the day as Dallas was now 1-for-4 on third-down conversions.

And so it would continue in the second quarter. Lawrence Taylor had a near interception and Gary Jeter dumped White for an 8-yard sack. Dorsett was making no progress. (See "Shut Down," page 204.) New York's best opportunity of the quarter came when the Cowboys' Anthony Dickerson plowed into rookie return man Leon Bright, who had signaled for a fair catch. The 15-yard boost gave them a start at the Dallas 37. New York was moving on the ground, but Ike Forte fumbled on the Dallas 22. The half ended with another stalled Cowboy drive followed by that rarest of NFL bird, the 60-yard field-goal attempt. Rafael Septien's boot fell short, however, and the teams went into the locker room without having scored.

For the Cowboys' offense, the second half was a continuation of the first. The Giants forced them to punt on their first two possessions. New York's second possession started with Beasley Reece recovering his own fumble on White's punt at the Giants' 38. After Leon Perry (7 yards) and Carpenter (4) got a first down, Brunner hit Young for 12, putting the Giants at the Dallas 39. The next play was a flea-flicker, with Brunner getting the ball back from Carpenter on a pitch. Cowboys linebacker D. D. Lewis got his hands up and tipped the pass at the line of scrimmage, but it found Leon Perry anyway and he was brought down after a 16-yard gain. Could the Giants get the rest of the way, or was it going to fall to Danelo to try to wrestle with the wind once again? On second down from the 20, Brunner hit Tom Mullady in the end zone and the Giants were on the board. "I'm still not clear what happened on the play," Mullady said later, claiming he didn't remember it at all. "I guess I was hit on the head on the touchdown."

Given the wind and the tenacity of the two defenses, it seemed like the sort of game where one touchdown might be the extent of the scoring. Keeping the Cowboys from answering was key for the defense, but the third quarter ended with Dallas's biggest play of the day, a 44-yard gainer on a pass from White to Tony Hill with Mark Haynes covering. Play started in the final quarter with the ball on the Giants' 11. Dorsett got 8 of his 39 yards (on 21 carries) on the next two plays, giving Dallas a third and 2 from the 3. The Cowboys finally got on the board when White hit tight end Doug Cosbie to the left.

With the score 7–7, New York's season almost ended on the very next play. Septien kicked off to Danny Pittman at the goal line, but

Pittman lost the ball. New York's season hung in the balance. If the Cowboys recovered, it would have been the end of the line for the Giants. Instead, it was an alert Beasley Reece who fell on the ball. The crisis was averted, but the Giants were pinned at their own 1-yard line.

Carpenter gave them some space with a 5-yard gain, but Young dropped Brunner's next pass. Brunner then hurled a bomb to Mistler at midfield, but it was intercepted by Downs. The Cowboys took over on the New York 47 and moved to the 17 where they stalled, in part courtesy of Terry Jackson spoiling a Drew Pearson reception. With 9:00 showing on the clock, the Cowboys opted for a 36-yard Septien field-goal attempt. It was good, giving them the 10–7 lead.

Pittman again had trouble with the ensuing kickoff. This time he failed to corral it at the 6, but it turned into a New York advantage when Leon Bright scooped it up and returned it 41 yards. The drive stalled, though, and Dave Jennings nailed the Cowboys with a punt to the 5. White got the Cowboys moving and, after a 23-yard completion to Pearson, they were nearly to midfield. On first and 10, Dorsett's bad day got worse. White pitched him the ball and he juggled it. Linebacker Byron Hunt, filling in for the injured Brad Van Pelt, hit him, and George Martin fell on the ball at the Dallas 45.

With two minutes showing on the clock, the Giants had field position and hope, provided Danelo could overcome his kicking woes. Those hopes were compromised when tackle Jeff Weston was flagged for holding, negating an 11-yard gain by Perry. After an incompletion, Brunner got 7 of the yards back with a pass to Mistler.

It was now fourth and 13 with 1:33 to go. Hopes for a return to the playoffs hinged on this long-shot situation. Could the Giants dig themselves out of this hole and gain redemption?

Brunner took the snap and did his dropback. Very quickly, the pocket disintegrated around him. Downfield, Mistler broke to the middle. Brunner stepped up, avoiding the oncoming rush, and hit his man. It was a 22-yard pickup, and it brought the Giants back from the precipice. A few plays later, on third and 7 with thirty-five seconds to go, the Giants went for the win with a pass to Earnest Gray in the end zone. It fell to the grass, overthrown.

It was time for Danelo to face the music again, this time from 40 yards out. If he missed, there would be no time left to get the ball back again for another chance. It was now or never. With the clock showing just twenty-five seconds, he swung his leg back and let fly. This time he was true, and the game was tied 10–10. The season had just gotten one period longer.

OVERTIME

New York won the toss but went three and out at their own 10. The Cowboys were cited for clipping on the punt return and started from their own 40. On second and 2, another pitch to Dorsett went astray. "It hopped like a knuckleball," Danny White said later, but Dorsett made no excuses for himself.

"I still had a chance to catch it," he said. "I had a chance to pick it up. It was a great play by whoever came down on top of me." That whoever was Lawrence Taylor, who came up with the ball and returned it to the Dallas 40.

On second down, Brunner pulled a nifty bootleg.

Billy Ard: At Delaware, Scott was allowed to always fake the play and run a naked bootleg, which they do all the time in the NFL now. So he decided to not tell anybody. He faked the handoff, kept the ball, and booted around the left side for over twenty yards. I didn't know about it. I said to Brunner, "You have such big balls. How the fuck do you do that?" He said, "Well, the play wasn't going to work." He's a really calm guy. I asked him, "So what did Perkins say?" He told me Perkins said, "Scott, you're lucky as all heck that worked because if that didn't work, don't even come to the sidelines." That was some pretty cool stuff.

"You don't tell anybody when you bootleg," Perkins said after the game, "It's ineffective if anyone knows." The play went for 23 yards, putting the Giants squarely in field-goal range. After a short run by Carpenter, Danelo was brought in on third down to win it. Before this game, he hadn't missed any field-goal attempts of less than 36 yards.

Joe Danelo: After I made that forty-yard field goal, my confidence was sky-high. Now I'm kicking in the same direction and I thought,

"This is gonna be a piece of cake." I had all the confidence and I nailed this thing—or so I thought. An image from the slide show in my head about that kick: There was a guy in a jacket and he threw his hands up in the air like he's the referee under the goal posts and I'm thinking, Wow, this is great. And then, out of nowhere, the ball just stopped and slammed into the upright. It was like watching the Fumble again. I kicked it exactly how I wanted to kick it. If you look at the film, the people right behind the goal posts are raising their hands like it's good. I went down. "*Noooo!*" I said in total disbelief. No way! Going off the field, the guys were trying to pick me up, and I could only look at them and say, "I'm sorry." Everybody was beating their heads against the wall trying to get this win and I went out there with the simplest job and didn't get it done.

George Martin: Joe is normally a sure-footed kicker but the elements are always playing tricks on you, and especially that wind inside the stadium.

Billy Ard: Hey, keep the ball between the uprights! I have no patience for that. You can't miss twenties, twenty-ones, or twenty-sevens and twenty-eights and thirties. Come on, you're a professional. That's my opinion.

Joe Danelo: Byron Hunt came walking by me and I grabbed him by the jersey and told him, "We gotta get this ball back—I gotta get another shot."

Perkins reassured Danelo that he would get another chance. It was then that the Giants' defense found another gear. On second and 8 from his own 20, White was dumped by Bill Currier on a safety blitz. He fumbled, but Dorsett was there to keep it away from the Giants. On third and 14, White tried to hit Pearson for the necessary first-down yardage. Instead he nailed Byron Hunt, who gratefully accepted the gift and returned it 7 yards before being brought down.

Joe Danelo: I couldn't believe it! I wanted to run on the field and kick it right then. A couple of downs later, I went in and made it good.

Danelo hit it from 35 yards out, 6:19 into overtime. The Giants had finished over .500 for the first time in nine years and their playoff hopes were very much alive.

Joe Danelo: They gave me plenty of opportunities. Thank God for Byron Hunt and the rest of the defense. I saw Byron about five years later at a players' convention. The first thing I did was jump up and give him a hug. I said, "Byron, I'll never forget you as long as I live."

George Martin: People just cheered their lungs out . . . we were so elated on the sideline, almost to the point of disbelief, that we had really beaten the Dallas Cowboys soundly in our own backyard.

Joe Danelo: After the game, a reporter pulled me aside and said, "Congratulations, you did it!" I said, "I didn't do a damn thing today. This is one of the worst games I've played. If you want to talk to somebody, talk to the defense. I'm embarrassed by the way I played." I had tears of sorrow for myself. That was one of the most horrible games, and then one of the most uplifting games. After having two field goals go awry, I'm thinking, What do I have to do? It's not that difficult.

Billy Ard: It was a big thing. The Giants were shitty for seventeen years.

Ray Perkins: It was a big game and we rose to the occasion and got a big victory.

Brad Benson: It was a beginning of things to come.

THE AFTERMATH

And so it came down to events beyond the Giants' control. They would make the playoffs if Philadelphia or Green Bay lost. The 9–6 Eagles were hosting the 7–8 St. Louis Cardinals while the 9–5–1 Jets were doing the same for the 8–7 Packers. Both the Jets and Packers needed the win to clinch a wild-card spot (although the Jets still had a back door in if the Chargers lost to the Raiders on Monday Night Football). For their part, the Giants trekked out to Queens and the swirling winds of Shea Stadium, dressed as spectators.

J. T. Turner: The next day we watched the Jets game in the press club.

Brian Kelley: Thank God the Jets came through for us!

The Jets did not burden the Giants with any drama. They completely stifled the Packers, building a 21–3 halftime lead. Green Bay managed just 84 total yards and eventually lost 28–3.

Joe Danelo: We were up in the stadium club. When the game was over, it was pandemonium again. It was a two-day high for the guys—it was fantastic.

George Martin: It was a big deal because for the vast majority of us, we never knew what postseason play was all about. If you were a Giant player, your bags were packed the week before the last game, and after that last game, you were on your way home for summer recess, as it were. This time was different! We were gonna play in the post-season and get that vital experience.

J. T. Turner: When it was over, we got ready for practice the next day. It was a very exciting weekend.

The Giants were in their first playoff game since losing to the Bears in the 1963 championship. The following Sunday, they traveled to Philadelphia and jumped all over the Eagles, running up a 27–7 half-time score. They then had to dig in their heels in the second half, when they stopped scoring and the Eagles crept to within 6. Rob Carpenter rushed for 161 yards on 33 carries, doing all of the clock eating himself on the Giants' final possession and getting the wind knocked out of him twice during the game. It was New York's first postseason victory since dispatching the Cleveland Browns in the 1958 tiebreaker.

In the divisional game a week later, the Giants' season came to an end. Playing the 49ers on the road, New York fell behind 24–7 but had battled back to within a touchdown. In the fourth quarter, they had forced San Francisco into a third and 18 when a lineman from each team got into an altercation.

Jim Burt: We were going to get out of the series and have a chance to tie the game, then have a chance to beat San Francisco out there.

Bill Ard: Gary Jeter punched Dan Audick in the head. Automatic first down, they scored—game over.

George Martin: I think it was a close call even that day. We had them on the ropes until the fourth quarter, until Gary Jeter got a personal foul and allowed them to keep possession of the football, and that was the difference in the game as far as I'm concerned. And had it not been for that personal foul, I think we would have gone deeper in the postseason, but, as history said, it wasn't to be.

APPENDICES

Shut Down
Best Giants Performances Versus Elite Backs Since 1960

Suppressing Tony Dorsett in this game helped keep Dallas off the scoreboard. Unfortunately, that is not always the case when a team stuffs a featured back, as other weapons are brought into play. Below are the Giants' best defensive performances against elite backs over the past fifty years. We are defining an elite back as anyone who is either in the Pro Football Hall of Fame or was ranked as one of the fifty best running backs of all time by Sean Lahman in *The Pro Football Historical Abstract*. The number next to their names is their yards-per-carry figure from that individual game. They were required to have at least ten carries to be eligible for this list. In this time period, the Giants have come up against these elite backs on about 250 occasions.

0.21: Tony Dorsett, Dallas Cowboys;
November 2, 1987 (14 carries, 3 yards)
New York had some great performances against Dorsett. They held him under 2.5 yards per carry on five separate occasions in sixteen meetings, this one being the most suppressive. Dorsett had just one catch for 2 yards in this game, too. It was only a moral victory, though, as the Cowboys prevailed 33–24.

0.64: John Riggins, Washington Redskins;
November 18, 1985 (11 carries, 7 yards)
This infamous game was the contest in which Lawrence Taylor ended Joe Theismann's playing career on Monday Night Football as millions cringed. While the New York D did a fine job tamping down Riggins (he also only caught one pass), Art Monk was catching 7 throws for 130 yards and Jay Schroeder racked up 221 yards as Theismann's replacement. Joe Morris had 3 touchdowns, but Washington got the 23–21 win.

1.10: Earnest Byner, Washington Redskins;
October 27, 1991 (10 carries, 11 yards)

While Byner didn't get the most Redskin carries this afternoon (that was Ricky Ervins with 22), this was in the midst of a 1,000-yard campaign, so attention must be paid. The Giants stopped scoring after the second period and saw their 13–0 lead turn into a 17–13 defeat.

1.18: Emmitt Smith, Dallas Cowboys;
October 18, 1999 (22 carries, 26 yards)

Like Riggins, Smith scored a touchdown in this one—the Cowboys' lone touchdown, as it turned out, and the Giants prevailed, 13–10. His longest run from scrimmage was 5 yards, and he had no receptions. He rushed for 1,397 yards in 1999, so this was, by far, his worst performance of the year.

1.30: Edgerrin James, Indianapolis Colts;
December 22, 2002 (10 carries, 13 yards)

True, 2002 was a down year for James, not being one of the seven seasons in which he rushed for 1,100 yards or more. The Giants swamped him—he was also held to 2 yards receiving on three catches—and won 44–27.

1.59: Herschel Walker, Dallas Cowboys;
September 20, 1987 (17 carries, 27 yards)

Walker did have 50 yards receiving on three catches (he led the league in yards from scrimmage in 1987), but got completely jammed up at the line by the Giants. They also intercepted four Danny White passes. Too bad for them that Phil Simms threw four picks, too, and Dallas won, 16–14.

1.64: Emmitt Smith, Dallas Cowboys;
November 24, 1996 (11 carries, 18 yards)

New York held Dallas to just 33 yards rushing, but the Cowboys had better luck in the air, as Smith had four catches for 24 yards. It was nowhere near enough; New York won 20–6. On December 17, 2000, the Giants held Smith to under 2 yards per carry for a third time.

1.69: Hugh McElhenny, San Francisco 49ers;
September 25, 1960 (16 carries, 27 yards)
In this 21–19 Giants win, the King was stymied time and time again at the line. He did catch four passes for 79 yards, however, which, arguably, should be enough to buy his way off this list. San Francisco quarterback Y. A. Tittle, not known for his dash, actually outgained McElhenny in this game 48 to 27. They would be reunited as Giants three years later.

1.73: Tony Dorsett, Dallas Cowboys;
October 5, 1980 (15 carries, 26 yards)
Conspicuous by their absence from this list are games from the Wilderness Years of 1964 to 1980. This would be the only exception, but it came in a 24–3 loss to Dallas, so it was a pyrrhic victory at best. Dorsett had four catches for 30 yards.

1.83: LaDainian Tomlinson, San Diego Chargers;
November 8, 2009 (12 carries, 22 yards)
This 21–20 defeat was the Giants' fourth in a row after starting the season 5–0. They held the Chargers to just 34 yards rushing, their best run-suppression job of the season. Tomlinson, who also caught two passes for 8 yards, had a significantly reduced role in 2009, the first time in his career that he didn't rush for four figures.

Denver Broncos vs. New York Giants

SUPER BOWL XXI
January 25, 1987

	1	2	3	4	F
New York Giants	7	2	17	13	39
Denver Broncos	10	0	0	10	20

It's rare that a game, especially a championship game, truly turns on just one play, but Super Bowl XXI may well have been one such game. Furthermore, the play in question occurred because of one of the gutsiest coaching calls in the history of professional football's championship games.

That play was called not by Ray Perkins, but by his successor, Bill Parcells. In the winter of 1982, after four seasons, the last of which was marred by a players' strike, Perkins answered what was, for him, a higher calling.

Ray Perkins: Call me crazy, I'll admit, but for several years it had been in my mind that I would like to follow Coach [Bear] Bryant at Alabama. When I talked to Wellington Mara and George Young about it, they understood it. They were just wonderful about the whole situation. I didn't leave or anything because of the strike or anything like that. I mean, the strike hurt my feelings a little bit, but it wasn't because of all that. It was my love and just desire, strong desire, to become Coach Bryant's successor, to just follow him at Alabama.

Harry Carson: Quite frankly, I didn't know what was going on with George Young's thinking. Apparently he knew something that we didn't know. Bill Parcells was a good linebacker coach. Apparently, when that whole situation took place, George looked at Bill as an obvious person who could take over. Nobody really expected any changes in the head-coaching position to be taking place during that time, but they did, and Bill was caught off guard as well. I was happy for him. I got to know Bill on a different level because he was my position coach before he became the head coach. We now had to show Bill Parcells a certain amount of respect, because he was no longer one of us, he was one of them—head coach. We couldn't address him in the same manner we addressed him when we were in a meeting room by ourselves with him. If we had done that, then it really would have set the wrong example for some of the younger guys, who would have probably done the same thing. So we had to look at him in an altogether different light, but we always knew that we were his guys. We had a special and unique relationship with him and we wanted the best for him. Unfortunately, that first year that he took over, so many things went wrong during the course of that season, that he almost got booted before he even got started.

Jim Burt: Coach Parcells was a fundamentals guy: block and tackle. Do those things. Basically a vanilla guy as far as scheming goes. He wanted the guys to be fundamentally sound. He wanted them to be a certain size and he wanted guys he can trust and count on. The way he did that was by his personality—the way he finessed people. He was a master psychologist. He was great at knowing who to kick in the ass—then, later on, he would put his arm around them and say, "You know I really love you." He had a tremendous amount of wit, and motivational skills that not too many guys have. That was his MO. He was very witty with the press, knew how to handle them, deflect things.

Parcells's first season resulted in a 3–12–1 record.

Ed Croke: He had players getting hurt—it's amazing he got through that first year. George Young considered replacing him with Howard

Schnellenberger, one of George's connections with the Colts. Schnellenberger had been head coach in Baltimore.

Brad Benson: It was the talk everywhere that Howard Schnellenberger was going to replace Parcells. So, Parcells had a parking place down in the tunnel, and over his name I put white trainer's tape with "Schnellenberger" written on it.

Billy Ard: Bill would yell at Brad everyday, but he did that out of habit. It's not like he hated him. Freaking Benson loved it even though he got ragged on every day. Benson would say every day in the locker room, "I tell you what, if that Parcells says one more thing to me, I'm going to let him have it." We just rolled our eyes. One day Benson came walking into the weight room and he said, "Fucking Parcells." Someone said, "What do you mean, Brad? He didn't yell at you today." Brad said, "Exactly, he's writing me off."

Very few of those losses were blowouts, however, and the Giants' point differential suggested a better team—a sure sign that improvement was likely to follow. Sure enough, the improvement did come. The Giants grabbed a wild-card spot in 1984 on tiebreaking procedures with the Cardinals and Cowboys and beat the Rams in the playoffs before being upended by the eventual Super Bowl champion 49ers. In 1985, the Giants were a wild-card team once again. This time they dispatched the 49ers in the wild-card game before running into a Bears team that is very much in the argument as the best of all time: They beat the Giants 21–0. While there was no shame in being shut out by a Bears team that held fourteen of its nineteen opponents to 10 points or fewer, it didn't make it any easier for the Giants.

Leonard Marshall: We knew we were just as good if not better than the Chicago Bears. They had enough schemes and trick things in their bag. They were a little bit better than us on that day.

Carl Banks: They had yet another gear that we had yet to achieve. So actually, that was kind of a blessing in disguise, the fact that we

actually went up against a team that could match us in the tough-
ness category and the physicality category and still come out on top
and be as dominant as they were. It showed us that we had to be, as
a team, of the same mind-set. I thought individually we had those
guys. But as a team, we found out that there's a whole other level
that we could get to, and we did.

Joe Morris: We were a pretty intense team. We thought we were on
the right track, but then we saw the intensity level of the Bears and
what they brought on defense to their game and how they went about
things. They were on such another level, one that we could step up to.

Harry Carson: Well, when we went through the '85 season, we thought
that we were pretty good. We thought we were better than the Bears.
We went into Soldier Field and, obviously, we were not ready for
prime time. We committed some errors, made some mistakes, basically we shot ourselves in the foot and the Bears won the game. We all
tasted the same bitter pill and we said in the locker room, we rededi-
cated ourselves at that time. We said when we got back on the field
things were going to be different. We were going to be certain to be
in control of our own destiny.

Bart Oates: I remember talking to Phil Simms about that game and
he was saying how close we were, because we could've won that game.
My response to him was, "What are you smoking?" We weren't even
close to winning, they dominated us. It was a game that we learned
from.

Joe Morris: We realized the importance of the fact that in the playoffs, we've got to have home games. We've got to have home games
as opposed to going on the road to Chicago or a place like that. We
couldn't control the winds, you can't do this. We wanted to be at
home where we knew what went on in our games.

Phil Simms: From there we knew we were close. We saw what the
Bears were and how it was playing them. We knew it was going to

take a lot of hard work. The team stayed together. I could see the difference in our football team the following year. We were a notch above what we were the previous year.

AFL and NFL finalists began meeting in the game that would soon be called the Super Bowl after the 1966 season. From that moment on, previous champions were secondary. It was no longer a question of when a team had won its last championship, but when they had won the Super Bowl. The Packers, famously, got their first out of the way from Jump Street while the Steelers, who hadn't won jack in the old system, eventually took to the new one with a vengeance. The dominant teams of the early fifties, the Browns and Lions, are still waiting (unless you're in the camp that counts the Ravens' 2000 championship as part of the original Browns lineage). For champs of the pre–Super Bowl era, like the Bears and Giants, there would be a considerable wait as well. It was the misfortune of both teams that they went into eclipse right around the time the Super Bowl was launched.

Chicago got the monkey off its back with its devastating 1985 season that saw them nearly run the table en route to their first Super Bowl win and first championship since 1963. By 1986, the Giants had showed they belonged in the playoffs and that they could succeed there up to a point. Now they were in a position to get to the next level.

THE GIANTS

A year after the Bears won it all, the Giants really *were*, arguably, the best team in the league. Their only real competition came from the defending champions, who, at 14–2, had the same record as New York, not to mention a better point differential. This was mitigated by one of the easier schedules in the NFL, however.

Only those Bears allowed fewer points than the Giants in 1986. Lawrence Taylor was awarded the Bert Bell Award as the NFL Player of the Year. In the fifty years the award has been given, he—along with Andy Robustelli in 1962 and Merlin Olsen in 1974—is one of only three defensive players to win it. Harry Carson, Jim Burt, and Leonard Marshall accompanied Taylor to the Pro Bowl that year (as did Mark Bavaro and

Joe Morris from the offense and punter Sean Landeta, who averaged the second-most yards per punt in the league). The Giants allowed only 15 touchdown passes while intercepting 24. Teams also averaged only 80 yards per game on the ground against New York, nearly 40 yards below average. Of course, some of this was owed to the fact that their opponents were usually behind and forced to go to the air in an attempt to play catch-up.

Jim Burt: We didn't slant. We played a three-four. We played a Cover Three ninety percent of the time on first down. We'd get to third and eight just knowing that LT was coming off the corner. We were going to get George Martin coming from the other side and a good push in the middle.

Leonard Marshall: I can recall Bill Parcells telling me that off-season, "Leonard, this is why we lift all these weights, this is why we run all these laps, this is why we hit these dummies. This is why I have [defensive line coach] Lamar Leachman up your ass ninety percent of the time, because I want you to realize that you can be that player. You know I am getting all this accomplished. I'm playing this college three-four defense. You guys have got to buy into this." Kudos to Bill Belichick, the guy was an amazing teacher. The guys Parcells surrounded himself with were amazing teachers and made me become more of a student of the game. They taught me how to look at guys with square body types like mine and watch them and how they rush the passer, and mimic some of the things that they were doing, and watch some of the guys that they played against.

Jim Burt: When Belichick came in, he just wanted to learn. He was special-teams coach. He would sit right next to Parcells in the meetings. He'd listen to everything and take it all in. When Parcells got the head-coaching job, Belichick became coordinator. Playerwise, Belichick was pure film. It was preparation beyond preparation. We had five different game plans. We'd call them "defending the ghosts." We would prepare for things that he'd think we'd be weak on. Belichick's preparation was invaluable to me because I'd see the formations—I'd see the splits. It took a real lot of work to dissect the teams and Belichick did it, so as players we never got caught with our pants down. He would try and get the edge. I thought he was amazing. To be a head coach, you need to manage people. Bill wasn't a people manager, but he was a great evaluator of talent. I loved Belichick because he gave me the chance to succeed. He and Parcells were interesting guys to play for.

Perry Williams: In the eight years that I played for him, I had just like one one-on-one session with him. He said, "I just want you to watch these films with me. I want to show you some stuff." He said, "I'm going to devise something for you. Everybody's going to be thinking Lawrence Taylor is going to be rushing from the short side of the field. We'll utilize your speed and you can get in and make sacks." So I was the one who revolutionized the cornerback blitz in the NFL, and Bill Belichick was the one who kind of invented that, coming off the edge. I'd look like I was playing man-to-man and then all of a sudden I'd come off the short side of the field and try to rush in and try to sack the quarterback. It was formed and developed when we were in that meeting on that particular day. I knew then that the way he was critiquing and breaking down tendencies and stuff for me, that this guy was amazing. The stuff that we talked about that day went on for the duration of my career.

Leonard Marshall: I can't say enough about our defensive coaching staff: Belichick, Romeo Crennel, Lamar Leachman, Al Groh. Offensive coordinator Ron Erhardt taught me how to read offenses and offensive schemes and help me understand protections at the pro level. He taught me to really study it and actually see it coming out of the huddle and play our defense.

On offense, Morris was at his absolute peak, finishing second in the league in rushing yards while scoring 15 touchdowns, the second most of his career. Phil Simms had not quite arrived yet. He was still throwing too many interceptions and was sacked frequently. His game would go to another level in the Super Bowl, though, and in the next phase of his career he would play much better.

Jim Burt: Bill Parcells was a defensive coach: sit on a lead, shorten the game. It worked, but it didn't make Simms look good. We were winning but his statistics weren't good.

Points-wise, the Giants got their worst defensive performance out of the way in the first week when Dallas came from behind to best them 31–28. Five straight victories followed, with only the Saints managing to break into double figures in the Giants' dramatic 20–17 comeback win. (See "The Largest Comebacks in Giants History," page 154.)

Unlike in baseball, midseason trades are rare in football, but the Giants managed to pull off two important ones in this span. First, they replaced the injured Lionel Manuel by getting back Phil McConkey (he had been released just prior to the season) from the Packers. Next, they landed Ottis Anderson in a deal with the Cardinals to shore up their running game. At the time of the swap with St. Louis, Anderson was eleventh on the all-time rushing-yards leaderboard.

The 5–1 Giants next traveled to Seattle, where Phil Simms had a rough day in the yard, throwing four interceptions in the 17–12 loss. New York built a 20–3 lead on the first-place Redskins the following week, only to find itself tied at the two-minute warning. Joe Morris, back from his ailments, tore off a 34-yard run, helping set up his own game-winning 13-yard scamper with 1:38 to play. The Giants then won three more, beating the Cowboys, Eagles, and Vikings by a combined margin of just 8 points. In the Minnesota game, Raul Allegre kicked five field goals, the last one giving the Giants the 22–20 lead with just six seconds left. It had been set up by a desperation Simms–to–Bobby Johnson pass on fourth and 17 from the New York 48 that got them the first down.

Leonard Marshall: Parcells used to tell the guys it's just like backyard-barbecue football. When you're in the backyard barbecu-ing, and you're playing catch while the chicken's cooking, that's what you go out there and think about on Sunday. You have to play

Frank Filchock demonstrates his passing form at Indiana University. In an era where forward passes ended up in the hands of the enemy nearly 10 percent of the time, Filchock was especially prone to getting picked off. His six picks in the NFL championship game versus the Chicago Bears on December 15, 1946, were cause for concern in light of the circumstances surrounding the game. (Courtesy of Indiana University)

Pat Summerall lets fly one of his two 46-yard field goal attempts in the first half against Cleveland on December 14, 1958 (with Charlie Conerly holding). Without his success on this kick, there would have been no opportunity for his dramatic "field goal in the gloaming" in the game's final moments.

(Courtesy of the *Cleveland Press* Archive at Cleveland State University)

Hell hath no fury like **Sam Huff** traded. Although he's smiling in this picture, Huff was by this time a bitter enemy of Allie Sherman when the five-time Pro Bowler was swapped to the Redskins by the Giants' head coach in 1964. Few traded players, however, have had sweeter revenge than did Huff on November 27, 1966.

(Courtesy of the Washington Redskins)

The Giants were 31–5–1 with **Y. A. Tittle** as their starting quarterback from 1961 through 1963. His greatest day—and perhaps the greatest game any quarterback has ever had—came against the Washington Redskins on October 28, 1962. Conversely, his most frustrating day would come a year later in the 1963 NFL championship against the Chicago Bears. (Courtesy of the New York Giants)

Had it not been for numerous debilitating injuries throughout his career, **Tucker Frederickson** would have had more outstanding afternoons like the one that helped the Giants achieve their greatest comeback ever on November 15, 1970.
(Courtesy of the New York Giants)

Joe Pisarcik, seen here in action early in the day against the Eagles on November 19, 1978, had previously been called on the carpet for calling his own plays in the huddle. When fateful orders came down from on high at the end of the game, it had been made clear to him that he better obey them. (Mike Malarkey)

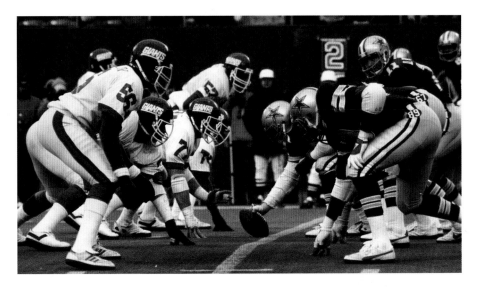

Rookie linebacker **Lawrence Taylor** (56) gets ready to run roughshod on Dallas quarterback Danny White and the Cowboys offense at the Meadowlands on December 19, 1981. The Giants' defense made an incredible leap forward when Taylor joined the team that season, enabling them to get to the brink of qualifying for the playoffs for the first time in eighteen years. (Mike Malarkey)

By this game, the final of the 1981 regular season, **Taylor** had already made his reputation in the NFL. He was a first-team All-Pro and was named Defensive Player of the Year by the Associated Press. Seen here rushing Danny White of the Cowboys; the Giants needed a victory to keep their postseason hopes alive. (Mike Malarkey)

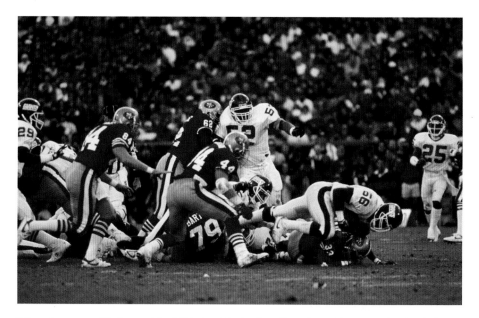

When **Lawrence Taylor** grabbed this fumble by San Francisco 49ers running back Roger Craig in the fourth quarter of the NFC championship game on January 20, 1991, the Giants were trailing and running out of time. Erik Howard's hit and Taylor's recovery gave them the chance to derail the 49er dynasty. (Mike Malarkey)

With John Elway watching from the Denver sideline, **Phil Simms** throws one of his 22 completions (in just 25 attempts) in Super Bowl XXI on January 25, 1987. At 150.9, his remains the highest passer rating in Super Bowl history. (Mike Malarkey)

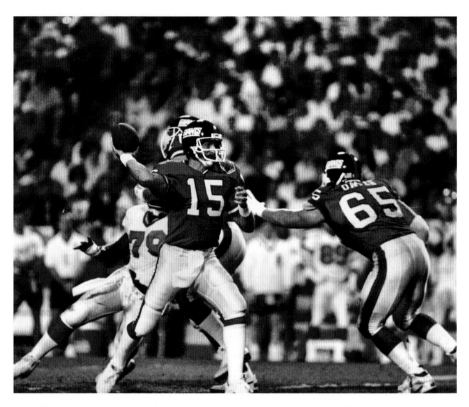

The Giants' game plan for Super Bowl XXV was to keep the Buffalo Bills' defense on the field by disrupting the team's famous no-huddle offense. Here, **Jeff Hostetler** has time to pass thanks in part to the efforts of center Bart Oates. First-ballot Hall of Famer Bruce Smith is kept at bay on this play at Tampa Stadium on January 27, 1991. The Giants needed maximum effort from everyone in a very close game against a very talented Bills team. (Mike Malarkey)

"Luck is finding a fifty-dollar bill on the ground." So said **David Tyree** when it was suggested it was merely happenstance that he made this spectacular catch against Rodney Harrison and the New England Patriots at a critical point in the waning moments of Super Bowl XLII on February 3, 2008. If the sobriquet "The Catch" hadn't already been taken by Joe Montana and Dwight Clark, this critical and amazing play would have legitimate claim on it. (Mike Malarkey)

it just like that. You can't go out there thinking about making this great glamorous catch—you just have to go out and play at a high level. Hope for the best, but play pitch and catch in the backyard. Just think of Simms being in the backyard with you throwing the ball, because that's what it's going to be like.

Phil Simms: It's interesting that was one of the first plays we put in every year at training camp. It gave me at least three options to pick up a first down. Back then, it was a much more down-field passing league. Now there'd be one guy down there. We had three people in position to get first downs. The first two were covered. I broke the huddle and said to Bobby, "Bobby be alert. I could come to you." I figured what the coverage would be. I thought there could be a spot along the sideline where I could bail out of the play and that would be it. How many times do you break the huddle and say things to guys? One out of a hundred it comes true. Bobby Johnson was the guy that was open and the defense wasn't ready for it.

Perry Williams: The turning point for the season for the Giants in '86 was when we came back against the Vikings at the Metrodome and Phil Simms threw that seventeen-yard pass to Bobby Johnson. The whole atmosphere changed. From that point on, we just knew that we were destined to do some great things and try to take this all the way to the Super Bowl.

Bart Oates: We didn't play our best and we won the game. It created a momentum that helped us carry through to the playoffs.

Phil Simms: From that game on, practices had a little spirit to them. There was an energy to the football team. It was a point where everybody just believed that anything short of winning the Super Bowl would be a big disappointment.

Brad Benson: The reason it was fourth and seventeen was because I jumped offside on third down. Parcells was gonna try to kill me and

I was mad because I could read his lips from the field and it really wasn't my fault because we were in a two-minute drill and all the plays start on the second sound. So for the first play we came up to the line of scrimmage and it was a ninety, which was a quick little pass across the middle, and Simms saw an opening there. Well, he wanted to run the same play, but we had a second play called. So he got up to the line of scrimmage and screamed, "Same play!" Well, all I heard were two sounds and, because it was a dome and because I was way out there at left tackle, I couldn't hear shit and I moved. I said to my buddy Phil, "You gotta tell Parcells." He said, "I ain't saying shit." We got on the airplane and I gotta go past him because he was in first class and I was glaring at him and he was glaring at me. I got word I was supposed to come up to first class. He wanted to talk to me. He said, "Are you still pissed off at me?" I said, "I would redirect that question." And he said, "Well, everything's all right, have a drink." He ordered me a seven and seven, which we were not allowed to have in the back. Then he said, "You know I love you." I said, "All right." He said, "Are we okay now?" I said, "Yeah." He said, "You can go back with the guys." I said, "Thank you." And I got up to walk back and he reached out and touched my arm and said, "By the way, if you ever fucking move like that again I'm gonna cut you."

In week twelve, the Denver Broncos came to town, sporting a 9–2 record, identical to that of the Giants. New York's offense was outgained 405 to 262 and failed to score a touchdown for the first time all season. Allegre had three field goals and George Martin added a 78-yard pick-six to account for the Giants' scoring. This left them tied at 16 when John Elway drove the Broncos downfield and Sammy Winder ran it in just past the two-minute warning. On the ensuing possession, Simms again found Bobby Johnson in a needy situation, converting a third and 22 to keep the drive going. The biggest play was a Simms-to-McConkey strike that covered 46 yards and set up Allegre's game-winning kick with, again, six seconds left.

The next victory required another substantial comeback effort (see "The Largest Comebacks in Giants History," page 154) to defeat a strong 49ers club on the road. New York fell behind 17–0 again.

Karl Nelson: All the plays were run through Parcells, so he went up to Ron Erhardt and said, "Ron, I don't give a shit what you call. Get me some goddamn points." So he let Erhardt call the game he wanted to call. We went down and scored three touchdowns. As soon as we got the lead, Parcells shut us down again.

It finally got easier after that. None of the final three wins provided the drama of the previous three. The Redskins fell 24–14, the Cardinals 27–7, and the Packers 55–24, although the last one was closer than the final score indicated. It actually got easier still in the playoffs, as the Giants—playing teams they had recently defeated in the regular season—produced one of the best back-to-back playoff showings ever. (See "Fewest Points Allowed in Back-to-Back Playoff Games," page 236.)

Carl Banks: It was a pretty incredible stretch for us. I don't think we had any more fear of losing to those guys. I think our confidence level was one in which we knew if we did everything we were supposed to do we'd have a pretty darn good chance of winning.

First up were the 49ers.

Joe Morris: Bill Walsh had two weeks to prepare for us. He was ready to go. He was going to make it this thing. We went out and made a statement.

Perry Williams: We dominated the 49ers. Fortunately, when Jerry Rice caught a ball running down the field and was going down the middle of the field with us in pursuit, he just dropped that ball out of nowhere. I think that was a turning point right there. It kind of let the air out of their bubble a little bit.

Bart Oates: He just fumbled as he was changing from one hand to another. It's probably the only time in his career he did something like that. It was nothing we did. It really set the tone for the game. I truly believe that had he scored there, I think it would have been a very different game.

Perry Williams: We were able to get the drive going and the offense clicking and the defense and special teams clicking. We were able to do some good things. More importantly, on our defensive side of the ball, when Jimmy Burt knocked Joe Montana out of the ball game, we knew we had them. I think that was a turning point also.

Jim Burt: When he was about ready to throw the ball, I caught him perfectly underneath the armpit. He didn't expect to see me, otherwise he would have ducked. I flipped him. It was cold and the turf was so hard. When he flipped his head hit first. I didn't want to hurt Joe, he was a good guy and a great teammate. I became good friends with him. It wasn't anything personal with him. We just hated the 49ers. We hated them because they beat us and won Super Bowls. We wanted to become the champions, and we knew we had to go through them.

With San Francisco dispatched 49–3, the 12–4 Redskins came to town for the NFC championship game.

Karl Nelson: I'm really ticked off that we didn't play the Bears, because I really had a bad taste in my mouth after that Bears game in '85 and I wanted to play them again. When I said that, the other four guys on the offensive line looked at me and said, "What? Are you nuts?" Well, see, I'm from outside Chicago, so I had a little vested interest in that I wanted to beat the Bears. I wanted to go back and play them again. But Washington beat them.

The week before, the Redskins had spoiled what many had hoped would be a Bears-Giants showdown by putting Chicago away with 20 unanswered second-half points, winning 27–13.

Ed Croke: Parcells had me find the direct line to the tower at Newark Airport. He called down there at ten o'clock in the morning. "This is Coach Parcells," he announced. Guy almost had a heart attack. Parcells said, "Here's what I want to know. At one o'clock this afternoon, which way will the wind be coming from and what degree is it gonna come from?" Who knows better than the tower at Newark? They know better than the weather forecasters. The guy gave him all the information. So he picked the coin flip, you know, which way to go in the first period and the fourth period, and it made a big difference. You know who won that game? You ask any player on the Giants who won that game. The one single player responsible for winning that game? Our punter, Sean Landeta.

Phil Simms: The fact that there were such tremendous elements that day kind of put me at ease. I was thinking, "Shoot, this is almost comical." For some reason that made me kind of relax.

Joe Morris: The Washington game was even harder, because the biggest decision we made was to take the wind. That meant something to us. That meant that Washington was going to have to run the ball into the wind. When we had the ball with the wind at our backs, we threw. If it was in our faces, we ran the ball. We were able to do that and get a touchdown rushing and add a touchdown in the air.

Perry Williams: We got that Redskin offense right back on their heels with the wind early in the game and never let up. They had Joe Gibbs—obviously a Hall of Fame coach there. They had a great core of guys: Art Monk and the other receivers like Gary Clark, Ricky Sanders, and the tight end Don Warren. They had good players and we just outwilled them.

Ed Croke: Landeta didn't miss one punt. Even into the wind, this guy was hitting shots while the Redskin guy was hitting knuckleballs. Parcells's hope in that game was to get an early lead and let our defense win the game, and that's what we did. We got up 10–0 right away with the wind, and then 17–0, and they had no chance after that.

Harry Carson: The weather cooperated with us that day. Everybody, I think, played their best game.

THE OPPONENT

The Broncos were led by quarterback John Elway, now in his fourth season in the NFL. While 1986 was not on a par with his later excellence, it was probably his best season to that point. Elway had made a reputation the year before as a master of the fourth-quarter comeback, driving the Broncos to no less than five of them in 1985. The '86 regular season saw only one aside from his late game-tying drive in Denver's loss to the Giants. In their opener, the Broncos scored 10 unanswered points in the fourth quarter to nip the Los Angeles Raiders 38–36. From there, Denver won its next five games and was off to an 8–1 record before faltering down the stretch. Big losses to Kansas City and Seattle as well as the squeaker to the Giants in week twelve dropped them to an 11–5 finish, their second in a row.

They revived in the playoffs, however, holding off a strong New England team, 22–17, in the divisionals. In the AFC championship game, Elway engineered his greatest comeback yet. Down 20–13 to the Browns with just over five minutes to play, taking over at their own 2, the Broncos went 98 yards to tie the game with thirty-seven seconds left. It was to became known simply as "The Drive." Denver won it on a Rich Karlis field goal in overtime.

Denver's offense was good, but not spectacular. They scored the sixth-most points in the NFL (378). Sammy Winder was their primary back, scoring fourteen touchdowns. He was named to the Pro Bowl in spite of a below-league-average 3.3-per-carry rushing average. Elway was himself a threat to run and had the best yards-per-carry mark on the team. His favorite target was Gerald Willhite, who caught 64 passes coming out of the fullback position. Downfield, Steve Watson, Mark Jackson, and Vance Johnson were his main receivers. As a unit, Denver had allowed 321 points in 1986, which was right around league average. In spite of the pedestrian showing, there were individual stars such as right end Rulon Jones, strong safety Dennis Smith, and left inside linebacker Karl Mecklenburg. All would make the Pro Bowl that year. In addition, linebacker and three-time Pro Bowler Tom Jackson and veteran safetyman Louis Wright (five Pro Bowls) were in the fold.

THE GAME

Carl Banks: After the national anthem, Bill Parcells looked back and I was standing right behind him and he had the look of a kid. And you could tell he got a real shiver up his spine. You could tell he was as giddy about it as anyone.

Joe Morris: Every game I've ever played and I've ever been around Bill Parcells, he was always tight. He was always the one with the coffee cup, walking around, pacing. That day, though, he was the loosest I've ever seen in my life.

Phil Simms: Bill had a lot of great sayings. One of them was, "you can't be afraid to go down in flames." It's so true. You can't be afraid of losing. We were definitely not afraid of losing that day.

Jim Burt: It never occurred to us that we were going to lose in that Super Bowl.

Carl Banks: During that week leading up to the game, I was watching ESPN or something where Howie Long was being interviewed about the Super Bowl and preparation. He said if he could give anybody advice, it would be to look at as much film as possible, even when you don't think you'll see something, just watch film, watch film, watch film. And I took that advice and I spent days and nights just looking at film of the Denver Broncos and it was like everything they did, I kind of knew what they were gonna do or I had a feel for how they were gonna attack, and I was able to make some really good plays and I was ready to play that game. I don't even know if it was keys or tendencies, some of it had become so subconscious. That's part of being in the zone: I became part of everything that they were trying to do. So I was just in tune with it. It's not like I knew—I could say "Okay, here comes this play, here comes that play,"—but I think instinctively I had an answer for everything they could do.

Phil Simms: I never thought of it like we were going to go out and pass and really surprise them. That wasn't part of it. The last eight or ten weeks of the season we made so many big passing plays that it couldn't have caught anybody by surprise. I think everybody thought, "Oh the Giants, it's Bill Parcells, they're going to run it every play." That was typical dumb thinking. I think my first thought was not about going to the Super Bowl, it was that we were going to get to play in good weather. It was exciting. I think the other thing was we really played such a conservative game against them the first time. I knew that we'd open it up and do different things. It gave me confidence knowing that they were going to see a different team that had a different feel to it.

Bart Oates: It was a beautiful day. No wind. The field was just in perfect condition. It was a comfortable, relaxed feeling. It was almost like a leisurely Sunday afternoon. We were gonna go out and have some fun. Let's go have a little pickup game—almost that kind of feeling. It really carried through into the game, too. Nobody was uptight. We were gonna play as hard as we could play and have a lot of fun. The more relaxed you play in a situation like that, the better you play.

Harry Carson: The thing that really stands out in my mind was the sea of blue and orange for the Denver Broncos and also the Giants. To run out into the Rose Bowl and see all of the pageantry—it's something that's really special.

The Giants had been playing in cold weather for the latter part of the season. With the temperature at 77 degrees at kickoff, Parcells was concerned about the cardiovascular aspects of being in the warmer climate.

Harry Carson: When we played the first half, it was pretty warm. The sun was bearing down on us. We knew how big the game was, but the weather was something that we were not that prepared for.

Things began well enough for Denver. On their first play from scrimmage, Elway was flushed from the pocket and rambled for a first down. A 24-yard pass to Mark Jackson got them to the New York 39.

Carl Banks stopped Winder on two runs and Denver faced a fourth and 2 at the 31. This brought on their barefooted kicker, Rich Karlis, who lofted one through the uprights for the 3–0 lead. The ensuing Giants drive was relentless, save for a holding call and a no-gain rush by Morris on a first and 10 at the Denver 23. Almost every other play would have to be qualified as a resounding success. Morris rushed for 19 yards on two other carries, and Simms hit all six of his passes, the last of which was a 6-yarder to Zeke Mowatt in the middle of the back of the end zone, giving New York the 7–3 lead.

Phil Simms: On that first drive I can remember the coverage on every play, and it was pretty much how I expected them to play us on every one of those downs. We knew they'd pay attention to Mark Bavaro in certain formations, which they did. On the opening play, I was beyond confident that Lionel Manuel would be wide open running that deep in cut. It was absolutely identical to what we had practiced.

On Denver's next possession, it was beginning to look like this would be a game without incompletions. Elway hit Winder for 14, rookie tight end Orson Mobley for 11, and then Winder again for 9. On that play, the Giants lost their composure. Harry Carson hit Winder when he was several steps out of bounds, resulting in a late-hit flag. Incensed, Lawrence Taylor picked up the flag and threw it, doubling the yards penalized to 30. Denver was now in business at the Giants' 6-yard line.

Banks and Elvis Patterson penetrated, dropping Steve Sewell for a 3-yard loss. On second and goal from the 9, Elway took the snap from a spread shotgun formation and hit Johnson over the middle, down to the 4. To illustrate how well the Giants' defense had done to this point, this was the farthest anyone had come against them in the playoffs so far—and it took two major penalties to make it happen. (See "Fewest Points Allowed in Back-to-Back Playoff Games," page 236.) The Broncos then sent four men wide, spreading the defense. Elway took the snap from the shotgun, hesitated a beat, then sprinted right up the middle through a gap that was about 7 yards wide for the TD.

The first incomplete pass of the game occurred on the next possession as Simms's throw to McConkey on third and 3 fell into an empty
space in the field. The crowd of 101,000 groaned as though collectively
wronged; McConkey protested vigorously that he had been interfered
with, but to no avail. Landeta punted it away. Taking over on the 20,
Elway hit 5 of his next 7 passes. The biggest among them was a 54-yarder
to Johnson on third and 12 from the Denver 18. On that play, Elway
sprinted right through a disintegrating pocket to find Johnson across
the field at the New York 28. From there, Denver worked its way to a
first and goal at the New York 1.

In his book, *Reeves: An Autobiography,* Denver coach Dan Reeves dis-
cussed his play calling on this series. He liked his first two calls in spite
of the outcome, but took himself to task on the third one.

- *First down: Rollout 'A' Corner:* The scheme on this play was for the
  halfback to get to the back of the end zone on the right side as Elway rolled in the same direction. This meant the cornerback would
  either have to cover the halfback or come up to meet Elway, who was
  running behind the fullback. Reeves liked that it gave Elway the option of throwing or running it in. Winder picked up two defenders:
  the corner and Harry Carson dropping back. Normally, this would
  have cleared out the goal line for Elway, but Carl Banks got penetration, disrupting the whole process. Taylor exploded from the middle
  in a burst of speed and ran all the way to the sideline, knocking Elway out of bounds for a loss of one.
- *Second down: Pitch 31 Trap:* Reeves was anticipating a blitz and thought
  this was the perfect counter for it. If no blitz came, a trap would develop. Harry Carson completely defeated this play himself, moving
  too quickly for the pass-over block to take place. Instead, Willhite
  was jammed for no gain up the middle.
- *Third down:* Reeves wrote of his third-down call, "I should have gone
  to four wides, four receivers. I should have gone to a play where we
  spread the defense out and give John some room to either find a
  receiver or run." That was the play that so effectively thinned out
  the Giants' defense in the first quarter and resulted in Elway's un-
  scathed romp into the end zone. Instead, Reeves called a play that

they had used to score on the Giants in their November meeting. Elway pitched back to Winder, who took the ball all the way back at the 10. By the time he caught the pitch, Perry Williams had already penetrated to the 7. Although he was blocked and didn't make the tackle, Williams's presence in the backfield slowed Winder and forced him back inside into the waiting arms of Carl Banks for a 4-yard loss.

The Giants had made a determined stand, keeping 4 points off the scoreboard in the process. That 4-point salvage job turned into a full 7 when Karlis missed the predictable 24-yard chip shot wide right. The Giants' next possession resulted in a punt after Simms had just his second incompletion of the day, a low pass that was trapped by Stacy Robinson.

Phil Simms: Rulon Jones had a hold of my leg and I couldn't quite get it to him.

After a fair catch, Denver started from their own 15 and immediately began going backward. On first down, Elway dropped back all the way to the 3 but was scrambling forward when Marshall caught him from behind for a 2-yard loss. The next play appeared to be a completion to Clarence Kay at the 28. Kay dove for the ball and plucked it from the air inches off the ground, rolling over with it in hand, then popping up without losing possession, but it was ruled incomplete by the officials. The play was reviewed, but the decision on the field stood. It would prove to be a call of no little impact.

On the next play, third and 12, Elway did a deep drop back to the 1 as the Giants came with a four-man rush: Martin, Marshall, Taylor, and Erik Howard.

Erik Howard: I broke up the middle and chased John out of the pocket and George was out on the end and Elway just kind of ran into his arms. The both of us brought him down. George hit him and I kind of jumped on, piled on there.

George Martin: It was a trick play, actually, that resulted in a safety. I told Howard to disregard what we call a dummy call that I was gonna give during the course of that play. Sure enough, as the offense broke the huddle I made out this dummy call and Howard didn't react to it. As we faked this stunt, the offense overreacted and I came around the corner virtually with John Elway running right into my arms, and it was a safety.

Erik Howard: There was a two-page photo in *Sports Illustrated* of me standing there celebrating the safety. While George got credit for the safety, I ultimately got credit in the pictures. That was a typical experience at nose tackle. To make plays and not get credit for them: That was the life of a nose tackle.

Leonard Marshall: The safety on Elway set the tone for us going into the locker room at halftime. It really said a lot about our football team.

Joe Morris: I said to George Martin before the game, "Make a play to get me a Super Bowl ring. That's what I want you to do. I'll take care of the rest, you make one play today."

George Martin: It's the highlight of my professional career.

With the score 10–9 and 2:46 left in the half, the Giants received their free kick at the 22 and got a 3-yard return from Tom Flynn after the ball sailed past the entire return team. From there, they went three and out as Simms missed his third pass of the day, an overthrow of Bavaro that was very close to being catchable. It was to be Simms's last incomplete pass of the day. (See "The Highest Completion Percentages in Playoff History," page 237.)

Denver had two time-outs and 1:05 with which to work. On second and 10, Elway rolled to the left, getting great protection. He fired one all the way across the field to Watson at the far sideline, down to the Giants' 32. On the next play, Elway shoveled one to Willhite for 11 more yards. Elway missed his next three passes and Karlis came in to try a

34-yarder with thirteen seconds left. For the second time in a row, he pushed it to the right. New York could have very easily been down 20–9 or 16–9; instead, they took a knee on the final play of the half trailing by just one point.

"Shit was happening so fast that we couldn't settle down and get our minds straight. That's the worst feeling for a defensive player," Lawrence Taylor would write later. "I was saying, 'Whoa, whoa, whoa! Settle down.'" In the locker room, Taylor addressed the team. "I felt it was my duty to say something, so I said, 'Listen, guys: We didn't play no type of football . . . we played no Giant football whatsoever, not one iota of Giant football. We're about to go out there and kick these sonuvabitches dead in the ass.'"

Perry Williams: They called Bill Belichick the Boy Genius back then. I always said he was one of my all-time favorite coaches I ever had, as a Little Leaguer all the way through high school, college, and all the way through the pros. He made some little adjustments at halftime. We were down, but didn't lose confidence. We knew they had us on our heels a little bit, but that's the nature of the game. That's why it's called pro football—just the best against the best in the world. We knew they weren't going to lie down and die and that we had to keep pounding and keep our poise.

Karl Nelson: Ron Erhardt came in and said, "Everything's working. We just missed a couple of little plays here. Don't panic. We've got them right where we want them. What we're doing is working." Reeves was not known for making adjustments at halftime, even when he was with the Giants. So Erhardt didn't anticipate making any changes.

Dave Anderson: The Giants came running out on the field for the second half and the music playing was the Sinatra version of "New York, New York." I tell you, every New Yorker had to get a chill with that one. I think this was before the Yankees adopted "New York, New York" at the end of each game. It got all the New Yorkers in the crowd all wound up, and the Giants just took it from there.

Harry Carson: We came back out after the halftime show. The sun had gone down behind the stands. It turned cool very quickly. There was a chill in the air and I think, as a result, that was when we turned it up a notch. It felt kind of wintry to us. The weather was a little chilly and we were playing Giant football in Giant-type weather. We all felt better once the sun had gone down.

Jim Burt: All of a sudden, that sun went down and things changed.

Brad Benson: Now, we did not know this at the time, but when we were coming into the locker room through the tunnel, Rulon Jones—who was the defensive end playing over me—looked at the television camera and said, "We got 'em now." I later saw it on the replay of the game. At the time, at the end of the first half, I knew the game was over. Even though we were a point behind, I knew the game was over. I could feel them physically fading because we were beating on them and we were just a physically superior football team at that time.

Ed Croke: I put a quick call to my wife back home to New Jersey and she said, "What are we going to do?" I said, "Listen, let me tell you something. The game's over." She said, "What?" I said, "This game is over. Denver just played the best half of their season and we played our worst half of the season and they're only up by a point. This game is over." She said, "Are you sure?" I said, "I'll talk to you at the end of the game."

On the opening possession of the second half, Louis Wright blasted Joe Morris on a third-down run, leaving the Giants just shy of a first down at their own 46. Sean Landeta came on, as did reserve quarterback Jeff Rutledge, who lined up as a blocking back.

Billy Ard: Let me tell you something that no one talks about: Perhaps one of the greatest calls in the history of the Super Bowl was Parcells going for it on fourth and one, being down ten to nine with like thirteen minutes left in the third quarter. Fake punt. Unbelievable—it was the play of the game.

Bart Oates: We ran a fake punt. I was the snapper for punts and field goals as well, so I stayed in. They brought in their little guys, the punt-return team. They didn't catch that Jeff Rutledge was lined up in our backfield. Direct snap to Jeff, and he just ran the ball. We took out some of the guys, but most of the line stayed in. The defensive backs and linebackers weren't looking. They weren't gonna defend the run, so we just steamrolled them. Had they known, they could have submarined and kind of created piles. Our thought was kind of hit them up high and block. We got the first down, and from there I don't think we had a punt the rest of the game. I don't think Sean Landeta got in the whole second half.

Phil Simms: That was a big play. The Super Bowl is about big moments. We'd already said you can't be afraid. Play on the edge, coach on the edge; Bill did that. We'd done that fake punt so many times during that year; had so many plays out of it. I didn't look at it saying, "Wow we're taking a big gamble."

It wasn't like most trick punts in that the ball was not snapped suddenly and directly to the blocking-back position. Instead, Rutledge sauntered up to take his place under center and did a very long count, hoping to draw the Broncos offside. They didn't bite, so he took the snap and slammed off right for the necessary yard and a bit more. As John Madden pointed out on the CBS telecast, "Everyone wants you to go for it when you're a coach, but then when you do go for it, that takes a lot of guts to call it. It's easy to put in, hard to call."

Billy Ard: Tremendous. Great call.

Bart Oates: It was a gutsy call by Parcells. That was critical for our offense.

Phil Simms: When Dan Reeves became our coach in 1993, we talked about that drive. He said on that fake punt, their plan was for both linebackers to get up near the center to stop the quarterback sneak. And there it was in the Super Bowl and both those linebackers were

229

four and five yards off the line of scrimmage and never got up to it. Was it the reason we won? I don't think so. It was a damn good play. It was a mistake by them and we took advantage of it.

From there, Simms moved the Giants directly downfield, connecting on four passes, the longest of which was a 23-yarder to Lee Rouson. The drive was capped when the Giants overloaded the left side with three receivers and Bavaro caught one over the middle from 13 yards out. Raul Allegre's extra point made it 16–10. The Broncos went three and out on their next possession as George Martin knocked down one pass, and the Giants may have gotten away with a late hit by Harry Carson that was not flagged. McConkey returned Mike Horan's punt 25 yards to put New York right back on the doorstep of scoring position at the Denver 36.

In spite of Simms's success in the air, the Giants now switched to their ground attack. Morris had runs of 7 and 9 before Simms threw his sole pass of the drive, a 9-yarder to Lionel Manuel that gave them a first down at the 12. Simms did drop to pass on second and 8, but quit the pocket when everyone was covered and rushed to the 5. When Morris was stopped after a 1-yard gain by a determined Denver defense, New York found themselves with a fourth and 2 at the Denver 4. This time there was no thought of going for it: Parcells went for the points, and Allegre made it 19–10.

Whereas Simms was on a tear, Elway threw his eighth incompletion in his last eleven tries on first down. After Elway hit Willhite for 8, Carl Banks smothered Mobley on third-down pass coverage and Horan had to punt again. McConkey called a fair catch at the New York 32. They moved across midfield on a 17-yard pass to Manuel, and then, on second and 6 at the Denver 45, Parcells called for something a little different.

Joe Morris: We had run that flea-flicker play every week in practice. And let me tell you, I said, "We'll never call this play in a game." When Bill sent the play in with me, Phil Simms looked at me and said, "He called that play for real?" I said, "Oh, yeah, he called it. We're gonna run it."

McConkey started on the left and went in motion, turning upfield at the snap on the right side of the line. Simms took the snap, handed off to Morris, then retreated deeper into the backfield. Morris hit the line, turned, and tossed it back to Simms. Meanwhile, McConkey had cut all the way across the field without picking up a defender and was open at the 20, where Simms hit him on the left sideline. If it sounds like a time-consuming operation, it was; Denver got no penetration on the New York line.

Ed Croke: Phil had four guys open on the flea-flicker and didn't know who to throw it to.

With ball in hand, McConkey approached the goal line. Sensing a scoring opportunity, he tried to hurdle Mark Haynes, but Haynes cut his legs in midair, resulting in a spectacular near-Immelmann that landed McConkey on the 1-yard line. He thrust his arms in the air in a mixture of triumph and frustration for not having gotten the extra yard.

Phil Simms: I remember thinking it was the perfect call. To say it worked perfectly was an understatement. Phil McConkey was wide open and tackled on the one. I was jogging down there and I really truly remember this and said it, and thought it and believed it. I thought that was the game. We'd be up twenty-six to ten and no one is going to score three touchdowns on our defense in one quarter.

On first and goal, Morris ran around the right end untouched, sprung by a Chris Godfrey block on Dennis Smith. Simms said after the game that the flea-flicker had been a staple play in practices, but that "We've never hit on the damn thing."

Joe Morris: That was the beginning of the end for the Broncos. We started running the ball effectively and doing the things we needed to do. Phil was just on fire that day, on fire.

Now trailing 26–10 after 17 unanswered points and being outgained 163 to 2, it had been a disastrous third quarter for the Broncos, but it nearly ended with even more bad news. On the last play before the gun, Elway dropped back to pass and had the ball swiped out of his hands by

George Martin. Elway was able to pick it up and start scrambling, but he was dropped for an 11-yard loss at his own 9 by Leonard Marshall.

It was only a disaster delayed, however. Denver was called for illegal motion and then Elway committed the first turnover of the game. Throwing from deep in his own end zone, he was picked off by Elvis Patterson at the 30. New York ended up 25 yards farther back, after a negative return and an illegal block.

It was only a temporary setback, however, as Simms found a wide-open Stacy Robinson on the Denver 20, who advanced it to the 16. It was his ninth straight completion, a new Super Bowl record. He then tried to hit Bavaro in the end zone, but Louis Wright blocked Bavaro's view and wiped him out, resulting in a pass-interference call that put the Giants on the threshold. On third and goal, Simms tried Bavaro again, but it went off his hands. McConkey was in the immediate vicinity, though, and came down with the ball, making it 33–10 after the extra point.

Karl Nelson: Everything was clicking, and even when things didn't go exactly as planned it still worked out, like when the ball off Bavaro's shoulder landed in McConkey's hands. It was just one of those days.

Elway took advantage of a Giants defense willing to trade yards for time and hit on his first five passes of the next drive. After twelve plays, the Broncos found themselves with a fourth and 6 on the Giants' 10. Trailing by four scores with just six minutes left, a touchdown was in order, but Reeves opted for three and Karlis hit one from 27 yards out. From that point, it was academic. While each team scored again, the most intriguing aspect of the game's final moments was watching Harry Carson don a disguise so that he could sneak up on Parcells to douse him with the Gatorade bucket, a tradition he had popularized.

For the first time in thirty years, the Giants were champions of the NFL. Simms was named MVP.

Dave Anderson: Simms was twenty-two out of twenty-five for two hundred and sixty-eight yards, three touchdowns, no interceptions. That's still the closest ever to being a perfect Super Bowl.

Phil Simms: When it was over and they announced I was MVP, I looked up and saw my stats and was like, "Oh wow." I didn't know I hadn't thrown an incompletion in the second half; didn't know I had such a good statistical day.

If a defensive MVP was named, it would have had to have been Carl Banks, the most disruptive force on the field that day.

Leonard Marshall: I think Banks and I had probably two of the better days as defensive players as any other defensive players would have in a Super Bowl game. Probably as good as the Cowboys had back in the days when Harvey Martin and Randy White were playing on the same defensive line and dominating people in playoff games and Super Bowls. So I look back at Super Bowl XXI as a game I'll never forget.

George Martin: I think if there was ever a deserved MVP that day, it was certainly Phil Simms, who had nearly an unblemished record. He had such ball control, such execution. They played like an offense with a lot of confidence and I have to credit the offensive coordinator because he called a very, very good game and kept that defense on its heels. Joe Morris, Phil Simms, McConkey, Bavaro, that offensive line—to say that they were near perfect would be close to a true statement. They were pretty near perfect.

Phil Simms: People said things to me then about how it would change my life and I didn't believe it. Well, they were right: It's been a huge part of my life. It's done a lot for me. I always laugh, I say if I'd have known the game was that big maybe I'd have choked. The whole week was funny. I was loose. My teammates were loose. We practiced hard. There was so much attention heaped on John Elway. It was a different game then. Now everybody gets tremendous praise heaped on them. I really truly was the other guy. I was having fun with it. I respected him but it all worked out.

Leonard Marshall: Nobody was better than Harry Carson, Lawrence Taylor, Leonard Marshall, Jim Burt, Carl Banks, George Martin, and

Pepper Johnson in terms of a front seven. I don't think there will ever be a front seven like that again in pro football.

THE AFTERGLOW

Bart Oates: The Rose Bowl was built a long time ago, so the locker room was cramped with a bunch of sweaty guys, but it was pure emotional relief. Just the relief of being able to relax because we were the favorite and it would have been an upset to lose that game.

Billy Ard: My dad is a pretty proper guy. He's not your typical jock parent. My father wasn't even an athlete. So this was all new to him. He's a *New York Times* crossword-puzzle kind of guy. One day he got a call from a friend who said, "Hey, Phil. I'm doing the *New York Times* crossword puzzle—perhaps you can help me? Three letters: Super Bowl XXI guard."

Harry Carson: It really did erase all those other bad games we played as a team since I'd gotten there. You have a tendency to not even focus on what happened prior to then, but just enjoy it from that moment on. So as a result, having won that game, you're at the mountaintop and you see what it truly is like to be a true champion. You remember all of that stuff like when people were burning their tickets and planes with banners were flying overhead and people were complaining, but it sort of goes out the window when you're standing there holding a World Championship trophy.

Phil Simms: Bill Parcells had a knack for saying the right things at the right time. He grabbed me in the locker room and said, "Simms, you were magnificent." I think Bill understood the moment better than we did, or at least better than I did. I think about that moment in the locker room and him saying nice things to me. That was the only time in my career he said it to me. It was pretty special.

Karl Nelson: People ask me, "What's your greatest thrill about winning the Super Bowl?" I say winning the Super Bowl is great, but that's not what it's about. It's about the climb. I say it's like climbing a mountain. Once you stand on top, you look around and say, "It looks nice. Now what?" I'll have this ring on my finger forever, showing people what I was able to accomplish. After winning the game, it really was anticlimactic for me.

Bart Oates: You dream about it as a little kid, but to actually do it is indescribable. The sense of accomplishment and satisfaction—it was pure enjoyment at that moment.

Perry Williams: One day when I was a kid I told my mother and grandmother I was going to play pro football and before that, I was going to win a scholarship to go to college. Not only was I going to play pro football, I was going to play in the Super Bowl. So this one particular afternoon I was telling my grandmother this. She went into one corner of the house and I could hear her talking to my mother, saying, "You hear this boy talking about how he's going to play pro football, much less he's going to be playing in the Super Bowl? The only kind of Super Bowl he's going to probably end up playing in is the Toilet Bowl." Yet, it still gave me the incentive and gave me the motivation and drive to get there. I guess she used kind of reverse psychology. I believed that I could do it. Fifteen years later, I was playing in my first Super Bowl, so I called my grandmother from Pasadena the night before the game when we were getting ready to play the Denver Broncos and the great John Elway. She said, "Good luck tomorrow. I'll be watching you." I thanked her, but before she hung up I said, "What do you think about that Toilet Bowl kid now?" That's the story I use for a lot of my youth programs. The believing-is-achieving concept is my motto. I believe that anything is possible. And that dream became a reality in 1986 and January 1987.

APPENDICES

Fewest Points Allowed in Back-to-Back Playoff Games

In 1985, the Chicago Bears established a mark that can only be tied. The following year, the Giants came very close to doing just that. Since the advent of tiered playoffs in the mid-sixties, those Bears remain the only team to pitch consecutive shutouts in playoff contests, while the '86 Giants remain the only team to allow just one score over the course of two consecutive games. If not for a Ray Wersching field goal, New York would be at the top of this list as well. These are the teams that allowed the fewest points in consecutive playoff games in the same season.

Points	Year	Team (Opponents and Scores)
0	1985	Chicago Bears* (Giants, 21–0; Rams, 24–0)
3	1986	New York Giants* (49ers, 49–3; Redskins, 17–0)
6	1971	Dallas Cowboys* (49ers, 14–3; Dolphins, 24–3)
6	1972	Washington Redskins (Packers, 16–3; Cowboys, 26–3)
9	1996	New England Patriots (Steelers, 28–3; Jaguars, 20–6)
10	2000	New York Giants (Eagles, 20–10; Vikings, 41–0)
10	1985	Chicago Bears* (Rams, 24–0; Patriots, 46–10)
10	2000	Baltimore Ravens* (Raiders, 16–3; Giants, 34–7)
10	1970	Dallas Cowboys (Lions, 5–0; 49ers, 17–10)
12	1988	San Francisco 49ers* (Vikings, 34–9; Bears, 28–3)

Indicates Super Bowl winner.

While the vaunted 1985 Bears' suppression unit appears in the top ten twice, the 2000 Ravens are notable for appearing in the top twenty-five *three* times. With their 21–3 win over the Broncos and 24–10 defeat of the Titans, they tied for eleventh with two 13-point combinations, in addition to their 10-point combo seen above. The '71 Cowboys also tied for twenty-second. The other two teams that had three consecutive great defensive efforts are the 1969 Kansas City Chiefs and the 1977 Cowboys.

The Highest Completion Percentages in Playoff History

Phil Simms's completion performance in Super Bowl XXI broke a three-year-old playoff record held by Joe Theismann. Simms's reign as the record holder was to last much longer, as it was twenty-one years before it fell to Tom Brady of the Patriots. Given yards per catch and yards per attempt, Brady's effort was a much more ball-control-oriented effort than some of the others on this list. Peyton Manning appears twice, and those two performances polarize as the best- and worst-rated among the top ten. His 2004 game had a perfect 158.3 passer rating, while his 2006 effort (71.9) is the only non-triple-figure effort on this list. Simms's rating was 150.9, second-highest among this group.

93% - Tom Brady (26–28, 262 YDS, 3 TDs)
New England Patriots 31, Jacksonville Jaguars 20 (2007 AFC divisional playoff)

88% - Phil Simms (22–25, 268 YDS, 3 TDs)
New York Giants 39, Denver Broncos 20 (Super Bowl XXI)

88% - Kurt Warner (29–33, 379 YDS, 5 TDs)
Arizona Cardinals 51, Green Bay Packers 45, overtime (2009 wild-card game)

87% - Joe Montana (26–30, 262 YDS, 2 TDs)
San Francisco 49ers 30, Los Angeles Rams 3 (1989 NFC championship game)

82% - Drew Brees (32–39, 288 YDS, 2 TDs)
New Orleans Saints 31, Indianapolis Colts 17 (Super Bowl XLIII)

82% - Peyton Manning (27–33, 458 YDS, 4 TDs)
Indianapolis Colts 49, Denver Broncos 24 (2004 AFC wild-card game)

82% - Kurt Warner (27–33, 391 YDS, 5TDs, 1 INT)
St. Louis Rams 49, Minnesota Vikings 37 (1999 NFC divisional playoff)

79% - Peyton Manning (30–38, 268 YDS, 1 TD, 3 INTs)
Indianapolis Colts 23, Kansas City Chiefs 8 (2006 AFC wild-card game)

79% - Rich Gannon (23–29, 294 YDS, 2 TDs)
Oakland Raiders 38, New York Jets 24 (2001 AFC wild-card game)

78% - Joe Theismann (18–23, 302 YDS, 2 TDs)
Washington Redskins 51, Los Angeles Rams 7 (1983 NFC divisional playoff)

78% - Brett Favre (18–23, 173 YDS, 3 TDs)
Green Bay Packers 42, Seattle Seahawks 20 (2007 NFC divisional playoff)

It should probably be noted that in three of these games, the high-percentage completers were relieved because of the one-sidedness of the scores, and their replacements—Bob Holly for Theismann, Hunter Smith for Manning in '06, and Steve Young for Montana—were a perfect 4-for-4.

The Much-Maligned Mr. Simms

From now until the last football game is played, the quarterback will be a team's lightning rod. Quarterbacks will be categorized as winners and losers regardless of the talent around them. How many have made Pro Bowls and set records because they were blessed with brilliant offensive lines? How many did not because they were in a scheme that did not suit their talents?

Football is rarely black-and-white, and nobody knew that better than Phil Simms, the oft-criticized Giants quarterback. From the moment he was drafted to this day, his ultimate value has been questioned. While there was redemption at Super Bowl XXI (Dave Anderson wrote the day after that "Never has a quarterback done any more to win the Super Bowl than Simms did"), it did not truly quell the criticism.

His biggest defenders are those who played and worked with him:

Ed Croke: He was the toughest quarterback I ever saw play in my life, and I saw a lot of them. The thing I remember about beating the 49ers on the way to that Super Bowl was that he threw four touchdown passes in that game and never saw one completion. He was flattened on each of the throws. He hung in knowing he was gonna get nailed and he waited until the last second to throw the pass and then he got killed. He didn't see any of the four touchdown catches—he had to wait and watch them on the replays. He was a tough son of a bitch.

Joe Morris: I remember having a reporter ask me, "Joe, what if the Broncos stack the line against you?" I said, "If they stack the line against us, Phil Simms will kill them. You do not know what a gutty player he is like I do. We believe in Phil Simms."

Jim Burt: He had his thumb detached from his arm. He had his shoulder and his knee injured and about every injury known to mankind. He was Mr. Adversity. You could put adversity on his forehead. He was a guy that took hits. Him not being in the Hall of Fame is actually stupid. You can't go by the statistics. He was coached by a guy who was a defensive coach that was going to leave it up to the defense because he's not going to put the ball in the air. Parcells would get a 3–0 lead in the first quarter and start milking the clock. Simms was never going to be a Peyton Manning, but let me tell you something: If Phil Simms was with the San Fransisco 49ers, he would have set every record known to mankind. I'm not saying he was better than Montana, because you have to give Montana his due with the four Super Bowls, but if you put Phil Simms in the West Coast offense with Bill Walsh, and he stays healthy? We had a front seven that would kick ass, so Parcells played to that strength.

Joe Morris: We lost Phil Simms a couple of times when he hurt his knee and some other things. I would rather hold people than let him go down and get hurt again, because I knew that for us to be a success, that guy's got to play.

George Martin: To literally add insult to injury, he got injured several times and we all thought that perhaps that number-one draft choice was a bust. But, thank God, history has proven us wrong and Phil turned out to be the real deal. Had nearly a perfect Super Bowl and that just shows you the caliber of athlete and competitor and professional Phil ultimately grew to be.

Jim Burt: Look at where he played: the Meadowlands. Before they put that extension on, that wind would howl through there. Other teams would come in there and wonder how we played in it. Simms had a ball he could throw through the wind. That's how we would play. When we got good, it was to our advantage. Simms was a product of that. When Hostetler came in and won that second Super Bowl, Phil Simms started them out at 10–0! Phil Simms was forgotten about in that second Super Bowl.

Joe Morris: People seem to keep forgetting in 1990 when that team went to the Super Bowl, that team was 10–0 when he was starting at quarterback . . . I don't understand why people have that feeling about him.

Jim Burt: I respect Phil so much that when I was with the 49ers, I wanted to beat the Giants, and I got those guys so fired up. I knew, even with Ronnie Lott, that if Phil Simms got a chance he'd light us up. I didn't want to be embarrassed. That was the only guy I was afraid of on the Giants. If Phil Simms caught fire and got confident and we didn't put pressure on him, he'd throw for five hundred yards. I told Ronnie Lott. I told him all of this crazy stuff. I only did that because I felt that if Phil Simms got a chance, he'd light us up. He's a competitive guy. I don't know if a lot of quarterbacks would have been able to stand up to the punishment he did. Not only the punishment physically, but the mental stuff with the press. They used to yell down from the stands. It was ridiculous. I used to scream back at them. I said, "It's not his fault." I knew what he was working with. I knew the restraints that were put on him. He had a lot of great seasons after that.

Never used

Joe Morris: There are people in this area, unfortunately, that just don't get it. They still hate Phil Simms to this day. I was at a dinner one night and this guy was telling me why he really didn't like Phil Simms. I said, "Why don't you step away from me, because if you say another bad word about my teammate, I'm going to punch you in your mouth."

Bart Oates: I do remember, even in '86, a group of Giants fans in the first- and second-row seats behind the bench busting on Phil all the time—nobody really cared what I did unless I got called for holding. You never saw him turn around and look at them. I remember one time he did turn around, though, and then threw a touchdown or something. From that point on they knew that Phil was listening to them. I laughed. He proved them wrong.

New York Giants vs. San Francisco 49ers

NFC CHAMPIONSHIP
January 20, 1991

	1	2	3	4	F
New York Giants	3	3	3	6	15
San Francisco 49ers	3	3	7	0	13

New York Giants vs. Buffalo Bills

SUPER BOWL XXV
January 27, 1991

	1	2	3	4	F
Buffalo Bills	3	9	0	7	19
New York Giants	3	7	7	3	20

The 1990 NFC championship game and the Super Bowl the following week had a lot in common. Both games were played against the backdrop of the first Gulf War, both were rematches of regular-season games the Giants had lost, and the Giants were not supposed to win either one of them. The Giants' opponents in the championship game were the two-time defending Super Bowl champion 49ers.

Bill Romanowski: When I got to San Francisco in '88, we beat Cincinnati in the Super Bowl, and what did we chant in the locker room? We chanted "Repeat." We beat Denver in the Super Bowl the next year and what do we chant? "Three-peat."

If not for a questionable call in the divisional playoffs the previous season, the Giants and 49ers might have met in the NFC championship game that year, too. But the Rams went on to have that honor.

Ed Croke: Yeah, what killed us in that [divisional playoff game against the Rams] was that horrendous pass-interference call. The side judge was named Al Jury—who was a cop in Los Angeles. He ran over to the guy that called the pass interference and said, "Are you sure? This is fucking championship time and that's a borderline call." And the guy wouldn't change it, wouldn't pick the flag up. Sheldon White had hardly touched Flipper Anderson. Minimal contact. It's a championship game, you don't call that. In fact, the guy felt so guilty about the call, the next day he called Parcells, tried to apologize, and the Tuna hung up on him and told him, "Fuck you." The 49ers breathed easy. They didn't want any part of us in 1989.

Howard Cross: Understanding how close we'd come in 1989, we had a premium on perfection the whole year. Coach kept saying, over and over again, "You're good, but you're not as good as I want you to be yet." The team got out of the gate the next season and won ten in a row and surprised themselves a little bit as to how they handled the adversity.

But the season started with a bump in the road.

Leonard Marshall: In 1990, half of our pass rush held out of training camp. Lawrence and I were away. I was in Florida, fishing and playing golf. Every now and then I'd run into Lawrence and ask, "What do you think they're thinking?" And he'd say, I don't know what they're thinking, but I'm itching to go back. I wanted to go back, too, but I wanted some money for it. I played like Howie Long, Richard Dent, Jacob Green. Come Sunday at one o'clock, I wanted them to pay me like them. I'd been Defensive Lineman of the Year twice, I've been MVP of the team a couple of times. As my momma always said, if they pay you, son, they've got to respect you—if they respect you, they've got to pay you. That's just how it works.

Fortunately for Taylor, Marshall, and the Giants, general manager George Young was able to work out deals with both defensive stars.

Leonard Marshall: We didn't get deals done really until the last preseason ball game. It took us a little while to get into the flow of things. I worked my way back into shape as the season went on. Thank God we were able to win ten ball games all the way up to San Francisco. I got a chance to start again as a force at right end. We knew we had a nucleus to be a team of destiny that year and to challenge for the championship. But we really didn't know how good we could be because we really didn't have a chance to have all eleven pieces working together in training camp that summer.

Greg Jackson: When we got on that run of 10–0, it got to the point where we never had any doubt in our minds that we were going to win. The chemistry was so perfect. It was just unbelievable. I think the biggest thing that made us so good was the guys we had up front then: Leonard Marshall, Pepper Johnson, LT, Gary Reasons, Eric Dorsey, Erik Howard, Carl Banks. I mean, you talk about a front seven. The other team had to get the ball out in two point seven seconds. Our normal pass rush was like a blitz. When we rushed four guys, it seemed like five were coming, because LT counted as two. That made our job a lot easier back there in the secondary.

Leonard Marshall: We were a team of destiny in '86. You knew what kind of product you were going to get. But this team, this nineteen-ninety team, we had no idea what we had as a football team until the season started to progress. We put together five, six, seven, eight, nine, ten wins and we're saying to ourselves, "We're pretty damn good. We've got something kind of special here. We've got to run with this thing." That's when we really started to believe a little bit.

In those ten games, the Giants trailed only three times. They held their opponents to 10 or fewer points in six of the wins. New York was especially adept at not turning over the ball. They would go on to give up only fourteen turnovers in the regular season, becoming the first team in NFL history to average less than one turnover a game.

Another NFC team was also 10–0 to start the year: the defending Super Bowl champion 49ers. And the two NFC powerhouses were slated to meet in a Monday-night game that some in the press dubbed Super Bowl XXIV½. Both teams lost their week-eleven games (the Eagles downed the Giants and the Rams bested the defending champs), but there was still plenty of hype surrounding the Monday-night matchup.

Erik Howard: I grew up out there in the Bay Area. That was a big deal for me to play in my hometown. The 49ers had a great squad. It was an extremely close game and we battled it out.

Perry Williams: They had outstanding players without a shadow of a doubt. You got all the favorites, Joe Montana, even his backup Steve Young. Jerry Rice and Roger Craig, I mean, you could go on and on. They had a good defense as well. It was always a dogfight. You knew it was going to be a long, drawn-out, hard-fought battle. With them, it was always survival of the fittest.

Bill Romanowski: You knew it was gonna be a who-was-going-to-knock-the-crap-out-of-who? kind of game. Every time we played them, that's what it was like.

Howard Cross: We were playing on probably the muddiest field in history. I remember sliding and digging out big chunks of turf the whole game, and there weren't many explosive moments.

The 49ers accounted for the game's only touchdown on a 23-yard pass from Joe Montana to John Taylor.

Greg Jackson: Joe Montana was an unbelievable quarterback. He was so tough to read. He was so good at looking you off. On that touchdown in the Monday-night game, Everson Walls was playing free safety. Joe looked to the curl route and Everson broke—Joe looked right back and threw it to the post. It was there, and you couldn't react fast enough, and that ball was already gone. I said, That's just Joe Montana for you.

The Giants had a chance to win the game in the fourth quarter but were stopped on four straight passing plays from the 49ers' 9-yard line, causing some people to question the Giants' choice of play calls.

Ed Croke: People asked Parcells why he chose to pass there. "I was trying to win the fucking game, that's what I was trying to do!"

Greg Jackson: I never thought that with the weapons they had on offense that we could hold them just to seven points. Who would have ever thought that we would hold the 49ers to just seven points and come out losers on that Monday night?

Ed Croke: People said, "Seven to three: What a boring game." Boring? It was one of the greatest games you'll ever see in your life. After the game we were a little bit depressed, and we were trying to get out of the locker room. But Parcells was always great to the visiting clubhouse guys, who were usually local guys. He tipped them fifty bucks or something for getting the coffee. The clubhouse guy looked at Bill and said, "You know what, Coach, I got a feeling you're gonna be back here before this year's over. And I hope you are."

Jeff Hostetler had been a backup with the Giants for five seasons and he hadn't seen much action. In week four against Dallas, the Giants were up 24–10 when Parcells did something unexpected.

Jeff Hostetler: He liked to play mind games. He liked to see if guys are ready. Out of the blue, he just started yelling my name and the offense is going out. He said, "Hey, you're in." No warm-ups, no preparation, no nothing. I'm in. We ended up scoring a touchdown. He was testing me. I had a great preseason and Bill had told me that I deserved to be out on the field. He said he was going to find a way to get me out there and he kept his word.

Hostetler saw action again in week seven.

Jeff Hostetler: I had another opportunity a little later on when Phil Simms got hurt in the game against the Cardinals. We were down nine points with maybe six minutes to go and we came back and won that one. I felt really comfortable and really good. I knew my teammates felt really good when I was in there.

Howard Cross: Hostetler was one of those guys who was a backup but always wanted to be a starter. He wasn't very public about it. So when he came into the game, he wasn't coming in wide-eyed. He was coming in to lay his claim to what he felt like he should have been the whole time.

Bart Oates: I knew Jeff's frustrations. He wanted to get in there and play. If Phil played well and stayed healthy, he wasn't gonna beat him out. Phil looked like he was gonna be there five more years. So there wasn't that urgency from the organization at the time to trade him. He wasn't going anywhere as long as the Giants wanted him. He was fairly cheap. Jeff was frustrated. He wanted to get in there and play.

Karl Nelson: There was a play in the San Francisco game back in 1986, Hostetler actually broke his leg on a special-teams play. I used to kid him all the time; there was a guy in the league, Jim Jensen, they called him Crash, down in Miami. So I had one of the equipment guys get one of the neck collars, one of the horse collars, and put it on his shoulder pads. Then I wrote "Crash" above his nameplate on his locker. He told me, "This isn't funny, man, cut it out."

By late in the season, Hostetler was on the verge of giving up.

Jeff Hostetler: That week, I sat at my table with my wife and told her that at the end of the season, I was done playing. I was so frustrated with the game. I was frustrated with the fact that I never got an opportunity. It seemed like when I did get an opportunity, I played well, but it just never looked or seemed like I was ever going to get a chance. I'd had it. I told her, "After the season, we're going to head back to Morgantown, West Virginia, and I'm going to find something else to do. I just can't do this anymore."

In week fifteen, the Giants were home against the Buffalo Bills. Led by Jim Kelly and Thurman Thomas on offense and Bruce Smith on defense, the 11–2 Bills projected to be a tough matchup for the Giants. They used a high-powered hurry-up offense that gobbled up yards and points and exhausted opposing defenses in the process.

Marv Levy: We felt we were a very well-rounded team. We went into that season running a no-huddle offense. Cincinnati had run something similar in previous years, but ours was different from what anyone had really run before. This was really based on what a two-minute drill would be except you had only three downs, not four. It was very quick paced. We probably had the smallest playbook in the league. Jim Kelly was calling the plays at the line of scrimmage and doing it well. It was the type of offense that gets you off the field in a hurry because you're either going to score or punt or give up the ball. It was an advantage that we had.

Greg Jackson: When we got prepared to play the Bills, we watched film that whole week and we were like, "Man, we got to find a way to stop these guys." Because in the NFC East it's all about pounding the football—we weren't used to an offense being spread out like they were.

Jeff Hostetler: It was a cold, wet, rainy, miserable afternoon. It was later in the game and I'd been standing around and doing nothing and was tight. I was the coldest I'd been in a long time. All of a sudden, Phil went down. It didn't look like it was anything major. He came off and he didn't really say much. I thought, Well, I've seen this before. He'll suck it up and he'll be right back out there.

But that wasn't the case this time. Simms had broken his foot and was done for the year. The Bills held on to beat the Giants 17–13 despite a couple of fourth-quarter drives by the Giants deep into Bills territory. But Hostetler's spirits were buoyed.

Jeff Hostetler: After the game, I realized that things were going to change. My opportunity was coming.

Not everyone was so sanguine about the Giants' chances of winning with Hostetler at the helm.

Ed Croke: As soon as Simms went down, a lot of people started getting doubts.

Jeff Hostetler: At that point we had lost three out of the last four games—everybody had jumped off the bandwagon. Here I was, the weakest link, and some people thought the Giants were done. At a point like that, your team can either go one way or the other. They can either pack it in and that's it, or they can rally around themselves and come out and dig their heels in and get the thing done.

Jeff's teammates chose the latter option. They had faith in Hostetler. For one thing, they knew how good he was from practice. Hostetler would run the scout team during the week, impersonating the coming opponent's quarterback.

Leonard Marshall: We respected the hell out of Jeff because he worked hard in practice. He was Joe Montana when he had to be. He was Jay Schroeder when he had to be. He was John Elway when he had to be. You almost hated him in practice because he was as good if not better than some of the quarterbacks we were going to face on Sunday. You could live with some of the looks he'd give you

THE MOST MEMORABLE GAMES IN GIANTS HISTORY

during the week because you knew he'd have your ass ready to play come Sunday. He made me earn it.

How did the Giants' offense change when it was Hostetler instead of Simms?

Erik Howard: Bill and the coaching staff adapted our offense to Jeff's style. Jeff was a superathletic guy. He'd even played wide receiver. He wasn't a pocket passer. I remember lots of rollouts and play-action passes that let Jeff use his athletic ability. He stepped in strong and did a great job. I think the whole team kind of rallied around him. All of a sudden he was the quarterback and I don't remember ever really thinking that we had a big challenge to overcome because he played that role so well.

Greg Jackson: I think the biggest thing that helped us with Jeff Hostetler was that Jeff was so athletic. Our opponents were used to Phil. Phil was a big, strong, pure pocket passer. Phil would sit in there and throw that football and let a three-hundred-pounder knock him down. Jeff would do the same thing, but he was also mobile. He could get out of the way of those guys. Our offense didn't totally change, but Jeff changed it just by moving around a lot more.

Bill Romanowski: There was something relentless about him. He had the fight that Phil Simms had, but then he had that added dimension of being able to run with the football and make things happen with his legs. He was a really good football player.

The Giants won their final two games on the road, defeating Phoenix 24–21 and New England 13–10 in what was a de facto home game: The 1–15 Patriots were not pulling in the locals. The close margins in those wins didn't exactly erase all the doubt about Hostetler's ability to get the Giants to the Super Bowl, but they certainly helped solidify his status among his teammates.

Jeff Hostetler: My teammates rallied around me. We were out to show some people.

The first playoff game was in the divisional round, at home against the Bears. Bill Parcells and the coaching staff did everything in their power to make sure the team was ready.

Erik Howard: The week before the Bears game, Bill had us do live nine-on-sevens. Usually at the end of the season, you're letting up on yourself during the week, trying to take care of yourself to play your hardest on the weekend. Bill had us all go back to fundamentals. Tackling, blocking, all that stuff. We had a real physical week of practice before we played the Bears.

The Giants put aside their usual 3–4 defensive set for much of the game in favor of a four-man defensive front. Parcells set the tone early, going for it on a fourth and 1 in Bears territory with a cheeky play call: a Hostetler pass to third-string tight end Bob Mrosko. On the next play Hoss hit Stephen Baker, Touchdown Maker, in the end zone. The Bears drove all the way down to the Giants' 1-yard line but were stymied on fourth down, and it was off to the races for the Giants from there. They won going away as Chicago could never establish a ground game. The Giants rolled up 194 yards rushing, by far the most the tough Chicago run defense allowed that year, and won, 31–3.

Greg Jackson: It was odd, because we thought Chicago was going to give us a much tougher game than that. Just like Coach Belichick always does, we were prepared defensively and we did a lot of good things to confuse the quarterback. We started to get back together that week. I think the one big thing that helped us through that year was we always communicated with one another.

Ed Croke: Hostetler started getting better into the playoffs. He played well against the Bears.

Hostetler threw for two touchdowns and added another on the ground. The brilliant defensive game plan that held the Bears became a hallmark of the Giants during that playoff run. The coaches and staff were constantly changing and evolving. Defensive coordinator Bill Belichick is often credited for their success during that run, as, of course, is the defensive-minded Bill Parcells. Notably, Belichick got nearly as much screen time as Parcells during the NFC championship-game broadcast and, at one point, John Madden said of Belichick, "This guy is a very good coach. And they're talking about him as a possible head coach in the National Football League this year. He's only thirty-eight years old." Pat Summerall added, "Very intense." While both Belichick and Parcells gained the respect of their players and opponents alike, neither man was necessarily easy to work with.

Erik Howard: Bill Belichick is one of those guys it takes some getting used to him. He was so dry and such a cynical bastard I think he could set guys off the wrong way if you didn't understand him. He was sharp as a tack. He always put in a great game plan for us. We had supreme confidence in both him and Parcells.

Greg Jackson: I learned so much from Bill Belichick. He always prepared you for each and every game and gave you tip sheets and everything. I always tell the guys who I coach now at Tulane, never take for granted what a coach is giving you, because you don't realize how much the coach prepares himself and watches film. I thought about this later on in my career. I said, man, if it wasn't for Belichick, I wouldn't have been able to make those plays. I heard stories when I was playing that Belichick used to sleep in the office overnight. I used to say, man, he must be crazy to do that. Now, being a coach, I can see it's necessary to do that sometimes. You feel there's always something you can add or there's something that you're missing.

Howard Cross: Well, I only got to play for Bill Parcells for two years. I was a young player, and he had a little bit of the red ass for young guys. He stayed after us pretty good, trying to make sure we stayed grounded. And I got a pretty big kick out of it because I was a hog farmer from Alabama. They're paying me to play football! He was big on motivation, trying to challenge guys. One thing about Bill was you almost never saw him happy. He always had an edge to him. I remember one funny story about Bill. I don't remember who we were getting ready to play, but he was talking to me and he said he was gonna put a rock in his shoe and walk around with a sore foot to make sure he didn't let up on us all day long. I thought that was the dumbest thing I had ever heard. After practice he came over and sat on a stool right beside me, took off his shoe and dropped a little rock out of it, and put his shoe back on and got up and walked away.

Greg Jackson: Parcells was very good at picking on guys. He would pick a certain person out during that week of practice and stay on him all week long—if he had to motivate you or make you concentrate or whatever it might be. He did the same thing with me.

Perry Williams: Parcells had an unusual way of doing things, and I didn't particularly care for that. I didn't like some of his tactics and how he handled people. Hey, that's him, that's how he wanted to do things.

Not all the news from that week was good. Rookie Rodney Hampton, who had shared backfield duty with veteran Ottis Anderson throughout the season, got hurt. Against the 49ers, special-teams ace and third-down back David Meggett would see more action, and it would be up to the thirty-four-year-old Anderson—the oldest running back in the National Football League to get the bulk of the carries—especially in crunch time.

The next week it was off to San Francisco for the rematch. The 49ers finished the season 14–2 and were 8-point favorites against the Giants.

Bart Oates: San Francisco was supposed to be the better team. If we played ten times, they'd probably beat us seven.

Leonard Marshall: We wanted to go out and prove to the 49ers that we were just as good if not better than they were. And we knew we were a better team than the team they beat on Monday night. We just had to go out and prove it to them.

Steve DeOssie: For our defensive game plan, we were told that two thirds of the catches their receivers made whether it was the tight ends, running backs, receivers, whatever, would occur in a certain, easily defined area and that they got that receiver there through a thousand different formations. There were a hundred different personnel groups and fifty different types of motion. They told us that we shouldn't get overwhelmed by all the different looks that we were going to see because they're basically trying to get to the same place on the field every single time the 49ers just want you to think about a thousand things before they do it. They want you to sit there and think about what's the formation. Once we saw film that week we knew they were absolutely right.

Bill Parcells brought an extra suitcase with him to San Francisco.

Carl Banks: There was a confidence that he wanted us to have going into that trip. Not as in, "Let's hope we win, come home, and then go to the Super Bowl." More like, "It's all or nothing. We're packing for two trips and we're not coming back home. Pack, and we'll make the arrangements with the families after the game is over with. We're not coming back home. We're going from there to Tampa."

Steve DeOssie: Instead of that being a psychological bump it was just the way Parcells thought and wanted us to think and perpetuate that. And that began way back well before the season started and that was the ultimate, very matter-of-fact scenario. It wasn't like "Ra! Ra! Ra! Lets bring an extra suitcase." It was, "Oh, and by the way, make sure you pack for Tampa."

Erik Howard: I was at my locker that week after practice. I was feeling particularly loose and there were a bunch of reporters standing around. We were all just kind of shootin' the breeze. And I guess I didn't really realize that I was on the record. I just really didn't think about it. I got to talking about how I grew up out there and I could remember going to 49ers games and how you could yell across the stadium to your buddies because there was nobody there. And how all of a sudden there were all these lifelong, die-hard 49ers fans when the Niners started seeing some success—fair-weather fans.

Somebody asked me about the 49ers' chances of winning again. And I said that it was my obligation to history not to let the 49ers three-peat. And they asked me if Montana could be rattled. I said, "Sure. Any quarterback can be rattled. You hit him enough, he's gonna be rattled." And the next day the cover of one of the papers said, ERIK HOWARD: 'MONTANA CAN BE RATTLED.' And then they went on to take everything I said and put it in the paper.

Leonard Marshall: I told Jeff before the game, "I am going to harass the shit out of Montana today. I hope he's ready to play like I am, because I am going to be on him like a gnat on shit. He is going to have to deal with my ass today."

Bill Romanowski: We didn't know a lot about Jeff Hostetler. There wasn't a lot of film on him. We couldn't study a whole season of game tape on him. So we approached it like we were playing a Giants team that was manned by Phil Simms. We thought they would pound the football. They weren't going to have the quarterback try and win the game for them.

There was a unique atmosphere surrounding the game that had nothing to do with football.

Ed Croke: It was the first Gulf War, and I served two years during the Korean War. And when they had all those patriotic songs before the game even started, that got to me. I thought that was fabulous. It was a very patriotic environment. I was all pumped up.

There were signs of the war throughout the CBS broadcast. An unusual number of fans—not just Giants fans—were seen wearing red, white, and blue. The Giants wore yellow armbands to honor the servicemen and women abroad. At a couple of points, the broadcast was interrupted for special reports from CBS News, though viewers missed only one play.

Joe Montana—arguably the greatest quarterback of all time—had missed two days of practice with the flu but was ready to go at game time. His first pass looked iffy, but he soon settled down into a rhythm, marching the 49ers down the field for a 47-yard field goal from Mike Cofer.

The Giants answered on their first possession with a long drive highlighted early on by a huge 20-yard third-down completion to Mark Ingram, made possible by Jeff Hostetler's scrambling ability. Meggett was the featured back early in the first series, running the ball to the outside. Once they got down to the 49ers' 30-yard line, it was Anderson running up the middle.

In the previous meeting with the 49ers, the Giants had done a good job moving the ball from their own 20 to the 49ers' 20; it was the red zone where their offense completely stalled. Parcells had a nifty trick ready for the Giants' first red-zone appearance in the championship rematch. Meggett took the ball from Hostetler and swept outside as he had done with some success earlier in the drive. But this time he was meant to throw. Sure enough, a wide-open Maurice Carthon was there in the end zone, with only run defender Matt Millen chasing him one-on-one. But the ball slipped through Carthon's fingers and the Giants had to settle for three—a 28-yarder from Matt Bahr. The drive took fifteen plays and ran seven minutes and eighteen seconds, keeping the potent 49er offense off the field, but the 4 points left on the table would haunt the Giants until the very end of the game.

In the second quarter, the Giants produced another long drive, spanning fourteen plays and consuming eight minutes and thirty-two seconds. Once again, though, they stalled out and had to settle for a Bahr 42-yarder. They left only one minute on the clock, but one minute was all that Montana needed to answer with another field goal, this one from 35. The teams went into the half knotted at 6.

Greg Jackson: Coach Belichick always had something up his sleeve as far as different defenses—a look that would confuse the other quarterback.

Part of the Giants' game plan was to attempt to contain receivers Jerry Rice and John Taylor while allowing Montana to complete shorter passes to the likes of tight end Brent Jones and fullback Tom Rathman.

Greg Jackson: We wanted him to check the ball down a lot and try to cover their receivers on curl routes and in cuts and take those things away. We knew if we could pass rush, we could definitely get to Montana and make him uncomfortable. We tried to close the middle up on them, the deep middle, and make them check the ball down a lot. We just made the looks a little bit different for him than what he was used to seeing.

The plan had worked well in the first half, with Mark Collins in particular doing an impressive job against future Hall of Famer Rice. But when the Giants were forced to punt on their first drive of the third quarter, John Taylor showed off his game-changing skills. Punter Sean Landeta delivered a booming 55-yard kick to inside the 49er 10-yard line, but Taylor got to the outside and returned it to the 39.

Everson Walls was the man in charge of covering Taylor in his role of wide receiver. For Walls, San Francisco's Candlestick Park was a house of horrors. Nine years earlier in the NFC championship game, Walls was a member of the Dallas Cowboys, playing against these same 49ers. He had had a big game that day—two interceptions and a fumble recovery—but that's not what haunted him about that game. It was Walls who was covering Dwight Clark on what would become one of the most famous plays in NFL history and one of the signature moments of Joe Montana's career. Clark snared the game winner that day, just over the outstretched hands of Everson Walls. A dramatic play that came off a Montana scramble in the game's final second, it was already known simply as the Catch.

On the next play, Montana targeted Taylor. On the broadcast, John Madden said, "Everson Walls is a gambler, always has been."

Ed Croke: Everson Walls went for an interception. Just missed getting it.

Instead, with Walls out of position to make the tackle, the play went for a 61-yard touchdown and San Francisco took the lead, 13–6. The Giants followed that with another clock eater of a drive, taking up more than six minutes before Bahr made it 3-for-3 on the day with a 46-yard field goal.

On the ensuing possession, the 49ers went no-huddle. They got a quick first down, but then went three and out from there, with a key sack coming from Lawrence Taylor and Erik Howard. The Giants started their next possession at their own 45. A couple of big runs from Ottis Anderson, including a 27-yarder on third and 2, brought them all the way down to the 49er 20-yard line. The quarter ended after a 1-yard run by Meggett, with Parcells on the sideline screaming for his team not to run another play. Along with all the short gains and long drives, this was just another way to shorten the game and keep the 49er offense standing over on the sideline.

The fourth quarter began with a familiar scenario: the Giants offense stalling in 49er territory. Two batted passes later and it was time for Matt Bahr once again. Only this time he seemed to rush the kick, missing a 37-yard attempt to the left. It was 3 more points left unclaimed by the Giants.

The 49ers' defense that day was a classic example of bend but don't break. The Giants moved the ball downfield seemingly at will with long scoring drives, and yet the 49ers hadn't allowed them to cross the goal line in nearly two full games. A huge part of their success that day was Jim Burt, the Giants legend. Among his claims to fame from his time in New York was knocking out Joe Montana and causing an interception in the 1986 divisional playoffs—but he'd been forced out after the 1988 season.

Jim Burt: I got asked during the summer to play for the 49ers, and I said, "I can't play for them. I just can't." I just couldn't do it because we were rivals, and we really didn't like each other. But I wasn't ready to stop playing, so I said, "I'll give it a shot. I have to win another Super Bowl to validate the first one." We did.

Naturally, Burt's emotions ran high when he played the Giants.

Jim Burt: Obviously I wanted to beat them. They wanted to get Erik Howard in the game. They used the excuse of my back to get rid of me. It was a business move by them, but I wasn't happy about things.

Bill Romanowski: It was an enormous football game for Jim Burt—to be able to beat his Giants and advance to the Super Bowl.

During the next Giants possession, on a 14-yard completion to Mark Ingram, Burt made his mark on the game.

Jim Burt: Bart [Oates] was blocking me on that play. He lunged forward a little bit. When he lunged forward, I got around him. He missed the block, and I think the guard was fanning out. When Eric Moore came to fan back out, he was late. I knew he was going to come back and cut me. I stayed low. I had to get myself down low, otherwise he'd take out my knees. So I came in almost like a submarine because Bart was going to cut my legs. He had to do that or grab me. These guards were going to do the same. They tried to cut me the series before that, so I knew I had to stay low once I got past them. So I came in low, and I hit Hostetler low. I had to protect myself. They made a big deal about it.

Bart Oates: Jim Burt was out there at nose tackle. He got around the edge and I ended up pushing him into Jeff where it hurt Jeff's knee. That was my fault, that wasn't Jim's fault. He got blamed for it—people thought it was a cheap shot. But he got my edge and I was just trying to do what I could and I pushed him. I wound up pushing him right into Jeff's knee. Jeff, fortunately, only suffered a partial tear.

Bill Romanowski: That's who Jim Burt was, that physical guy in the middle who was going to use really good technique, brute strength, and desire. It wasn't going to look pretty—on some level he wobbled to the quarterback—but he was able to put a good hit on him.

Jeff Hostetler: The one hit that stood out was Jim Burt coming in and taking a shot right at my knee sometime in the fourth quarter. I knew my knee was gone. I had excruciating pain and a burning sensation. I just knew it was gone. The pain wouldn't go away. I'd waited so long for this opportunity and I was done.

Howard Cross: Jeff Hostetler got knocked out and Matt Cavanaugh came in.

Cavanaugh was a thirteen-year NFL veteran, and he had a championship ring for backing up Montana in Super Bowl XIX. In the following sequence, however, he appeared to be caked with rust.

Howard Cross: There was a pass play. I shook the defender—I was open down the middle of the field and he threw it almost a few rows up in the stands! After that, we're like, "Okay, Hos, time for you to get back in the game."

Jeff Hostetler: I was over on the sideline and they were checking me out. I was trying to do a little dropback to see if I was going to be able to go. Parcells kept coming over saying, "Can you go? Are you gonna go? Can you go?" Every time he'd say that I'd say, "I'm going, I'm going." Finally, one time he came over and said, "Can you go?" I looked at him and said, "I'm going!" That was it.

The 49ers got the ball back with 10:50 remaining, still up 13–9. The Giants' defense was more focused than ever.

Leonard Marshall: I'm not going to lie to you: That Burt hit motivated the hell out of me. I wanted to be a guy Jeff could count on. The guys were very upset because Jimmy Burt was one of ours. When I say it was a dirty hit, it very well could have been one of the cleanest hits in football. We kind of took personal offense to it because Jimmy was one of our own. If it had been another guy on the team, maybe it would have been a different deal.

On the next series, the 49ers faced a third and long from their own 23. What followed was another one of the game's signature plays.

Dave Anderson: Leonard chased Montana all the way to the sideline and just wrapped his arms around him like a grizzly bear would. And they both went crashing down and Montana couldn't get up.

Leonard Marshall: People ask me about that play all the time. I'd hear statements like, "Leonard's only as good as he is because he's lined up next to Lawrence Taylor." They have to realize that in a three-four defense, I'm blocked ninety percent of the time by two blockers. A guard and tackle would be on me ninety percent of the time, so whenever I had to make a play, I had to work twice as hard. I never gave up on plays. I tried to play every play. I have over eighty-five quarterback sacks, not including the playoffs. With a three-four defense, that's unheard of. You go back and look at that play. I was blocked. I'd been cut at my feet. I was crawling. Joe Montana rolled off to the right, telling Jerry Rice to keep running. As he pulled up, I dove, trying to strip the football.

Marshall hit Montana from behind and the ball went flying forward—a fumble.

Greg Jackson: I was back in the secondary and I could see it coming. As Leonard hit him, it was like slow motion, because I was trying to get to the ball and I could never get to the football.

The officials called "Red's ball." Somehow Steve Wallace of San Francisco got it back. Replays show the ball bouncing right off the chest of Giants cornerback Mark Collins.

Erik Howard: That still bugs me from time to time. Most of the game, I was just beating these guys in the pass rush, but every time I'd quick-swim the guard or the center, the ball was already gone. On that play, Montana lingered back there and I got tied up with Guy McIntyre. I tried a quick swim or something and he got me. And I've seen that played back and I'm like, Jesus! I was tied up and I could've hammered Montana because he threw the ball in three steps every time. Leonard actually fell down, got up, and still hit him. The one time he hung back there because he couldn't find an open receiver, I'm tied up with McIntyre!

Even though it was still San Francisco's ball, they had to punt, and Montana was done for the afternoon with what proved to be a broken hand.

Greg Jackson: Finally, I looked and I saw Joe down and I said, "We're going to the Super Bowl." That's the first thing that hit my mind. I said, "We're getting ready to go to the Super Bowl, guys."

On the next sequence, Hostetler came back in and, incredibly, looked none the worse for wear. He deftly avoided a sack and scrambled for 6 yards on second down, setting up a huge third and 1 near midfield, but Anderson was absolutely stuffed by Michael Carter, losing a yard. With the Giants trailing by 4 and less than eight minutes on the clock, the punting unit came on the field.

Parcells had a reputation for being aggressive on fourth downs—he'd gone for it on fourth down (and failed) at a key moment in the fourth quarter in the first meeting against San Francisco. Early in the second quarter of this game, he'd punted on a fourth and 1 in 49ers territory. Again, in the third quarter, the Giants chose a Bahr 46-yard field goal instead of going for it on fourth and 5 when down by 7 from inside the 49ers' 30. So, given that there was enough time on the clock for the Giants to get the ball back and sustain another drive, when they lined up in punting formation, all of the 49ers had every reason to believe Sean Landeta was going to kick it away—but that's not what happened.

Ed Croke: That's the famous Arapahoe call. A run, a pass, a hit on the enemy. That's what it stands for. Gary Reasons is the guy that caught it. He's the one that yelled it. And the villain on the 49ers' side was Romanowski. He was supposed to be on the field. He's supposed to be on the punt-return team—he's sitting there on the bench. They only had ten guys out there. Reasons saw the spot and yelled Arapahoe. Sean should have won an Academy Award jumping in the air like the ball sailed over his head.

Howard Cross: I was on the field and I saw that they were in the right position for the fake-punt call and I thought, "We should call it." But I didn't hear the fake-punt call. So I was blocking my guy, but I didn't hear the ball kicked. And then I saw Gary running down the field and I thought, "Uh-oh, he's gonna get a flag." Turns out he had the ball!

Reasons rumbled 30 yards and nearly broke the play for a touchdown, but he was tackled by John Taylor. Bahr added another field goal, bringing the Giants to within one.

With Montana done for the day, Steve Young trotted onto the field. Young was no ordinary backup: He'd done extremely well filling in for Montana and was clearly poised to be the team's starter of the future. On the very next drive he showed why the Niners didn't miss a beat when he came into a game. He threw a 25-yard strike to Brent Jones close to midfield. Two rushes from Roger Craig brought another first down, and, despite all the hard work the Giants had done on the day, it was now looking as though their numerous red-zone failures were going to kill them. The 49ers certainly appeared to be headed to Tampa for a chance at the three-peat.

Bill Romanowski: At that point, the game was ours to win. We have the ball. Two and a half minutes left. We're going to win.

Ed Croke: Timmy Mara said to me, "We came so far and we're going to lose like this. What a shame."

Erik Howard: I remember a feeling of desperation before that play. I said to myself, "Somebody's gotta come up with a big play." And there's Lawrence Taylor right there, there's Leonard Marshall over there. Carl Banks over there. One of these guys has gotta make this play. When I walked up to the line it was one of those slow-motion moments. I was never really a big film guy. I played by instinct. Ninety percent of the time I knew what the play was a second before the snap. You can read stances, formations. You're playing Dallas. They're in the Power-I. The guard and the center got their stances cheated together. You know it's an inside run. Very similar situation here. As I walked up to the line, Jesse Sapolu and Guy McIntyre walked up and they had their stance just cheated real tight. I got down to the three-point and they were getting settled in. They're real heavy on their fingers. I'm going to get double-teamed: I know it. So I went through the process in my mind of playing this fundamentally correct. Go back to basics: Just stab the center. Drop the knee and squeeze through the chute. That's the way we've practiced it a thousand times. I knew it was coming at me. I stabbed Sapolu and McIntyre came at me hard and I leaned into it and dropped a knee and squeezed right through. As soon as I squeezed right through, there was Roger Craig in my face. I popped out and my helmet hit Roger in the breadbasket. I grabbed his leg. I knew I had him in my grasp. I grabbed him and tackled him for the loss. I didn't know that the ball had actually popped out until later.

Dave Anderson: Erik Howard tackled Roger Craig and the ball popped into the air and who was there to grab it out of the air? Who else? LT.

Jim Burt: Craig didn't even get hit. He was fumbling it before he got hit. On the series before, he almost fumbled because he was a little tight. They should have gone with two tight ends, and ran the ball inside the tackles with Rathman. On third down, you can do many things. You've got the fastest guy on the field in Steve Young. He'll break containment or maybe throw a little short pass and win the game. Maybe he'll hold on to the ball and stay in bounds and pooch-kick it. That would have made them drive the field with no time-outs. But Craig fumbled, and they had the whole two minutes and didn't have to worry about time or anything like that.

Greg Jackson: Everybody just looked at one another. I know me and [Myron] Guyton just looked at one another and we're like, "We're going to Tampa." It was funny because it seemed like it was destiny because we were playing the two teams that we lost to during the season. When we beat San Fran to go to the Super Bowl, that's the most memorable game for me because of how it was won. That NFC championship game was unbelievable.

Erik Howard: When the play was over or during the play I realized there was a fumble and we had gotten it. This is what we needed: a little bit of relief after a feeling of desperation.

Ed Croke: Then boom, all of a sudden the fumble. I said to Tim Mara, "This isn't over yet, Timmy." That's a big play in the history of the Giants, Erik knocking that ball out. We get the ball back like that, you say to yourself, "You know what? We've got a chance here."

The Giants took over at their own 42, needing only a field goal to win. The defense was left to sweat it out on the sidelines.

Erik Howard: As a defensive player, you're helpless on the sideline. I was over there just talking to myself, "C'mon, c'mon, c'mon, c'mon." Willing the ball down the field. You mentally sit there and will it to happen. "Here we go. We're gonna do it!"

On first down, Hostetler narrowly avoided another sack and found Mark Bavaro for 19 yards to the 49er 38. Two plays later, he found Stephen Baker inside the 30 on a rollout pass. Then, on a pivotal third and 1, running back Ottis Anderson got a huge couple of yards, ensuring that the Giants could run out the clock if they wanted to. There would be no more Montana, no more Young. The Giants would either win or lose on Matt Bahr's sixth field-goal attempt of the game. It was from 42 yards out. During the time-out called by the 49ers to ice him, he stood alone, yards behind his teammates. There was a slight wind at his back.

Steve DeOssie: Matt had had to make a tackle or two in that game on kickoffs and his head was ringing. He might've had a concussion or something. He wasn't completely of sound mind. When they called the time-out to kind of slow him down at the last field goal, I came up to him and he was a little woozy because of the kickoff tackle that he made. Matt was as cool as they come. He was my best friend on the team, so I could goof around with him a little bit. I said, "Matt, you're the coolest kicker around, they can't freeze you with a time-out." He looked at me and said, "They're not trying to freeze me they're trying to freeze you. You have to snap the ball." I said, "You gotta be kidding me. I can't believe you just said that."

Jeff Hostetler: As a holder, the only time you get noticed is when you screw up. So here I was, having driven us down to a point where we're on the verge of knocking off the defending Super Bowl champions, the guys that are going for the three-peat. All I could think about was catching the ball and getting it down. Just catch the ball and get it down. I can still see it. I can still see the rotation of the ball coming back. If I got it down, Matt Bahr was kicking it through.

Greg Jackson: I was on a knee. We were all holding hands. I could not look and my head was down. The first person I heard was Pepper Johnson. I heard him scream and I didn't even look at the field goal. I just started running on the field.

Steve DeOssie: As soon as he kicked the ball I knew it was good. My first instinct was to run back to Matt because I knew he was hurt and I knew guys were gonna mob him. So I had to run back to Matt and make sure guys weren't smacking him on the head and tackling him and throwing him to the ground.

There was no time left on the clock. For the fifth time that day, Bahr had done his job. He had provided the Giants with all of their points.

Jim Burt: It came down to who was going to blink first, and we blinked. We made the mistake, and they capitalized on it. You hold a team to fifteen points, and eighteen points in two games, you expect to win both of those games, especially with the offense the 49ers had.

John Madden told a story that has been often repeated. During his speech to the team the night before, Parcells told his team that the 49ers had already moved their stuff to Tampa, and, according to Madden, concluded by saying, "They think they're going to three-peat, we'll show them what a three-peat is."

Jim Burt: They made a big thing that we packed our stuff for Tampa, but they came with their stuff packed, too. They left right from there to Tampa. Parcells said, "Listen, they think they have already gotten to the Super Bowl because they have their stuff packed." All of those things don't even come into play if Roger doesn't fumble that ball.

Bill Romanowski: Parcells had given them a talk before the game and told them, "They're so confident they're going to beat us that they already have their staff down at the Super Bowl. They've moved in. That's how confident they are." But he didn't tell them that the Giants had their people in Tampa, too! It was the only way you were going to be able to pull something like this off without having the two weeks to prepare for it.

Just because he'd just won one of the biggest games of his career didn't mean that Bill Parcells was going to miss an opportunity to mess with one of his players.

Jeff Hostetler: Bill Parcells didn't draft me. We didn't have the best of relationships. Bill liked to play mind games and I didn't like mind games. I knew that I needed to be on the bus. So I answered all the media questions and was ready to go and someone said I needed to come down and do an interview on the field with John Madden. I said, "Listen, I'm not doing any interview down there unless you make sure that they're going to hold the bus for me." As I'm walking down, I was assured, "No, no, we'll have a bus there." As I was walking down to the field, Parcells was walking up from the field. He just kind of looked at me. I went down and did the interview with Madden. I told John that Bill was going to leave without me. He just laughed and said, "Nah." I headed back to where the buses are supposed to be. All six buses were gone. I had no idea where the team was. All of a sudden, here comes John Madden. He laughed and said, "Listen, I'll get you there." I hopped on his bus and he had guys making calls and, the next thing I knew, we had everything taken care of. We pulled into the airport. We drove right up to the plane. I thanked Madden, walked up the steps and got in that plane, and Parcells looked at me and just gave me a little smirk and nodded his head like, "Okay, that's not bad." I felt good that he put me on a spot and I had to figure out a way to get there and was able to do it.

Ed Croke: That might have been the greatest plane ride I've ever been on. Because it was a short week that week, all the brass went back to New York the next day, but we flew to Tampa right after the game. We got to Tampa about two thirty in the morning. One of the great plane trips of all time.

The party didn't last long. Just one week later, the Giants would be facing another, arguably even tougher rematch: this one against the Buffalo Bills in the Super Bowl. New York opened as 8-point underdogs again and were still 7-point underdogs by the kickoff.

Bart Oates: The Bills were just a juggernaut that year. They just steamrolled through the season. They beat the Raiders 51–3 in the game before. Their offense and defense were great. I think pretty much the whole team went to the Pro Bowl. They were another team that was better than us. We play ten times, they probably beat us eight times. But we knew the more time we ate up, the less time they got on the field.

The Bills had led the league in scoring in 1990 with 428 points. Their victory over Los Angeles in the AFC championship game is the third-largest margin of victory in playoff history. (See "The Most Resounding Playoff Victories of All Time," page 311.) Quarterback Jim Kelly had the highest passer rating in the NFL while Thurman Thomas was in the second of four consecutive years leading the league in yards from scrimmage. So loaded with talent were the Bills that they even sent a special-teams player to the Pro Bowl, gunner Steve Tasker.

Greg Jackson: It was great that we played them before, because we knew what to be prepared for. One of the things Coach Belichick said was that we had to discourage these guys and make it hard for them. Usually, when you play a spread offense, it's easy for the receivers to run routes. When the timing routes are two seconds, two point five seconds, they want to get that ball out. When you get up there, jamming in their faces, it makes their routes hard to run. It makes the receivers press a lot more. That's what we wanted them to have to do.

Perry Williams: Bill Belichick has always been a great coach as a defensive-minded guy. For the Bills, he came up with a perfect game plan. Bill had put together nickel and dime packages where we had five or six defensive backs out there the whole game, basically.

Erik Howard: The big nickel. That's what he called it. It was a great plan. They had spanked the Raiders. That's what we were faced with going into that game. The no-huddle offense. For me, I dreaded it.

Belichick's concept was a revolutionary way to defend the hurry-up, pass-happy Bills that no one had tried before.

Leonard Marshall: We knew what the tempo of the game was going to be like. What we didn't know was how we'd match up with a two-five-four scheme. Two down linemen, five linebackers, and four defensive backs. We didn't mind Thurman Thomas getting a hundred and fifty yards running the ball.

Belichick's idea was that the Giants had to give them something while taking something else away. He'd give them Thomas and take away the quick-strike, downfield passing game.

Leonard Marshall: We didn't care about their running game because we knew that they were going to have to pass the ball to get in the end zone. That's what they were all about all year long. We wanted to take control early on and make them earn everything they got.

Carl Banks: Our first meeting before that game was interesting because we put the film on first, and we saw this high-flying offense that was just putting a ton of points up. And then Bill Belichick put the lights on and told us we're going to allow Thurman Thomas to gain one hundred yards. And for a prideful defense, that was a hard pill to swallow. And the genius behind that is that his ability to analyze the opponent was incredible. I don't think many teams or coordinators would have come to the same conclusion and had the courage in his convictions to stay with the game plan. Because he took a sampling of the Buffalo Bills' last eight games of the season, including the playoffs. They ran the ball about ten percent of the time. And their running plays had become swing passes to Thurman Thomas. And he had enough of a sampling to believe that they weren't going to deviate from that. So as teams would line up to play them traditionally, they were getting torched. He said, "Okay, we're going to defend the pass first, if he gets a hundred yards that means they're not passing the football." And what we had to do was devise a way to disrupt their passing game. Couldn't get there [to the quarterback], the ball was out of his hands too fast to get a sack, so we decided it was going to be in our best interest to beat the heck up out of their receivers. We proceeded to beat the hell out of Andre Reed on his crossing routes. We gave them a lot of speed bumps, and it was an effective game plan.

Steve DeOssie: The emphasis was beating up the receivers and not letting the receivers kill you. And that was something you noticed right from the get-go. Guys were so physical with the receivers. These weren't tiny little receivers either. The other part of the game plan was the idea of slowing down their offense whenever we could. Unpiling slowly, accidentally kicking the football after it got set— anything that could be done to slow down the rhythm of that offense. So instead of running a play every twenty-four seconds it took them thirty-two seconds or whatever. Anything you could do to disrupt the rhythm and slow down the quick-strike capabilities was pretty much the strongest part of that defensive game plan.

In the book *Tales from the New York Giants Sideline*, Mark Collins details another aspect of Belichick's defensive game plan: "To get used to the no-huddle offense we actually watched the NBC coverage, the game itself, with Dick Enberg announcing the game so we could see how much time it would take to run a play. Never been done before. Bill Belichick said, 'Okay, guys, watch this film, let your clock run in your mind to see how much time you got to gather and call a play.'"

As it had been with the conference championships, the atmosphere surrounding the Super Bowl was very patriotic. Flags were ubiquitous in the stands. Frank Gifford welcomed fans to the broadcast with a message of support for U.S. armed forces abroad.

Dave Anderson: There were snipers on the roof of the stadium. There was serious concern about a terrorist attack.

During the broadcast, Al Michaels said, "Of all the people interviewed [this week], the Ottis Andersons, the Jeff Hostetlers, and the Bruce Smiths, I think a guy named Robert Smith was the most interviewed man in town this week—the Tampa safety director." Dan Dierdorf added, "The Super Bowl has never seen anything like the security in place right now, and I for one am very much appreciative."

Erik Howard: One of my most prevalent memories of that game was the trip to the stadium. It was a sea of red, white, and blue as far as you could see. Driving in, they had to take the buses against traffic because it was gridlocked getting in there. And we had the police escort and we were driving in the oncoming lanes of traffic for several miles. People were standing on the sides of the road waving flags. It was just red, white, and blue everywhere.

Dave Anderson: Whitney Houston sang the national anthem. I tell you, it was the greatest national anthem I've ever heard. She didn't just sing it, she belted it. It was spectacular. And it still gives me chills to think about it.

Erik Howard: The culmination of all the patriotism surrounding the event was when Whitney Houston sang the national anthem. It was one of those chills-up-your-back moments.

The Bills got the ball first and they lined up once again in their trademark hurry-up offense, dubbed the K-Gun. Kelly's first pass was incomplete. He threw again on second down.

Karl Nelson: The first thing the Giants wanted to do was stop the crossing patterns by the Buffalo receivers. In the first crossing pattern, Andre Reed came across the middle and Greg Jackson just leveled the crap out of him. They didn't want to come across the middle again. That kind of set the tone for the whole game.

Greg Jackson: When they caught that ball across the middle, we wanted to let them know we were there. One thing about the no-huddle, the ball has to come out quick. If it didn't come out quick, they were in trouble. Plus they couldn't hold number fifty-six on the corner off the football. So we went up and challenged them. We went up with different looks. A lot of times during the season, guys weren't playing up in their faces. We started getting up in their faces and making their routes a lot tougher to run. That's what I wanted to do there. I was trying to make him reroute and run a tougher route.

Sure enough, on the next play, same thing: a short crossing route complete to Reed. But he was short of the first down and got tagged by the Giants' D once again. You could hear the amazement from the broadcast team about the Giants' unusual scheme. Frank Gifford predicted, "Kelly will have a lot of time with that kind of defensive alignment."

Erik Howard: The first defensive series where we got them to go three and out was big for us. It was an instant momentum killer because those guys thrived on the no-huddle and moving the ball downfield and controlling the tempo of the game. They went three and out and all of a sudden it was our offense out there. They were big ball-control guys and totally upset the tempo of the game.

Steve DeOssie: I don't know if that had happened all year. For a few seconds they all kind of looked at each other. It was almost like they didn't know what to do and then they realized it was fourth down and they had to get off the field. It was a very unfamiliar situation for them.

The Giants' first drive highlighted the dichotomy between the two offenses. The Bills played every drive as a two-minute drill; the Giants played every drive as if they were killing the clock at the end of the game—runs and conservative passes.

Carl Banks: What we did there was make every possession by Buffalo an important possession. By us shortening the game and getting something out of it every time we had the ball, there was more of a premium on them trying to get something done. They could never enjoy their cushion and that was to our advantage defensively; we were able to at least contain them.

On a first down from their own 43, Hostetler hit Howard Cross for 12 yards on a rollout pass—and got the Giants into Bills territory.

Howard Cross: Bavaro was a strong blocker on the edge. That caused teams to cheat inside. They did everything they possibly could to stop the running game because they didn't want to give the edge up to Bavaro or me. So the bootleg became a big part of the game plan.

Hostetler had a nice completion to Ingram on the drive but looked a little choppy, too. He overthrew an open Bavaro on one play and underthrew Ingram on a key third down, leading to a 28-yard field goal from Matt Bahr, leaving many Giants to think, "Not this again . . ."

On the Bills' next offensive series, the Giants used six defensive backs, but that still couldn't keep Jim Kelly from getting on track. He hit the venerable James Lofton on a 61-yard pass that was tipped and nearly intercepted by Perry Williams, but Lofton couldn't get in the end zone.

Ed Croke: There was nobody between Lofton and the goal line and Everson Walls came out of nowhere and got him by the ankles and tripped him. And then they had to settle for a field goal [a 23-yarder by Scott Norwood]. Saved four points for us right there.

On their subsequent drive, the Giants drove to midfield before punting. The first quarter ended with the score knotted 3–3 and the Bills on the move once again. Notably, this wasn't a Bills-like drive. It was a much more methodical, balanced, dribs-and-drabs, down-the-field, Giants-like drive. This worked well with the Giants' overall game plan, but, as Gifford had predicted earlier, Kelly was having an inordinate amount of time to throw back there. Leonard Marshall thought something had to be done.

Leonard Marshall: I took a late hit on Jim Kelly. I hit him in the back. I wasn't trying to hurt him. I was just trying to get his attention, to get him to focus on me. We knew what kind of a player he was. We knew he was a great leader. And he was taking control. We knew we had to rile him early. It was the second quarter and he didn't have any dirt on his uniform. He'd get the snap, complete a pass, call a play, complete a play. We didn't want that to be like that. We wanted him to be out of rhythm, to have him wonder what's going to happen next. Are they going to blitz? Who is going to hit me? Where are they coming from? We wanted his mind to go other places. My thing that day was just try and be as relentless and to be in his head as much as possible. And that's what we tried to do.

Don Smith capped off the drive with a touchdown from the 1. The Giants were quickly thwarted on their next drive: Leon Seals landed a massive hit on Hostetler, set up by an impressive inside move from defensive end Bruce Smith, who was described earlier by Al Michaels as "the dominant defensive player in the NFL right now."

Thurman Thomas broke a 14-yard run early in the next sequence. Now the pressure was really on the Giants' defense. They didn't have the type of offense to come back from far behind against the Bills. They needed to hold. Myron Guyton crushed Andre Reed, causing a second-down incompletion. Then, on third down, on another crossing route, the usually sure-handed Reed dropped a pass from Kelly. The Giants' plan was working.

Jim Burt: Anything that came across, they were clocking. That's what the Giants did with the Bills. The Bills did those five-yard crossing patterns, and they tried to kill Andre Reed.

On the next sequence, deep in Giants territory, Bruce Smith sacked Hostetler for a safety. But it was nearly a lot worse.

Jeff Hostetler: They had been physical against our offense up to that point. They put a lot of hits on me. I think what happened there was it was a two-five-eight, where you drop straight back and then roll to the right to get me out of the pocket a little bit and out to the corner, and I could have the option of running or throwing. I think Ottis sensed the fact that these guys were coming after us. He stepped up a little close to the line, caught my foot. I can remember stumbling and then it was like slow motion. I was trying to keep my balance. Then boom! I just felt this big old mitt on my hand. It was everything that I had in me to try to get my body turned, to pull that ball in and just protect it. We were just real fortunate to be able to hold on to the ball and live for another day.

Marv Levy: That was a big play, Hostetler holding on to that ball, a five-point difference. There are a million ifs in a game and that's one of them.

As Leonard Marshall had hoped, the Bills looked out of rhythm on their next possession. Reed dropped another ball, and the Giants' pass rush had more success in getting to Kelly. The teams traded two more ineffective possessions and the Giants got the ball back deep in their own territory with 3:49 left in the half, down 12–3.

The Giants stuck with their game plan: bootleg pass to Bavaro, Ottis Anderson up the middle. Hostetler found Ingram on the sideline in Bills territory. Meggett broke one for a big gain to the 25 right at the two-minute warning. Giants fans held their collective breath. Their previous seven possessions in the red zone had yielded six successful field goals and one missed field goal. Could this be the time they finally punched one in?

It didn't look like it. Hostetler underthrew Cross on a first-down catch that might have been a big play. Then Bills linebacker Cornelius Bennett spiked a pass out of the air like a volleyball. On second down, Hostetler missed Stephen Baker in the end zone on a perfectly run route, bringing up third and 10. But this time, when hope was fading, Hostetler came through.

Jeff Hostetler: Lots of times, there is a receiver that has the same mind-set as you and you can kind of read him. Certain routes that they run you have a better feel for than others. We were able to hit on a big play there for a touchdown right before the half. It was just huge for us because not only did we bring the score closer together, it just showed all of us that, hey, we can move this ball, we can control the ball, we can attack these guys and keep them on their heels. It gave us a little bit of confidence. We may not be the flashiest, but you're going to have to be able to stop us.

Bart Oates: It was not flashy. But Jeff made some tremendous plays there.

Thanks to that pass to Baker, the Giants went into halftime trailing only 12–10, and they got the ball again to start the second half. Once again, they started to drive the ball downfield. On a third and 8 from their own 25, Meggett made an amazing run after a catch. He got the ball at the 30, broke a tackle, and scurried for the first down. Ottis Anderson began to assert his authority on this drive, as great work by the O-line—and the Giants' tight ends in particular—opened up some impressive running lanes. He gained 24 on one play to take the ball down to the Bills' 29.

After a penalty, on third and 13 from the 32 Hostetler got the ball to Mark Ingram at the 26. Ingram proceeded to juke and jive and break no fewer than five tackles as he made the first down. It remains one of the great plays in Giants—and Super Bowl—history. Dan Dierdorf commented on the broadcast, "Every now and then in a football game, you can look back to a play and it might set the tone for everything that happens after that. If the Giants win this game, they may look back to this catch—and run—by Mark Ingram."

Jeff Hostetler: We were going to get the ball to Mark Ingram underneath because they were dropping back. It was third and long and they wanted to make us kick the field goal. The effort, not only by Mark Ingram but other guys just down there throwing blocks and getting in people's way and nobody giving up, that just really epitomized our whole team. We weren't going to give up.

On the next third down, Hostetler again got the conversion, this time with a bootleg pass to Howard Cross.

Howard Cross: Buffalo was keyed in on the fact that we were really crushing the edges of the defense, and Parcells and the offensive coaching staff figured, "Let's dump it to Howard out in the flat. They'll be so far inside that he'll be able to get five yards before someone even notices he has the ball." They were overpursuing to the ball, trying their best to keep Ottis Anderson from running it. Coach Ron Erhardt did a great job of figuring that out.

Jeff Hostetler: We knew what we were going to do. We were going to throw some bootlegs. We're going to come out and move the pocket around. Stop us.

Bart Oates: Jeff was phenomenal on third-down conversions.

Indeed, he was 7-for-11 at that point. Two more runs from Anderson and the Giants had their second touchdown of the game. Dierdorf declared the Giants' nine-minute-plus drive "one of the greatest drives in Super Bowl history."

Greg Jackson: You have to give a lot of credit to our offensive line, Maurice Carthon, and O. J. Anderson for the way we controlled the time of possession. Anderson was a bruiser, man. He was one of the main reasons why we made it that far during the whole season with him running that football. He was unbelievable.

Leonard Marshall: Well, we looked at Ottis almost like James Brown returning to the Apollo Theater. I used to tell him that. I'd say,

Ottis, just think of James Brown returning to the Apollo. Give them that one last hit to show 'em you still got it. You know, Papa got a brand-new bag!

Jeff Hostetler: Ottis and I, we spent lots of time together, frustrating time together. He was looking for another chance when everybody told him he was done. I was looking for my first chance, so we had a lot in common. During practice, during scout-squad stuff, we would do everything that we could to better each other and to pick each other up and support each other. Throughout that season, he was an awfully important cog for me as far as support and experience, so it was great to see how well he did and to be a part of that with him.

Bart Oates: It was a long halftime anyway, so between the drive to end the first half and the drive to start the second half, the Buffalo offense was off the field—for over an hour they didn't get to play.

Marv Levy: The disadvantage to running the no-huddle is that you are exposing your defense to a tremendous amount of time on the field by virtue of your quick-paced offense.

Steve DeOssie: At the end of that drive I looked down at the end zone and saw Bruce Smith with his hands on his knees. He wouldn't get into his stance until the very last second, then you saw the back of his jersey was all grass and field chalk. Jumbo Elliott had been abusing him the entire game—even though he was the one that got in on the safety. That was it. For the rest of the game he was useless. Jumbo pretty much dominated in that scenario.

The Bills' Al Edwards ran the kickoff out to the 40, but penalties on Buffalo and a Leonard Marshall sack meant the Bills had to punt. The Giants looked as if they might score on a third consecutive drive but Buffalo got a huge stop of Anderson on fourth and 2 by an increasingly exhausted-looking Bruce Smith. The Giants braced themselves for another K-Gun assault, but the Bills went back to taking what the Giants were giving them. A couple of short passes and a huge Thurman Thomas 31-yard touchdown run later, and the Bills were in the lead once more.

Marv Levy: Thurman could do so many things. He wasn't a big running back. He was five nine, just under two hundred pounds. He had the best balance that I've ever seen other than Walter Payton. He was a superb receiver out of the backfield. He was the second all-time greatest receiver in Buffalo Bills history behind Andre Reed when he retired. Thurman could do a fantastic job of picking up the blitz. He could have been MVP of that game.

On a big third and 7 early in the next drive, middle linebacker Shane Conlan was lined up one-on-one with Mark Bavaro. Hostetler hit him for the first down. Later Hostetler hit him again, bringing the Giants down to the 27, still trailing by 2 points. Hostetler found Ingram to make it first and 10 at the 14 and Meggett converted another third down on the ground, giving the Giants first and goal.

Bart Oates: On first and goal, we had a sweep to the left. I overstepped it. The defensive tackle stepped inside. William Roberts, the left guard, was pulling and I had to reach and cover his space at defensive tackle. I thought he was slanting outside so I overshot the gap. He slanted inside and wound up adjusting and tackled Ottis for a three-yard loss. You remember the plays you miss. I'll tell you why I remember it—because we had two incompletions and kicked the field goal to go up.

Bahr's 21-yard chip shot gave the Giants the 20–19 lead, but it could have very easily been 24–19. The Bills got the ball back with 7:19 and began another drive that was atypical for them: a slow and methodical advance down the field. The Giants' defense was starting to wear down a bit.

Erik Howard: It was extremely difficult to play a two-man defensive scheme against a no-huddle offense. It was me and Leonard the whole game, two-on-five essentially. And it was ninety-something degrees and one hundred percent humidity. It was brutal.

Parcells would instruct his troops on various methods to slow down the game.

Erik Howard: Bill would do the "kill shot." He would take his finger and his thumb and make a gun and fire the gun. That meant for us to stop the tempo of the game. And the way we did that was before the huddle, a guy would "accidentally" kick the ball and they had to reset the ball. If you go back and watch, I don't know how many times I accidentally tripped over the ball as they came up to the line, but the refs eventually warned me. The other way was that a guy would go down with cramps. I couldn't do that. That was one of my deals. I was never gonna lay on the field. But there were a couple of guys that didn't mind. They'd go down and yell, "Oh, cramps!" And they had to stop the clock and the trainers had to run out and check 'em out.

The Giants got a key stop on a third and 8: Perry Williams laid a huge hit on Al Edwards to force a punt.

Perry Williams: You come across here, you will be hit. That's what our game plan was—we had a seek-and-destroy mentality. If anybody came into your particular area, you struck him and you let him know that we were there. We hit them and hit them all day.

The Giants got the ball back with 5:25 to go. Hostetler tried to drain the play clock as much as possible, and Ottis Anderson pounded the ball up the middle. New York had a chance to seal the game on third and 3 from right about midfield with 2:41 left. Hostetler set up in the shotgun and ran the ball up the middle on a designed play but was stopped short. The Giants—who had held the ball for an incredible 40:23 in the game—would have to punt.

Edwards made a fair catch at the Buffalo 10. For any team down by just one point, 2:22 would be plenty of time to get into field-goal range. For the hurry-up Bills, it was practically an eternity.

Jeff Hostetler: It's a lot easier being out there offensively and having it in your control. Given the effort and preparation that all come into play, there, you just have to sit back and say, "Okay, defense, just hold them one more time."

Once more the Giants' game plan gave them a chance. With all his receivers covered, Kelly scrambled for 9 total yards on the first two downs. Then, on third and 1, Thurman Thomas broke one to the Buffalo 40. It was nearly more.

Ed Croke: Late in the game, Thurman Thomas was wide open around the left side and Walls came out of nowhere to tackle him. He was the last man between him and the goal line. It was the kind of play you don't think about until you watch it on film.

Meanwhile, the Giants' pass rush was nearly nonexistent by this point.

Erik Howard: I suffered from exercise-induced asthma. It was really my biggest opponent my whole career. I don't know if it was the humidity and stuff in the air. It was murder for me. I had to come out of the game there at the end. I thought I was literally gonna die. I was blurry-eyed and seeing spots and I just could not catch my breath near the very end of the game. Bill came up to me and he asked, "Are you ready to go back in?" And I just kind of shook my head. I couldn't go in. I was completely spent. I'd given everything I could give.

Carl Banks: I think both teams played to the point of exhaustion and I give the Buffalo Bills a great deal of credit because they played like champions that day. We were the better team, but they gave it everything they had on that last drive.

Leonard Marshall: We played those guys with two down linemen the whole ball game. I lined up with probably the biggest lineman they had, Howard Ballard. They called him House. This guy was probably six six or six seven, three hundred seventy-five, three hundred eighty pounds—biggest man I ever dealt with my entire life. I was so exhausted from playing against this kid.

Another big Thomas run got the ball down to the Giant 30 with 0:08 showing on the clock. Scott Norwood came on to try the 47-yard field goal. It was a big ask. In his career, Norwood was 0-for-6 from 50-plus yards, and 1-for-5 on grass from 40-plus yards. Still, to many Giants fans it seemed almost like poetic justice that, after breaking the hearts of the 49ers last week, they'd get their hearts ripped out with a last-second field goal this week.

Greg Jackson: It was the same thing as with San Francisco, but now we were on the other side. That's what I was nervous about. "Please, man, don't let this happen to us. We've come too far for this to happen!"

Jeff Hostetler: I can remember kneeling down at the end of our bench. Everybody was down closer to the action. I said to myself, this is one of those games where it's a shame that there's going to be a loser. Everybody's been out here busting their butts. There's going to be a lot of sore guys the next day. We left it all out on the field. That's how we felt. We couldn't have done anything more and we just had to watch to see what happened. I wanted to watch everything, whether he made it or not. I can still hear the thump of the football.

Leonard Marshall: I'll never forget it. I was like, "Damn, we worked our tails off today." I recall looking up at my pops and I said, "Dad, I gave it my best shot, pal, I gave it all I had. If we come up short today, if we lose this one, I know I gave it all I had. And if we win it, we're going to have a great time tonight." That's what I recall about it—my teammates standing there, holding hands. The fact that we were even there at the Super Bowl—we were a team that was totally counted out.

Bart Oates: I was standing there on the sidelines looking at Norwood ready to kick the game-winning field goal, and I was the only one who knew why Ottis got tackled [earlier in the game]. Had he not gotten tackled there, it was wide open. He would have scored. If the defensive tackle doesn't tackle him, he would have scored a touchdown. We'd have gone up by five and they don't even attempt the field goal. So I was sitting there going, "I'm going to lose my job." It won't be tomorrow. It will be Tuesday when they dissect the films and look at the deciding plays and see my missed block. I was thinking, I lost the Super Bowl. What am I going to do? Maybe I'll put my house up for sale. Maybe Wednesday.

Ed Croke: He hit it to the right and it never came back.

Jeff Hostetler: I can still see that referee under that right upright, signaling no good. Me and our guys just exploded all over the field. It was just an awesome feeling.

Bart Oates: Norwood was gracious enough, took a bullet for me. Nobody looked at the play because there was no reason to. We won the game. We don't go back to analyze why we didn't score there. If we'd lost, they would've cared. Instead of putting my house up for sale, I had a parade.

Marv Levy: It was a difficult field goal, which people don't recall nearly so well. During the course of that season Scott made three late field goals to win games for us. The next season he made two late field goals to bring us back into the Super Bowl. Several of his teammates after the game came by and pointed out a play they should have made which wouldn't have brought it down to that point. What was amazing was the people in Buffalo felt no malice toward him. They really encouraged him. A huge crowd was there in Niagara Square to greet the team. They chanted for Scott to come forward and gave him a rousing ovation. He told the crowd he never felt so loved. That provided the impetus for us to go back to the Super Bowl the following year.

Erik Howard: Super Bowl. Right there. Seconds to go. And the guy missed it. You gotta feel for the guy. I still have nights where I roll over in bed . . . you don't remember the good plays, you remember the bad ones. A guy like that [Norwood]—it doesn't matter how successful he was as a field-goal kicker. Every time he wakes up in the middle of the night, that's the one he's thinking about.

Jeff Hostetler: Here I was, six and a half weeks after deciding that I was going to quit football, and I'm standing on a podium with my boys in my arms with my wife there, having just won a Super Bowl. In a matter of six and a half weeks, I went from having decided that my career was over to having won on the biggest stage in football and standing there with my family—it was, without a doubt, one great feeling.

APPENDICES

Questionable Calls in the 1990 NFC Championship Game

Referee Jerry Markbreit told Bill Parcells after the game that it was the best one he'd ever refereed. This was in spite of the work of the officials that afternoon. Here are a few of the contest's questionable calls:

1. The 14-yard pass play to John Taylor on the opening drive was clearly incomplete. It was a huge play because it put the Niners into field-goal range. This was in the early days of booth-instituted instant replays. At first, the officials appear to be reviewing the play, but then referee Markbreit announced that "No replay was allowed on this play because the runner was down by contact." Never mind that he didn't have the ball.

2. On the Giants' first drive, they got a gift pass-interference call on a third and 8 in 49ers territory. Darryl Pollard got called for hitting Mark Ingram early, but the ball was already past Ingram and uncatchable. This was a critical play that led to a Giants field goal.

3. On a 49ers drive in the second quarter, Guy McIntyre was called for a false start when he didn't move a muscle and it looked as if Lawrence Taylor was in the neutral zone. San Francisco punted anyway, so it was of little consequence.

4. An unnecessary-roughness call on Eric Dorsey on the last drive of the first half was a little dodgy: He hit Montana a little late and came in a little low, but he really just fell, or was pushed into him. The 49ers ended up with 3 points—but even without the penalty, they may well have gotten the three. This *was* Joe Montana in a two-minute drill, after all.

5. The holding call on Bart Oates on the Giants' first drive of the second half was ticky-tack at best—you see worse go uncalled on just about every play in the NFL. The Giants got a first down on the next play anyway.

6. The 49ers' Johnnie Jackson could have easily been called for an illegal block in the back on John Taylor's big punt return in the

third quarter. The next play was the Montana-to-Taylor touchdown. Could that have just as likely been an 81-yard pass play as a 61-yard pass play? Probably.

7. In the fourth quarter, a false-start call on 49er Bubba Paris on third and 3 was completely phantom: He didn't even flinch! This turned a very makeable third down into a third and 8. Montana's pass was incomplete and the Giants got the ball back.

8. On Stephen Baker's huge reception on the Giants' final drive, he could have been flagged for offensive pass interference for a push-off. Then again, if the officials had made that call, it might have ended up on this list in the other direction.

The Stingiest Giants

This chart lists the Giants teams that allowed the fewest points in the NFL. For reference, the last column shows the average number of points a team was scoring in each given season. It is far more impressive to lead a league of twenty-eight teams than one of ten. (The 1989 team had the lowest points against in the NFC.) The old adage that defense can win championships is hard to prove by the Giants. While the '27 club predated such games and won the league title outright, and the '93 team was defeated in the divisional playoffs, 44–3, the other nine teams went 2–7 in championship games. In fact, these teams were outscored by a combined total of just under 100 points in the postseason.

Year	NFL Teams	Points Against	Points Per Game	League Average
1927*	12	20	1.5	9.1
1935	9	96	8.0	10.9
1938*	10	79	7.2	13.5
1939	10	85	7.7	15.4
1941	10	114	11.3	16.5
1944	10	75	7.5	18.0

Year	NFL Teams	Points Against	Points Per Game	League Average
1958	12	183	15.2	22.6
1959	12	170	14.2	21.3
1961	14	220	15.7	21.5
1990*	28	211	13.2	20.1
1993	28	205	12.8	18.7

*NFL Champion

Minnesota Vikings vs. New York Giants

NFL CHAMPIONSHIP GAME
January 14, 2001

	1	2	3	4	F
Minnesota Vikings	0	0	0	0	0
New York Giants	14	20	7	0	41

Some wins you grind out with endurance. Other wins are keyed by a big play or a great individual effort. Then there are the rare games where absolutely everything goes as planned. The 2000 NFC championship was such a game for the Giants: a rout of a well-regarded offense. It is the very definition of the term *complete victory*.

THE 2000 GIANTS

Greg Comella: At the end of the previous season, Mr. [Wellington] Mara came to address us. I guess he hadn't addressed the team in twenty-five years. It was the second subpar season on a team of really talented players. I remember he said, "You play this game in one of two ways: You love it and play it with a tremendous amount of enthusiasm and passion, or you hate it and you refuse to let it lick you." That was the story of our 2000 season.

At the start of the 2000 season, the Giants were coming off two disappointing years and there was much speculation among the media and fans about head coach Jim Fassel's job status. But things started off well for them. A big part of their success was Kerry Collins, who joined the team in 1999. Collins's early career was marked by both success and controversy. He guided Carolina to the NFC championship game in his rookie year, but soon after problems with alcohol led to a number of incidents off the field. He was waived by Carolina in the 1998 season and finished up the year with New Orleans. A free agent after the season, Collins did two things that changed his life. He signed with the Giants and got treated for alcoholism.

Kerry Collins: I came into the league in '95 and had some success early. I had a couple trying years there. I was really excited for the opportunity to play again. A lot of credit goes to Ernie Accorsi and Jim Fassel. I was trying to take advantage of a tremendous opportunity that they gave me.

Ernie Accorsi: You have to get the best you can possibly get of the people available. If you don't have a top quarterback in the draft or you're not in the position to draft him, then you have to get what you can get. I inherited [quarterback] Dave Brown. We were not going to win anything with Dave Brown. Now, somebody could say, "That's your opinion." It's not my opinion: It's a matter of fact. Nobody's ever won anything with Dave Brown, starting at Duke. We had to get to the next level somehow. Everybody in our organization liked Kerry as a quarterback. If I'm ever going to get sound information on an athlete, I'm getting it from Penn State. I trust those people. I knew that things didn't go well for Kerry Collins. He played pretty well, but personally he got off the track. But I've always believed two things. Number one, if you have a good kid and he gets off the tracks, you always have a chance to get him back. If he's always in trouble, you're kidding yourself. You're trying to hit it against the wind then. But he was a good kid. The Penn State people vouched for that. And I have to say this: I didn't hire Jim Fassel. We didn't see eye to eye on everything, but he did an extraordinary job with Kerry and straightening him out, smoothing his game out. Kerry was a great pure thrower and Fassel brought out the best in him.

Howard Cross: Kerry was a great quarterback at Penn State, a high draft pick. Had a couple problems, but he dealt with them. In our society today we really focus in on mistakes. We really don't give people enough glory, but we can't wait to kick them when we get a chance to take them down. And Kerry came to the Giants under the scrutiny of the league, people thinking he's a bad guy. But he came in, showed up, fit right in, and he could throw the football from any angle with a big arm. He would step back, he steps up in the pocket, and he puts it on you. He made all the receivers better receivers.

Ike Hilliard: People wrote Kerry off after some of the issues he went through off the field. Kerry's a heck of a guy. He's my favorite quarterback that I played with throughout my career, and I played with a number of good ones.

Jim Fassel: Somebody asked me, "If you're an offensive guru, how come we're changing quarterbacks?" We'd gone through Dave Brown, Danny Kanell, Kent Graham, then Kerry Collins. I got a little frustrated. I said, "We're getting better. I liked all those guys, but each one we lose is getting us better." Kerry came in and handled things well, made all kinds of improvements. I'm as proud of what Kerry Collins did as any player I've ever coached.

Tiki Barber was the featured back and a big part of the 2000 team's offense. He would go on to become the team's all-time leading rusher.

Jim Fassel: When we drafted Tiki, I liked him and I thought he could eventually become an every-down back. But in the meantime, he could be a third-down back and a punt returner until he learned the game and got used to taking the pounding. And that's what he did. He was right on target. In about his third year, I was ready for him to make the transition. I called him up to my office one day and I said, "I'm not happy with what you're doing." In his book he said that he left that meeting and was upset. But he also said that I said the right things to him. And that was most important. He said, "He woke me up." I did what I had to do and he emerged. I always knew Tiki had it in him.

Kerry Collins: Tiki was probably the toughest football player I have ever played with. He's not a big guy. He would run with authority. Smart as well. Good in protection. Very good in third-down situations. I knew that I had a great outlet with him. He's the kind of guy that you can throw a three-yard pass to and he could break one off for a big gain. Just an all-around complete football player.

Lomas Brown: And I think Ron Dayne helped us that year. Even though he didn't have the career that people expected him to have. I know his first year, with his addition of being able to run between the tackles and Tiki being able to go outside of the tackles, we were a dual threat on the ground. We had two running backs that gave us two different looks on the offensive side of the ball. That is really going to help your offense. Tiki had an outstanding couple of years. He really busted onto the national scene.

Like any good quarterback, Collins gives a lot of credit to the offensive line to explain why the 2000 team performed well.

Kerry Collins: Lomas Brown, Glenn Parker, Dusty Zeigler Luke [Petitgout]. They were all guys that had a lot of experience, very professional guys who knew what it took to be a cohesive unit. They were a tight group even though it was our first time playing together. Stoney [Ron Stone] was the guy who was just mauling people. He was our mauler. He was big and strong and when we needed to get yards we were going to Stoney. You look at different guys, all different personalities, but all very good in their own right of what they did and that made them a great unit. They really responded to [Coach] Jim McNally. They were the unsung heroes. Tiki was getting a lot of attention. I was having a good year. Amani Toomer and Ike Hilliard were guys who could make plays who were coming into their own at the time. But the offensive linemen were really the guys that were making it happen.

Lomas Brown: They had tried Luke over at left tackle and it just wasn't working out for him. With me coming out on the market, that gave them a chance to put Luke Petitgout at the right tackle position. That way he wasn't facing the best pass rusher and it would give him more experience. Once I was out of the way, he could move back over to the left tackle. It was just a great year teaming up with Glenn Parker and Dusty Zeigler. I had never played with Parker before. He's such a smart, crafty guy. There was never a problem with communication on the offensive line. As an offensive line, one of the hardest things is communication. Your center is your quarterback up front. Your center has to relay the calls. Or your guard sees a certain look that can change up a call, all that has to be communicated to the offensive line, and I thought that was one of the best things that we did that year. We were great communicators.

After ten weeks (including an open date), the Giants were 7–2 and appeared to be playoff bound. But two tough home losses to offensive powerhouse St. Louis and the last .500 Detroit Lions team made it look like it might be another lost season—and the likely end of Fassel's time in New York. For former Lion Pro Bowler Lomas Brown, the Detroit game was especially bitter.

Lomas Brown: That was one of my most disappointing moments in my career, losing to Detroit. We had been on a roll and then we lost to St. Louis. I took that Detroit game personally. I wanted to beat Detroit so bad! I couldn't believe they beat us. We shouldn't have lost to those guys or to St. Louis. At that point, a lot of people wrote us off.

Fassel had one last move to make.

Jim Fassel: I needed to do something to change the media's attitude about us. And I needed to be the one that stepped up to the plate. Probably before that, I did maybe the most important thing with the team. I pulled all the special-teams guys together because we played awful on special teams and I cut the MVP of a year before and I threatened everybody on the team, special-teams players mainly, that if we don't play better I'm cutting two of you every week. And boy, did they pick it up. I called [vice president of communications] Pat Hanlon and told him what I wanted to say and he said, "Jim, you don't have to do that. That's putting your job on the line." I told Pat, "I didn't call you for your advice—I called you to tell you what I'm doing."

In his weekly press conference, he made an unusual prediction, especially for a team that had just endured two excruciating home losses: "This team is going to the playoffs," a smiling Fassel declared. "I'm raising the expectations. I'm raising the stakes. I love it. Maybe I should put more pressure on myself. The way I feel right now, I really don't care."

Ernie Accorsi: John Mara called me and said, "Did you hear what Jim said?" I said, "No, what?" I thought it was bizarre.

Lomas Brown: After he did that, he called all the captains in. We didn't know what he'd done. He called in me, Strahan, Jessie Armstead, Ron Stone, Kerry, Tiki, maybe one or two other persons. He told us what he told the media. He said, "You guys are the guys I'm counting on to get this done. I'm putting all this on you." Then we had the big team meeting to let everybody know what he said. That was the boldest guarantee that I remember.

Michael Strahan: When he made his infamous "Put my chips on the table" speech we got a giggle at first. We said, "What is he talking about?" Then we looked at it that, hey he's really showing that he's in this with us.

Greg Comella: When you think of coaches over the years, Coach Fassel didn't have that sort of brass persona about him, but when he made that statement, that instilled a ton of confidence in me and a number of my teammates: "Hey, this guy really does believe in us." We knew we had to win to save his job and our jobs as well.

Kerry Collins: It was really a bold move by Jim. And one that was very strategic on his part. Not only was he sending a message to the rest of the world, he was really sending a message to us. That gave us the confidence to know that he believed in us and he knew we were a good football team regardless of the fact that we stumbled there for a couple of weeks. We needed that. Credit to Jim, it did take the heat off of us. He wanted us to go play and play freely and play loose and play the kind of football he knew we were capable of playing and that we knew we were capable of playing. It definitely was the catalyst for us to make the run that we did.

Greg Comella: At seven and four, we absolutely had to make the playoffs to save Coach Fassel's job. I don't think anybody was looking at it that way. But if you're not winning, changes are made. You'd rather win and keep things in place than lose and create a ton of uncertainty.

Luke Petitgout: He took the heat off of the players and put it on his shoulders. It was a do-or-die move. Fortunately, we did it.

Jessie Armstead: He had nothing to lose. And that brought that attitude to the team. We had nothing to lose, so we might as well go out there and throw it all out on the line.

Ike Hilliard: I was shocked, but at the end of the day we knew that to have the season we planned at the beginning of the year, we needed to pull up our sleeves and make it right. We went out there and won five straight and we ended up in the playoffs.

Jim Fassel: Wellington Mara told me, "I like my coach to stand up for his team and take accountability. I thought it was great." John Mara said the same thing, and so did Bob Tisch. That was important to me—those three guys backed me completely.

Not only did the Giants manage to make the playoffs, they ended up with home-field advantage throughout. There was no dominant team in the NFC in 2000. The team with the best point differential and probably the hardest schedule was the Tampa Bay Buccaneers, and they were wiped out in the wild-card game by the Eagles, 21–3, while the Giants enjoyed a week off.

Ike Hilliard: I think the bye really helped us. Everyone needs rest at some point after the grind of the year. We were fortunate enough to run off a few games at the end of the year, and the opportunity to get some rest really helped.

The first game was in the divisional round against the hated Eagles, a team New York had already beaten twice.

Kerry Collins: I'm a Pennsylvania guy and I grew up an Eagles fan, so I was well aware of the rivalry between the Giants and the Eagles. There are certain periods where teams just have another team's number, and it just so happened that at that time we had the Eagles' number. So for them to come to Giants Stadium in a divisional game, I think we all felt confident that we were going to have a good game plan. We knew how to beat them. I think a lot of that credit has to go to [offensive coordinator] Sean Payton and the offensive coaches. The Eagles' defense at the time was a great defense. We just knew what it took to be successful against them.

Lomas Brown: Philly had a good team. I remember that week of preparation, getting ready for [All-Pro defensive end] Hugh Douglas. I remember the coaches asking me, Can you handle Hugh Douglas? If not, we can do different things to chip in and help you out. I said, "I got it."

Bob Papa: I'll never forget the energy in the building. First of all, it was the Giants and Eagles' first playoff game since they had played in Philly in '81, so, despite the fact these teams were bitter rivals, they didn't have much of a playoff history. At that point the Giants had kind of dominated them in the head-to-head matchups, but you always had the fear factor against them because McNabb at the time was much more of a running quarterback. There was an electric feel in the stadium. Obviously, right before the kickoff everyone was charged up. Then for Ron Dixon to take the opening kickoff from coast to coast, the stadium was rocking like 1986. You got a sense the Giants were off and running.

Luke Petitgout: Everybody had the white towels going. It was an unbelievable start to a good day for us.

Lomas Brown: That was a great way to start that game. I still get goose pimples when I think of that game. It was an emotional win to beat those guys.

Keith Hamilton: Our corners were pretty good, so going into the game we really didn't think Donovan McNabb could beat us. We knew we had to stop the run, and the only way he could beat us was with his legs. The game plan was to stop the run and stop him from running. I remember coming in Wednesday before that game for the first team meeting. Coach said, "The only thing we gotta do is stop him from running—we got to stop McNabb from running." That was the game plan. We had Jessie Armstead spying on him the whole time, so when he tried to run Jessie was right there. I'll never forget that. Man, we put a hurtin' on them that day.

The final score was 20–10 but it wasn't that close. Other than Dixon's kickoff return, the game's signature play was a circus-catch pick-six by Jason Sehorn in the second quarter that made the score 17–0. Sehorn dove for the ball fully extended, popping it into the air as he hit the ground. As he lay on his back, he reached up and knocked it further into the air, buying himself time to leap to his feet and gather it in. From the Eagles' 32, he bowled over teammate Ramos McDonald and wended his way into the end zone. In 2009, it was voted the most memorable play in Giants Stadium history.

Kerry Collins: It was freakishly athletic. Those were the kind of things Jason could do.

Bob Papa: It was one of the most acrobatic, athletic interception returns for a touchdown you're ever going to see. The guy is on his back, tips the ball to himself, got up, and then had the ability to return it for a touchdown. It was a special-teams play and a defensive play that will always burn in your memory from that game—and you know Giants fans love their defense. That was just an incredible start to the playoffs.

Michael Strahan: We called him Sea Breeze. He made everything smooth and easy like the summer breeze.

Luke Petitgout: Jason Sehorn is obviously a great athlete. And it was just unheard of what he did. It just gave us more momentum to advance.

THE OPPONENT

The 1998 Vikings had been a devastating offensive team. Had they been able to go all the way rather than getting derailed by the Falcons in the NFC championship, they would be mentioned in the same breath as the all-time great clubs. Two years later, vestiges of their offensive greatness lingered. Dennis Green's charges had fallen off from 556 points to just under 400 in the next two seasons, but that was still good for fifth most in the league in 2000. The Minnesota offense was led by the hulking quarterback Daunte Culpepper, a rookie for all intents and purposes, having barely appeared in 1999. He had an outstanding passer rating and was named to the Pro Bowl, as were his favorite targets, wide receivers Cris Carter and Randy Moss, who caught 96 and 77 passes respectively. With 1,521 rushing yards, Robert Smith averaged over 5 yards per carry—as did Culpepper when he ventured past the line of scrimmage. Key blockers up front were Matt Birk at center and Korey Stringer at right tackle.

Minnesota's big issue was on defense. Only three teams allowed more total yards, and, while they were equally permissive against the run and the pass, they intercepted only 8 passes all year, worst in the league. In spite of these travails, the Vikings had run out to an 11–2 record before losing their final three regular season games, giving up 104 points in the process. It didn't cost them their first-round bye, however, and they turned it around in the divisional playoffs, racing out to a 24–3 lead over New Orleans before eventually besting them 34–16. This landed them in the Meadowlands for the NFC championship.

Kerry Collins: Coming into the game, you looked at the Vikings and they had Daunte Culpepper, Randy Moss, and were certainly a very prolific offense. No one really gave us a chance in that game, and we liked that. That's kind of the way we were. We didn't talk a whole lot. We weren't flashy and we kind of snuck up on people and earned their respect on the field. It was one of those things. We enjoyed that role. We relished it. While nobody thought we were going to win that game, everyone in that locker room was convinced that we were going to win. And their defense wasn't the best defense in the NFL, either.

Jessie Armstead: We wanted them. We wanted a piece of them. We felt we were the number-two defense in the National Football League behind Baltimore and we knew we could play with their offense. The Minnesota Vikings' power was their offense, not their defense. We knew if we could just contain their offense, our offense could overwhelm their defense.

THE GAME

Jim Fassel: I wanted to get as many of the old Giants players to come back for the game that wanted to come back. Phil Simms and Harry Carson and a lot of guys came back. And I asked Lawrence Taylor personally to come back to say a couple things to the team on Saturday. And you always worry about a past player that gets up and starts talking about what his team did and how good they were. Lawrence got up, and I thought he put things in incredible perspective. He said to the team, "You know, guys, remember one thing: We're here to honor you. We're not here to talk about what we did." And I went, "Oh, my God, thank you very much, Lawrence." I couldn't write a script better than that. And he got our players fired up.

Keith Hamilton: It was cold and a lot of their guys came out with long shirts on, and we went out there with no shirts. They were wearing long sleeves, and in my mind, right then I knew we were going to win that game that day. They were dressed for the cold, but we were ready to go.

Ike Hilliard: I think we felt like we had a slight advantage being an outdoor team—no discredit to Minnesota with what they accomplished that year or what they've accomplished as a franchise. It's a little bit tougher playing football outdoors in that kind of weather.

Michael Strahan: Before the game, we were in the tunnel and we couldn't see the crowd. They were introducing the Vikings and it was loud. Then when we [came out and] saw the towels waving. It sent chills up and down my spine. I realized before the game started that we were going to win. The twelfth man had shown up. It was intimidating to us—and they were *our* fans. So I knew that there's no way those guys weren't intimidated as well.

For those who remember the Viking teams that had a great home-field advantage playing their home games outdoors at Metropolitan Stadium (they won 80 percent of their home games in November, December, and the playoffs from 1969 to 1981), it is ironic to hear the latter-day team spoken of this way. And it wasn't even *that* cold: 37 degrees at kickoff, and Pat Summerall noted in the booth, "It feels warmer than that." But it was certainly a lot colder than Minnesota's dome. Other Giants remember other places where they found their motivation.

Lomas Brown: Minnesota hurt themselves. What happened was, we got wind that Minnesota had already made their travel plans to Tampa. Matter of fact, they had the T-shirt already printed out: NFC CHAMPIONS. We had that T-shirt hung up in the locker room that week of practice. They figured they were going to walk all over us. That was our motivation. They just disregarded that they had a game against us. We were motivated.

Tiki Barber would engage in some psychological warfare of his own. He would write later, "I got a Randy Moss replica jersey and had the logo of Super Bowl XXXV printed onto it. On top of that, I pinned a quote I cribbed from General Ulysses S. Grant: 'The art of war is simple enough. Find out where your enemy is. Get to him as soon as you can. Strike at him as hard as you can and keep moving on.' I left the whole tableau in the middle of the locker room where everyone could see it."

Bob Papa: I remember the week leading up to the NFC championship game, Giants fans and Giants media and everybody following the team were following the weather. There was a chance there was going to be bad weather. Everyone said that if the grass field got sloppy and there was wind and bad conditions and maybe some snow, it would give the Giants a chance. If the game was played straight up, people figured the Giants had no shot to beat the Vikings. Well, unbeknownst to everybody else, Sean Payton, who was the offensive coordinator for the Giants at the time, was actually rooting for good weather. When they went into the first player meeting, Payton said, "We're putting up fifty on these guys and we are going to steamroll them."

Howard Cross: Let me give you a little insight into that one. We sat down and watched tape as an offensive team. And the defense was watching Randy Moss, Cris Carter, Daunte Culpepper, and they were impressed. But the thing was, the Vikings would score a couple touchdowns and the other team would be playing catch-up. And when the other teams were playing catch-up, all the Vikings did was rush the passer. They sent everybody in. That's all it was: a big mosh of people on every play. So Coach Payton had us watch the games they played that were close games, the games where they had trouble. He looked at that, pointed out all the wide-open spaces and said, "We can score a hundred points on these guys." And I'm like, "What?"

Ike Hilliard: Coach Payton came into the meeting room on Wednesday and said, "If we don't score forty or fifty, I'll be pretty disappointed." Sure enough, we prepared all week and had an awesome game plan.

Bob Papa: I was in a great Italian restaurant the night before the game in New Jersey, and the Vikings owner was in there with a group. The weather forecast looked like it was going to be good for the next day and they were confident about their team. Even the waiters in the restaurant were saying, "The weather isn't going to be good for the Giants." All I could think of in the back of my head was, Just watch: They don't know what they've got coming. Hours before kick-off, I saw Sean Payton come out to look at the field and I said to him, "Pretty mild conditions." He just smiled and said, "Exactly what we were hoping for—we've got some things planned for today."

Jim Fassel: We had fun with the game plan all week. We knew we were going to throw the football. The weakness of the Vikings was their secondary, and that's what we wanted to attack. And the media kept asking me about all their offensive weapons, with Randy Moss and Daunte Culpepper and Cris Carter and Robert Smith. They said, "You probably want to slow the game down, you don't want to get into a shoot-out with them." Well, the whole time I'm thinking No, we *are* gonna get in a shoot-out with them. We *want* to throw the ball. But I didn't say that, and every press conference was laced with, "No, we're gonna slow the game down, we're gonna run the ball." And they kept writing it, and I'm laughing every day reading the articles. And I never like to mislead the media, but I misled them all week long.

Kerry Collins: The confidence was there that week. We had a great week of practice. All week we were talking about what we could do. Obviously, the premium is scoring points against an offense like that. Going through the week, we had that feeling that we could be the offense that wins this game. There was no secret we were going to throw the ball. We were going to throw it early and often and be aggressive. That tone resonated throughout the week. That was a big factor in getting us prepared. When Sunday came, that was the most electric atmosphere I've ever played in front of, without question. Giants Stadium was just on fire that day, and the fans were great and had the towels. They were all over. I remember standing in the tunnel and seeing all those towels right before we were about to run out. We were going to be hitting on all cylinders.

And hit on all cylinders they did, right from the start. The Giants' first drive took only four plays and covered 74 yards, culminating in a 46-yard strike from Kerry Collins to Ike Hilliard.

Kerry Collins: Ike Hilliard is probably the smartest football player I have ever played with. He had a tremendous feel for the game. He was not the fastest guy in the world, but he had tremendous change of direction. He worked the middle of field. He was really a matchup problem when we'd bring him in slot. He was matched up on nickel guys and they just couldn't cover him.

Ike Hilliard: I think we tried to catch them in a single high coverage. Coach Payton called an unbelievable game. Kerry dropped back. He looked off the free safety well. I beat the nickel corner and crossed the line of scrimmage clean. Kerry threw an unbelievably perfect football and hit me in stride. It was practically a walk-in.

Kerry Collins: It was a great start. The crowd was going crazy. Then they fumbled the kickoff and we got it right back.

Lyle West picked up the Moe Williams fumble at the Vikings' 19 and the Giants went to work.

Greg Comella: We broke the huddle. Everything was super-quiet. And as I went into the flat, I saw that the linebacker, Dwayne Rudd, had taken a bad angle. I turned upfield and looked behind me. Kerry literally stuck it right in my chest. Some people later remarked they never actually saw a ball knock a player down before. The following week I ended up with a nasty bruise on my backside as a result of how I landed. We run a play a zillion times in practice but only once or twice in games. You spend ninety-five percent of your time preparing for that sort of mountaintop experience.

Kerry Collins: I hit Greg Comella on the sideline on a little wheel route. That's as close to being in the zone as I think I've been.

Jim Fassel: Kerry was lights out. You dream about that type of game as a coach. Rarely do you get to experience one.

The score was 14–0 before the vaunted Minnesota offense even got on the field.

Jim Fassel: I looked at my son and I said, with the crowd in a tizzy, "They got no chance today. No chance. They have a lot of talent on that sideline. But they have no chance."

Bob Papa: They unleashed holy hell on Minnesota that day.

And the Giants never looked back. Minnesota did threaten to score on their second possession, getting as close as the New York 22, but Emmanuel McDaniel intercepted Culpepper in the end zone for a touchback. Kicker Brad Daluiso added a field goal on the first play of the second quarter, and New York's third touchdown came on a pass to Collins's old Penn State teammate, Joe Jurevicius. Hilliard got his second touchdown on the last drive of the half, a 7-yarder from Collins, and by halftime they were up 34–0. That was more points than they had scored in the entirety of any of their regular-season games.

Jim Fassel: I asked John Fox during the week, "How many points do you think we need to score to beat these guys?" And he gave me the number thirty. I said, "Thirty? I know their offense is good, but we've got a good defense, too. You gotta be kidding me. Are we gonna give up twenty-nine points?" He said, "Jim, they're really good. They've got a lot of weapons." I said, "I agree with you, I really agree with you." But now it's halftime, and it's thirty-four to nothing. And we're walking side by side into the locker room. I said, "John, it's thirty-four to nothing. We're okay, right?" He said, "Jim, I don't know. Man, they're good. They really got a lot of weapons." I said, "If they score thirty-five points, your ass is out of here! We better be okay. Don't tell me that crap!"

The only scoring in the second half was another 7-yard touchdown pass, this time to Amani Toomer. This was only appropriate, as in many ways Toomer was the linchpin of the Giants' offense.

Ike Hilliard: We leaned on Amani a lot. He was the guy that really made it for us on the passing game. Without his ability to get vertical downfield with his big frame and making some of those big plays, we wouldn't have been half the team that we were.

Kerry Collins: You go through each one of those receivers, they were all very different guys. Amani's a taller guy. Kind of a straight-line speed guy, down the field. He was really adept at making tough catches in traffic and had really strong hands. I knew with Amani I could fit the ball in there and he was gonna use his body—his size and speed—and go up and get it to make big plays.

Jim Fassel: I was proud because Amani was drafted number one the year before I got there and it wasn't working out. He had a terrible rookie year. My first year, he didn't do well. Coaching plays a part, but at the end of the day, being honest, he probably didn't like me very well because I pushed him hard—*really* pushed him. But at the end of the day he made some changes that allowed him to be a better player. And that year he really stepped out and got better.

Luke Petitgout: The game was decided by halftime. We had a whole half to celebrate that we were going to the Super Bowl. Lomas, I think, was in his fifteenth or sixteenth year in 2000—playing that long and never had a chance to go. As a second-year player, I was very fortunate.

In the end, Collins threw for 381 yards and five touchdowns. He did throw two picks, but neither led to anything.

Kerry Collins: I threw a couple interceptions in that game and it didn't faze me. I like to think it never fazed me, but in that game in particular I was like, "That's okay. We're gonna get it back again and we're gonna score." It's hard to get there, and then it just kind of happens. It was one of those days when everything was going right and guys were playing great. Everything was just kind of falling our way.

The Giants outgained the Vikings 518 to 114. Minnesota never got a chance to run the ball, rushing only seven times in the first half and then, in full catch-up mode, just twice more in the second half. Culpepper was picked off three times and the Vikings lost two fumbles.

Howard Cross: We called off the dogs: We could've scored seventy points on them. They were that poor on defense. The secondary was out of position. They were so used to being with such a big lead that teams would make mistakes pressing, trying to catch them. They had never been in a situation where they had to fight and make plays the whole game. And that's what happened.

The score prompted Randy Moss to say in his postgame press conference, "Man, forty-one to doughnut. I don't know if I've ever been a part of something like forty-one to doughnut."

Forty-one to doughnut indeed. Even though the Giants' offense grabbed the headlines, obviously, the Giants' defense came up huge all day.

Ernie Accorsi: Defensive coordinator John Fox's office was right next to mine, and every time I saw him that week I went in the opposite direction. Finally, on Friday, Fox said to me, "You've been ducking me all week." I said, "Yeah, I don't even want to look at you because in my apartment every night between midnight and eight o'clock, the Vikings have scored twenty-five touchdowns a night in my mind." He said, "Let me tell you something, Ernie. We might shut them out." And I said, "You're nuts!" and walked away. I knew their defense wasn't very good. I thought we were gonna have to beat them forty-one to forty. Not that our defense was that bad, but because of that offense they had. Of course, we shut them out. It was the perfect game. It was probably the best-played game by the Giants in that stadium.

Jessie Armstead: I was the captain, but when it came down to it, Keith Hamilton anchored that defense. Him and Strahan controlled things up front, Sam Garnes controlled the back, and I was the guy in the middle who made sure that everybody did everything. I checked on them, that's all.

Keith Hamilton: One thing about Jessie and Michael—they were never out of place. Jessie was like a coach out there on the field. He knew that defense inside and out. Sometimes when you play with guys, they talk about plays they missed or say, "My bad." I never heard that from the linebacking crew.

Jim Fassel: Jessie was a true warrior. He brought an attitude and exuberance to the defense. Jessie and Michael were vocal leaders, and it wasn't phony—they backed it up. Some guys don't get the respect of their teammates because they talk a good game but they don't back it up with a work ethic and the way they play. But those two guys, they did it. They practiced all the time, they concentrated, and they didn't make mistakes. They earned the respect of the team.

Jessie Armstead: Strahan always wanted to get better and would do whatever it took to get better. He never took a day off; he looked forward to being on the field. He had all the things you can't coach. Even at the end of his career, he was still dominant.

Jim Fassel: Michael Strahan is one of the greatest players I've ever been around. Denny Marcin, our defensive-line coach, did a tremendous job with him. Michael just got better and better and better. He's a rarity in the NFL. He's a defensive lineman but never once came out of the game, no matter what the score was. Never missed a day of practice, never wanted to take a play off even if he was hurt and we're rolling out to play again next Sunday on a Wednesday. He didn't want to miss practice. He wanted to practice every day. A lot of times those big guys inside need a little downtime, they get worn out a bit. Michael Strahan was not that type of guy.

Keith Hamilton: There is no question that John Fox is one of the greatest defensive minds in the game. He had the brains and we had the manpower to go with it. It was just a great combination—he knew how to get us fired up for the games, and we were always ready. When we went on that run, he was a key part to that.

Michael Strahan: John Fox was definitely a master planner. He understood offenses. He taught you the game. He didn't just say go out and run this defense. There was a reason behind it. There was a rhyme to it. You understood what formations were. You understood certain teams' nuances that would give away their plan for a play. That's what allowed us to play fast. You recognized those things because of the coaching you received, so there was no hesitation in the way you could attack. He was very good at that. It was one of his strong suits.

Ike Hilliard: I can't say enough about Jason Sehorn and the way he took Randy Moss out of the game.

Jim Fassel: John Fox did a great job that game, and the offense did a great job. When I came to the Giants, John Fox didn't have a job and neither did Sean Payton. Sean Payton had only been in the league one year when I hired him. They were both on the street, they weren't sexy hires. They were good football coaches. And that's the problem today: Everyone wants sexy hires. They want to hire somebody that's been somewhere. Like George Young said, "Sometimes it's the coach, sometimes it's the players. You have to determine the difference." I got questioned heavily on both of them, but those were my guys.

Ernie Accorsi: I remember Jason Sehorn breaking the huddle on defense and walking out there, one-on-one on Moss, and shutting him down. He demoralized Moss, and when Moss got demoralized, the whole team got demoralized.

Keith Hamilton: We had big, physical corners, which was good against Moss. He used to dominate little guys just by jumping over top, but the corners we had were six four and maybe two hundred and fifteen pounds, and that's very rare to see.

Collins, especially, was savoring the moment, having overcome his demons to enjoy a spectacular game on a big stage.

Kerry Collins: I was humbled by the opportunity, humbled by the success. I remember we played the Packers in Lambeau when I was with the Panthers and they won the trophy, and I saw Reggie White run around the field and I thought that was the neatest thing. I thought if I ever got the opportunity I was going to do the same thing. It's hard to believe that two years later it happened. It was a special time for me, but it had everything to do with the guys around me. What a great bunch of guys. It was a really emotional day. And for everything to go the way it went made it the most special day I've had as an athlete ever. Just a tremendous day.

Soft-spoken team owner Wellington Mara said after the game, "We were the worst team ever to get home-field advantage in the playoffs, the worst team ever to reach the championship game, now we'll be the worst team to win the Super Bowl."

THE AFTERMATH

It didn't quite work out that way. The 2000 Giants had to take their glory where they found it, and that was in the NFC championship game. For one of the many times in their history, the Giants came up against a historically ranked defensive juggernaut. In the past it had been the '62 Packers and the '63 and '85 Bears. This time it was the '00 Baltimore Ravens. After a defensive touchdown was taken off the board by a holding penalty that would have knotted the game at seven, Super Bowl XXXV was all Ravens. The Giants eventually lost 34–7.

Michael Strahan: It felt like they had twenty players on the field against us out there.

Greg Comella: I think they were the sixth seed in the playoffs that year. I think they finished the year at twelve and four. They had the same record as we had. We were a one seed and they were a six seed.

They were sporting one of the best defenses in NFL history. Our team that year had always done better against great offenses. The strength of our team was our defense that year—it just was. In some ways we were mirror images of each other. Baltimore had an okay offense that didn't make many mistakes and a great defense that gave them great field position and played great special teams. That's what we were. Everybody wants to play the game over again.

Ike Hilliard: It was a tough day. The Ravens had an unbelievable defense. They had the numbers for all the right reasons. Statistically, they were the best defense in football. They physically beat us up that day. We had a tough job running the football. If you cannot establish the line of scrimmage, you're going to have a tough time winning. They had Big Goose [Tony Siragusa] in the middle and Ray-Ray [Ray Lewis] and [Jamie] Sharper roaming around and [Rod]Woodson on the back end getting those guys organized. We were beaten by a team that played a lot better than we did.

But in order to get there, they very nearly threw a perfect game against the Vikings—and there was no denying that Coach Fassel's guarantee had paid off.

Jim Fassel: I talked to Joe Namath the next year. They had a big article in the *Times* and it was about players making guarantees. They had like seven of them in there. Joe Namath told me that mine was the best guarantee ever in New York. I told him I thought mine paled in comparison to his. He said, "You know what? Mine was fine, but here's the deal: Players make guarantees, coaches don't. And you made a guarantee as a coach. That's why I think it was the best one."

APPENDICES

The Giants' Largest Margins of Victory

56: Giants 56, Philadelphia Eagles 0 (October 15, 1933). New York crushed Philadelphia in the first game in Eagles franchise history. They recovered and actually beat the Giants later in the year, 20–14.

53: Giants 53, Washington Redskins 0 (November 15, 1961). The low ebb of the Redskins franchise in their long drought between championships.

53: Giants 53, Frankford Yellow Jackets 0 (October 19, 1930). The recently proud Yellow Jackets franchise got tanned in its penultimate season.

52: Giants 62, Philadelphia Eagles 10 (November 26, 1972). The most points ever scored by the Giants, albeit against the worst Eagles team since World War II.

46: Giants 49, San Francisco 49ers 3 (divisional playoff, January 4, 1987). An impressive takedown of a well-coached team and one of the biggest margins of victory in playoff history.

46: Giants 49, Green Bay Packers 3 (November 21, 1948). One of the many trouncings received by the Pack that year, the first in its long string of losing seasons—a string that would be broken only by the arrival of Vince Lombardi eleven years later.

44: Giants 51, New York Yanks 7 (December 3, 1950). The third time in four weeks the Giants broke the 50-point barrier. The other game in that quartet? A 7–3 win over Philadelphia.

43: Giants 49, St. Louis Cardinals 6 (December 7, 1969). One from the Department of Reversed Polarity: The Cards had won their earlier matchup 42–17.

41: Giants 41, Minnesota Vikings 0 (NFC championship, January 14, 2001). The 41 part was not as impressive as the 0 part, in that the Vikings were fifth in the league in scoring, but twenty-fourth in points allowed.

41: Giants 48, Cleveland Browns 7 (December 6, 1959). The Giants' most impressive win ever against the Browns.

40: Giants 47, Chicago Bears 7 (NFL championship, December 30, 1956). How much of a rout was this? Consider that the Giants put in Bob Clatterbuck at quarterback late in the game.

The Most Resounding Playoff Victories of All Time

Not counting the American Football League, the Giants own the fourth-, tenth- and twelfth-largest margins of victory in playoff history. These are the most one-sided playoff contests ever, going back to 1933.

The Shutouts

73–0: Chicago Bears over Washington Redskins, December 8, 1940; NFL championship

41–0: **New York Giants** over Minnesota Vikings, January 14, 2001; NFC championship

41–0: New York Jets over Indianapolis Colts, January 4, 2002; wild-card game

38–0: Dallas Cowboys over Tampa Bay Buccaneers, January 2, 1981; divisional playoff

37–0: Green Bay Packers over **New York Giants**, December 31, 1961; NFL championship

34–0: Baltimore Colts over Cleveland Browns, December 29, 1968; NFL championship

31–0: Miami Dolphins over San Diego Chargers, January 10, 1992; divisional playoff

The Non-Shutouts

62–7: Jacksonville Jaguars over Miami Dolphins, January 15, 2000; divisional game

51–3: Buffalo Bills over Los Angeles Raiders, January 20, 1990; AFC championship

49–3: **New York Giants** over San Francisco 49ers, January 4, 1986; divisional game

56–10: Cleveland Browns over Detroit Lions, December 26, 1954; NFL championship

55–10: San Francisco 49ers over Denver Broncos, January 28, 1989; Super Bowl XXIV

59–14: Detroit Lions over Cleveland Browns, December 29, 1957; NFL championship

51–7: Washington Redskins over Los Angeles Rams, January 1, 1983; divisional game

44–3: San Francisco 49ers over **New York Giants**, January 15, 1993; divisional game

47–7: **New York Giants** over Chicago Bears, December 30, 1956; NFL championship

52–14: Dallas Cowboys over Cleveland Browns, December 24, 1967; conference championship

New York Giants vs. New England Patriots

SUPER BOWL XLII
February 3, 2008

	1	2	3	4	F
New York Giants	3	0	0	14	17
New England Patriots	0	7	0	7	14

By the time Super Bowl XLII was played, the New York Giants and their fans had grown weary of hearing what a bloodbath the game was going to be. New England was installed as a 12-point favorite. It wasn't just popular opinion that had come to this conclusion: It was also backed up by modern analytics. Writing in the *Pro Football Prospectus 2008*, Vince Verhei crunched the numbers based on the two teams' regular-season performances and ran a thousand simulations of Super Bowl XLII. In only *seven* of those thousand did the Giants win.

Trotting out the handiest cliché for the circumstance, it's why they play the games. It is also why, in spite of their lack of statistical gravitas compared to some other great teams of all time, we must continue to genuflect in the direction of the 1972 Dolphins. If getting through an entire season without losing or tying a game were that easy, some other team would have done it before or since they did. (See "The Season Spoilers," 348.)

THE OPPONENTS
Had the 2007 New England Patriots been perfect, or even if they had lost the final game of the regular season to the Giants 38–35 and won

Super Bowl XLII 17–14, they would be considered the best team of all time. Instead, they reversed those two outcomes and will always be known as a great team that did not close the deal. Still, believe the hype: The 2007 Patriots were as good as all that. A team with more backstories than a telenovela, they didn't just beat their opponents as many previous great teams had done; they destroyed them. They played as though they came down from a higher league, for which the NFL was some kind of feeder. At least that was the case in the first half of the season, when they won by an average of 26 points with the lowest margin of victory being 17.

In the second half of the season and the playoffs, they were more human, having to sweat out a few games and generally not seeing their enemies run before them as they had in the first half of the campaign. In week nine, they had their first close game in a much-anticipated showdown with the Colts, who were also undefeated. Indianapolis went up 20–10 with just under ten minutes to play, but Tom Brady drove New England to two touchdowns for the win. It would be the first and only time the Patriots were outgained in the regular season. Their next game resulted in their biggest win of the year, a 56–10 thrashing of the Bills in which Brady hit Randy Moss for four touchdowns. There then followed two close calls. In week twelve, the Eagles were 20-point underdogs in part because they were reduced to using their backup quarterback, A. J. Feeley. With nothing to lose, they took a lot of chances and led 28–24 after three quarters before New England finally prevailed in the fourth. The 4–7 Baltimore Ravens gave the Patriots a time the next week with Don "Perfect Season" Shula sitting in the stands. Baltimore led 24–17 in the fourth quarter but gave the Pats life with mistakes on two fourth-down plays. New England won it 27–24 with forty-four seconds to go on a Brady-to–Jabar Gaffney pass that had to be reviewed. Things eased up again for the next three weeks as they dispatched the Steelers 34–13, the Jets 20–10 (their lowest point total of the regular season), and the lowly Dolphins 28–7. All that stood in the way of a perfect season was a visit to the 10–5 Giants.

In his eighth season as head coach of the Patriots was Bill Belichick, the architect of the Giants' defenses in the Parcells years. After cutting his head-coaching teeth with five years in Cleveland, he had come to the Patriots in 2000 and amassed a staggering 91–37 regular-season record through the end of the '07 season. His Patriots teams were also 12–2 in the postseason through 2006, a record that included Super Bowl wins after the 2001, 2003, and 2004 seasons. In 2007, Belichick had seemingly done the impossible: He had assembled a better team than the clubs that went 17–2 in consecutive years in 2003 and 2004. His was not a season free of controversy, however. Few stories in recent NFL history attracted more attention than the Patriots getting caught videotaping the Jets' signals prior to their season opener.

"Spygate," as it was called, personally cost Belichick a half million dollars in the form of a fine from Commissioner Roger Goodell. Like the Watergate scandal that inspired its name, it was an unnecessary breaking of the rules. Richard Nixon had the 1972 election sewn up without whatever intelligence was gained by breaking into the national headquarters of the Democratic Party. Likewise, the 2007 New England Patriots were good enough that they didn't need to resort to chicanery to succeed on a grand scale.

New England scored the most points ever in a season with 589 (although they did not break the record for most points on a per-game basis, held by the 1950 Los Angeles Rams). Tom Brady–to–Randy Moss became the most prolific touchdown-passing combo in history. Brady's 50 touchdown passes and Moss's 23 touchdown catches both set league records. Wes Welker led the NFL in yards after completion and caught 112 passes. Combined with Moss's 98, they were one of the most productive receiving tandems ever. Kevin Faulk caught 47 passes out of the backfield and Laurence Maroney averaged 4.5 yards per carry. The Patriots landed three offensive linemen in the Pro Bowl: left tackle Matt Light, left guard Logan Mankins, and center Dan Koppen. Moss and Brady were also so honored.

The defense was led by nose tackle Vince Wilfork and a group of veteran linebackers, including future Hall of Famer Junior Seau. They allowed the fourth-fewest points in the NFL and were sixth in passing yards allowed. (Considering the leads they had in many games, it's surprising they didn't allow more junk passing yards.) Left cornerback Asante Samuel and left outside linebacker Mike Vrabel joined Wilfork as Pro Bowl selections.

THE GIANTS

The 2007 Giants proved that there are many ways to the mountaintop. Coached by Tom Coughlin, who was in his fourth season with the team after building the expansion Jacksonville Jaguars from scratch, New York had made the playoffs the previous two seasons but bowed out in the first round both times. Coughlin was a notorious rules-and-regulations guy who had decided to soften his approach in 2007. He created an executive players council with whom he conferred regarding decisions that affected the rank and file.

Rich Seubert: Everyone made a big deal about how Coach changed. I think he made changes that were better for the players. He didn't become any lighter—he always expected the most out of all of us. He worked us hard. Training camps were always tough. He got us ready as a team. He was more open to us. He looked to his players for suggestions on how to improve the team morale. He opened up more to the players and he took the suggestions into consideration, but he always made the final decision on what was best for us.

Sam Madison: Coming from Miami playing with Jimmy Johnson my first three years, Coach Coughlin was like a cotton ball rather than steel.

David Tyree: It was a testament to the character of the man. There are always things we can do to improve our character. For a man of his age and level of accomplishment, it speaks to the measure of humility to be willing to learn and adapt to figure out what's best for the group of guys that he's leading. I was one that was firmly in agreement. He understood what was at stake: Obviously, it was his job. He wanted to have fun with it. He wanted to enjoy the preciousness of the moment. He wanted to coach hard but be able to relate to the guys much more. From a leadership standpoint, I appreciated it.

Michael Strahan: All players want to be coached and given direction. I think what he didn't understand at first was that players [also] want someone to care about them. He figured that out. He formed a player's council. More importantly, he allowed his leaders to lead. He allowed the veterans to lead. If there was an issue, he let us handle it. I think that was a smart way to do it. He became more human to us. And with that, the players felt like this is a great place to be; a fun team to play for. The guy definitely wants to win. It was always his number-one focus. There was no doubt about that. In the [new] way he went about it he allowed men to be men; the leaders to lead. He challenged us but gave us direction.

The Giants attack was led by Eli Manning, playing in his fourth year since being the first player named in the 2004 draft. Installed as the team's starter midway through his rookie year, Manning demonstrated many of the typical symptoms of a young quarterback who is required to come of age on the job. Consequently, he became a lightning rod for the frustrations of the fans and media who grew tired of watching him make ill-advised throws (he led the league in interceptions thrown in 2007 with 20) and occasionally lose his composure.

Manning's main target was Plaxico Burress, a veteran receiver who was so banged up that he did not practice for the entire season. His only time working with Manning came during pregame warm-ups. With that, they were still able to connect 70 times for 12 touchdowns. It wasn't Brady to Moss, but it was fairly remarkable given the circumstances. Manning's other go-to wide receiver was Amani Toomer, the Giants' all-time leader in reception yards. Tight end Jeremy Shockey caught 57 passes before being felled by injury. Way down on the depth chart was a special-teams player and occasional wide receiver named David Tyree, a player who was fated to burst from obscurity on the grand stage of the Super Bowl.

David Tyree: I think they understood that I was more than capable of making plays. For whatever reason, year to year, it was a role that I fit. I think they had the confidence in me from the top down, from the guys upstairs to the coaches on the field.

The Giants' main running back was Brandon Jacobs, a man who would have been the biggest player in the NFL throughout most of its early history. At six foot four, 255 pounds, he proved an effective force moving through the line, averaging 5.0 yards per carry. Derrick Ward was nearly as prolific in his 125 carries, posting a 4.8 average while also catching 26 passes. When Ward was lost to injury, Ahmad Bradshaw emerged as the number-two back and saw ample field time in the playoffs. As a team, the Giants were an impressive fourth in the league in yards per carry.

New York was ranked seventeenth in the NFL in points allowed with 351. Not all of that was on the defense, however, as 37 of those points were scored on the offense or special teams. They allowed the seventh-fewest yards from scrimmage in the league. Their D-line was a strength, with Michael Strahan and Osi Umenyiora especially effective coming off the ends. Third-year man Justin Tuck improved steadily as the season wore on, so much so that he was dominating in the Super Bowl. The unit was led on the field by middle linebacker Antonio Pierce and was coordinated by Steve Spagnuolo.

Steve Spagnuolo: Because our players in New York had gone against the Philadelphia Eagles twice a year for the prior eight years I was there, I had instant credibility. It was really unique. If I had come from a place that played so-so defense or was just a friend of Tom Coughlin's it would have been different. I was fortunate enough to walk into that first defensive meeting and have a little bit of credibility and that was very, very helpful. You don't realize that until later, but the defensive players bought in because they wanted what they saw another team execute for a number of years. I was putting in that defense with my little twist and I want to show examples of it, so I had to show them Eagles tape, so I worried about that. Yet, guys like Antonio Pierce, Michael Strahan, Osi Umenyiora, Sam Madison, and Corey Webster wanted to watch Philadelphia Eagles film because they had Brian Dawkins, Troy Vincent, Jeremiah Trotter, and Hugh Douglas play that defense. It was really interesting to me how much they embraced watching their peers and trying to replicate them. To the guys' credit on defense, they took it to a new level and were able to do a lot of different things.

Michael Strahan: I was excited about Spagnuolo [coming to the Giants] because it was something new and fresh and that reinvigorates you. The Eagles had so much success with him. If we had some of that we were going to be good. Did I expect it to happen as fast as it did? Absolutely not. I was excited about having him in because he came from a program with a proven track record and we wanted that. The first two weeks we gave up 80 points and he came into team meeting and said, "The foundation is there. Just trust in the system. Believe in the system. I wouldn't trade anybody here for anybody else." That made guys go, "Wow is this guys nuts?" or "I really like this guy." It might be a little bit of both. It worked out well for us.

Sam Madison: The good thing about Coach Spags's system was that it played right into my mind. I was used to being right up in receiver's faces; being able to use my hands, my quickness and my foot speed to control receivers. Whereas, in my first year, with defensive coordinator, Tim Lewis, I had to play twelve yards off the line. I was in no man's land. Even though I played well, people were like, "Oh this isn't the right person for the football team." When Coach Spags came in, we watched the Philly defense; those guys playing spreads. It played right into what I was used to playing. It kind of helped me. Coach Spags saw that I could play it. He felt comfortable calling a lot of different plays for me. Now the team and the fans could see why they brought me in here.

Perhaps the most curious thing about the Giants as a Super Bowl contender was their takeaway-giveaway differential: –9. Teams that give away more than they take are not often successful, but it is possible to slip into the playoffs with a negative count. What is very nearly impossible is succeeding in the playoffs while continuing to lose more fumbles and interceptions than are gained. New York reversed this flaw in the postseason, forcing seven turnovers while losing the ball only twice.

The Giants' season started 0–2. The defense had given up 80 points in those first two games and the New York media was calling for everybody's heads.

Steve Spagnuolo: The saving grace was that I got some great advice from, I think, [Philadelphia Eagles' head coach] Andy Reid, telling me never to read a newspaper during the season. All that was going on but I was oblivious to it. I have a great wife who didn't fill me in on any of it. What she did do, though, was save some of those clippings which she showed to me after the Super Bowl, so I knew what happened eventually.

Linebacker Antonio Pierce spoke up and calmed everybody down.

Justin Tuck: AP was always known for being the spokesman. When something controversial needed to be said, he was there. [For week three], the coaches did such a great job focusing on the Redskins. In the game we were down seventeen to three.

David Diehl: To start off that way was tough for us to handle, especially with all the heat. The media was saying that they should fire Coach Coughlin and start all over—get a whole new staff, do all this stuff. Throughout that time we still had confidence in one another.

Justin Tuck: The halftime speech from Spags really got us to start playing. The first two weeks we were trying to play the perfect football game. We got our reckless abandon back. We went out and just played football. One play turned into two, and before you know it we were back in the game. Other than playing New England at the end of the season, that Washington game was the most important game we played all season.

David Diehl: I think that turning point was at halftime of that Washington game. We said, "We're not going 0–3. We're not gonna lose this game. And we're gonna have to do whatever it takes." And you saw a completely different team come out in the second half of that game offensively and defensively. Offensively we started pounding the ball, we got the run game going, we started putting points on the board. Defensively, you saw big hits, and we ended up winning the game by a fourth-and-goal stop by our defense. And I think that was the thing—both offense and defense really rallied off of each other and fed off of each other. We kept saying to the defense,

"Get us the ball, get us the ball." And our defense kept saying, "Put it on them, put it on them."

Amani Toomer: There wasn't any fear when we were down fourteen because we knew we had a good team.

In the second half, the New York defense shut down the Redskins, including a heroic, game-saving goal-line stand on first and goal from the 1-yard line in the fourth quarter. Michael Strahan made the stop on running back Ladell Betts on third down, and Justin Tuck, assisted by Aaron Ross and James Butler, stuffed Betts again on fourth.

Justin Tuck: I was exhausted after those four plays. I remember saying these are four plays that can turn our season around. From that point on, it catapulted us as far as confidence. That goal-line stand goes down in history as the most important string of four plays for that year.

Meanwhile, the offense scored 21 unanswered points to record their first win of the season. Five consecutive victories followed, and, after a bye week following their trip to London to play the Dolphins, the Giants were 6–2, good for second in the division behind Dallas at 7–1.

From that point forward, there was no telling which Giants team would show up. They lost to the Cowboys for the second time that season (see "Super Bowl Champions Beaten Twice by the Same Team," page 349) and got by a fading Lions team, 16–10. Then came the low ebb of the season. The 4–6 Vikings came to town with one of the worst pass defenses in the league. All they did was run back three interceptions for touchdowns and beat the Giants 41–17. It was at this point that the fan and media confidence level in Eli Manning, which was never rock solid to begin with, dropped to perhaps its lowest point. (Never mind that no less a light than Joe Namath had done the exact same thing against Buffalo in 1968, the same season in which he delivered on his guarantee that the Jets would win the Super Bowl.)

Because of his laid-back demeanor, it was sometimes said Manning did not have the fire in the belly necessary to win in the NFL. What would be considered coolness under adversity in a more accomplished quarterback was often perceived as a lack of desire in Manning.

Amani Toomer: The thing a lot of people don't realize is how competitive he is. Sometimes, looking at his facial expressions doesn't show the type of burning desire he really has. I had a charity auction in which I auctioned off a throwing-skills camp with me and Eli up in the bubble we had at that time. The old practice bubble. We were out there doing some things and the kids were getting bored because they were really young. So we decided to play a game with me being quarterback on one team and Eli being quarterback on the other. We'd just throw the ball around and have a little fun with these kids. Eli was throwing up reverses and quarterback throwbacks and throwing down the field. I'm like, "This guy's crazy. What if he were to pull his hamstring or something?" He was throwing it like he really wanted to win, but it was just a little pickup game. That's when my impression of him really started to come to.

The Vikings debacle was followed up by a stirring 21–16, come-from-behind win in Chicago in which Manning led two fourth-quarter touchdown drives. They followed up with a win over Philadelphia but came out flat against the Redskins and lost 22–10. They also lost outspoken tight end Jeremy Shockey in that contest, a player who could be quite demonstrable about getting his share of on-field attention.

Amani Toomer: I think with Shockey getting hurt, that actually helped us. I felt that Shockey and Eli's personalities didn't really mesh that well. When he went down, I think Eli relaxed a little bit and took more ownership over things and wasn't worried about how Shockey was going to feel about different situations if he wasn't getting the ball and things like that. I think that really ended up being addition by subtraction.

In week sixteen, needing a win to clinch a playoff spot, the Giants traveled to Buffalo and quickly fell behind the Bills 14–0.

Sam Madison: Man, that game was one of the toughest. Playing with the Dolphins I was used to anything happening in that stadium. In Buffalo you can have snow, rain, and sleet coming at an angle.

David Diehl: The weather in that game was unlike any game I've ever played in my life. Everybody's gonna point the finger at, oh Green Bay, when they played in below-zero temperatures, but that game in Buffalo was the wildest thing I've ever been a part of. Before the game I think it was forty-five, fifty degrees and sunny. It started raining, then it started to sleet, then it turned to snow, then it turned to hail, then it turned to wind and snow. You watch the film of that game and it's completely sunny, then on our next series, it's completely black and it's pouring. I think that game was huge for us. That was a huge confidence builder for our team.

Michael Strahan: It was one of the few times that year that I absolutely flipped out on the sidelines at everybody, basically saying, "Get your head out of your ass and let's go. What are we doing?" We understood that the last week was gonna be a tough one to win if that's what was gonna be required for us to make the playoffs. So damn, let's try and get it done this week if we can.

New York battled back to make it 17–14, but lost the lead again in the third quarter.

Corey Webster: A couple of interceptions were returned for touchdowns. I had one myself, and so did Kawika Mitchell. So it wasn't one person in particular, but a lot of people rising up and never pointing the finger.

These pick-sixes off Trent Edwards were sandwiched around an 88-yard Ahmad Bradshaw scoring scamper. With the win, the Giants locked up the fifth seed in the NFC playoffs.

THE FIRST MEETING

With a playoff spot already clinched and many of their fans scalping tickets to Patriots fans who wanted a chance to see their team go 16–0 in person, New York gave New England all it could handle on the final Saturday night of the season. While there was some concern in the media that Patriots fans were going to turn Giants Stadium into their house, the Giants players joked that they welcomed the opportunity to play another "road game."

"We play well on the road," nose tackle Barry Cofield told the *New York Times*, referring to their 7–1 away mark, "If this is going to be Foxborough South for a week, we'll get through it."

Corey Webster: We started playing well on the road. Didn't know why, but a lot of other people said it was because we didn't have anything to worry about, everybody was already against us, our back was against the wall, and we had less to worry about, fewer distractions. We went out there and used that for motivation and it helped us and we don't like to play like that but for some reason it helped us that year.

Michael Strahan: [The home-road disparity] was something I couldn't figure out. We were one of those teams that liked to be somewhere where the odds were against us; kind of like us against the world. I don't know what happened at home. Maybe it wasn't that same type of mentality because you do have your home crowd, which is a shame, because you always want to play well in front of them.

Coughlin made the decision not to rest his starters. He later wrote, "Yes, it is a bit unusual to have an undefeated team as an opponent. Even so, it is a difficult decision. It becomes clear that the media and fans care about a playoff game and therefore don't want our first-teamers to play. But I feel differently."

The result was the greatest threat yet to New England's pursuit of perfection.

Steve Spagnuolo: You would have thought a bunch of guys who had fought through the season the way we did would want to kind of back off a little bit. But our team was so hungry to play the Patriots in that sixteenth game it was unbelievable.

Sam Madison: By week sixteen we knew the system and we knew we had a great football team. We knew what Coach Spags wanted from us. We felt way confident. We knew we had the talent.

Carl Banks: Bill Belichick told me, "Carl, if we play like we played in the Meadowlands, the Giants are gonna win the football game. They attacked us in every phase of the game. If we can't play any better than we did, we're gonna lose." I don't think he was predicting that, but he just acknowledged how good the Giants were.

Justin Tuck: We were going to play them toe to toe. We knew they were going for history and we wanted to make history by beating them.

Rich Seubert: I wanted to be the team to beat them.

Ernie Accorsi: The interesting thing about playing the regulars that last regular-season game against the Patriots—I was wrong about this—I was saying to myself that we shouldn't play anybody. Obviously I didn't say anything to Tom [Coughlin]. And yet that was the game that had made us believe we could beat them.

Michael Strahan: I think there were two plans. Obviously, we weren't gonna go into the game with a big game plan about stopping the Patriots, because we didn't want to give away what we were gonna do in the playoffs to Tampa Bay, our next opponent. But, we *were* gonna go into that game with a solid game plan and we were gonna play hard. And for us, it was a challenge because they asked us [and we told them], "Of course we want to go play. We want to be the team that beats them. We don't go out there to roll over and give them a perfect season. I don't want those guys to be perfect. Are you kidding me? Bragging rights, man."

After his subpar performances against Washington and Buffalo, Eli Manning got himself untracked and threw four touchdown passes while Domenik Hixon had a 74-yard kickoff return for a touchdown. The Giants had a 12-point lead with five minutes to go in the third quarter before the Patriots rallied, scoring 22 unanswered points. Their comeback was aided by Ellis Hobbs picking off Manning, but it was the only interception he threw on the night. The 38–35 final gave the Patriots their perfect regular season, but in the New York camp there was a feeling that it gave the Giants something more.

Justin Tuck: Our team that year was one that thrived in situations when people told us we didn't have a shot. It didn't matter who we were playing. We felt comfortable playing in adverse situations. We didn't prepare for the New England game. We were focused on the playoffs. So when we had the success that we did, we knew if we saw them again we had a shot at playing well against them.

Sam Madison: We tried to do everything we could to win that game. We didn't hold anything back. We were actually upset with ourselves not being able to do exactly what we were coached to do. We gave up a few big plays, not physically, but mentally. So we knew then, if we didn't give up those plays, we had a chance. So we went back to the drawing board to try and eliminate some of those mental errors that we made throughout that game. There were a lot of busted coverages. Going against an offense like that, they tried to manipulate and put us in positions to make that happen. Tom Brady being one of the best, and Randy Moss, I think that game right there, he broke the record in that game, and we were very upset about allowing that to happen on our own field. So that didn't sit too well with us, as players or as a staff.

Steve Spagnuolo: Justin Tuck said, "Coach, if we get to play them again, just let us line up and get after them." In other words, we don't need to blitz that much. After that game, the defensive line was convinced that they could just line up. Because I had blitzed a little bit and the Patriots hit us for a couple of big plays. Randy Moss got one. To the credit of the offensive line of the Patriots, they picked up a couple pressures and got some big plays, so Justin's point was that if we were to just line up with our four guys we could do some damage.

David Diehl: Even though we lost in a hard-fought battle, that game gave us complete confidence going into the postseason. We walked away from it saying, If this is the best team in the NFL that just went 16–0, we can beat anybody as long as we go out there and believe in one another and play smart football.

Michael Strahan: We had seen what they were about. We had no fear going into the game, which was not what everybody thought we were gonna have because we didn't care if they were the Patriots and they had beaten everybody else. They barely got away with beating us and we felt like we had a second shot.

Justin Tuck I'm glad we didn't [beat them] because that fueled us in the Super Bowl. At the end of this game, I said, "We're going to see these guys again and we're going to beat them."

Bob Papa: After the game I come down the elevator and bumped into [Patriots center] Dan Koppen and I congratulated him. He thanked me and said, "Let me tell you something: That was one of the toughest games we've had. That team is good! I would not be surprised at all if they run through the NFC playoffs and we wind up playing those guys again." And that wasn't in an interview setting, that's not a politically correct answer, that's one guy giving you the unfiltered stuff.

THE PLAYOFFS

Their romping days behind them, the Patriots did not steamroll their way through the playoffs. They dispatched a tenacious Jacksonville Jaguars squad 31–20 in the divisionals. The Jags kept it close throughout the game, as did the Chargers a week later. San Diego even intercepted three Tom Brady passes, after a season in which Brady had been picked off just eight times. Lacking the services of injured All-Pro running back LaDainian Tomlinson, San Diego could only manage four field goals, although they hung with the undefeated Patriots until Brady hit Wes Welker for a pull-away touchdown in the fourth quarter, icing the 21–12 victory.

As a wild-card team, New York's road to the Super Bowl was a game longer than New England's, and it would all take place on the road. As the regular season proved, though, traveling was not an issue for this team. They throttled the Buccaneers for their eighth straight road victory. It was their first playoff win since the NFC championship of 2000. Manning looked especially good, registering a 117.1 passer rating while the defense picked off Jeff Garcia twice and recovered a fumble. From that point on, the Giants would meet only teams to whom they had lost during the regular season, accounting for four of their six losses.

David Tyree: We really couldn't script it any better for us. From the moment we beat Tampa, it was all about redemption.

For the divisional playoff game, the Giants returned to the site of their only 2007 road loss: Dallas. Antonio Pierce characterized their next meeting with the Cowboys as ". . . an All-Pro team versus an all-Joe team," referring to the twelve Dallas Pro Bowl selections to just one for the Giants. Manning had an economical but effective outing against the 13–3 Cowboys, throwing only 18 times. He completed 12 of those tries, two good for touchdowns to Amani Toomer. The Cowboys outgained the Giants by 106 yards but were denied victory with nine seconds to go when R. W. McQuarters intercepted a Tony Romo pass in the end zone to preserve the 21–17 lead.

The NFC championship was a classic, played in a Lambeau Field that was so frigid, Coughlin claimed he could "see the cold" when the team arrived in Green Bay. No Giants team had ever encountered game conditions like this: a –23 wind-chill factor. In what proved to be Brett Favre's last game as a Packer, New York and Green Bay battled for sixty minutes to a 20–20 tie. Given the conditions and the fact that he was covered by Pro Bowl cornerback Al Harris, Plaxico Burress had a remarkable game, catching 11 passes for 151 yards.

Michael Strahan: I know Brett Favre was around a long time, and in my pregame speech to the guys, I said that everybody's talking about legacy and tradition and Brett Favre this and Brett Favre that. Well, fuck Brett Favre! This is *our* time. How about *we* make our legacy, *our* tradition today? [Brett:] we respect you as a man, and as an opponent, but we're here to beat you.

Amani Toomer: The heater on our bench shut down and we didn't know it. I was sitting there thinking I was getting warm and I was actually getting colder. I was running and parts of my body were shutting down. I'd try to react to the ball and my arms just wouldn't go there. So after that I decided I had to put on a jacket. It was the only thing that kept me going because I remember thinking my body is shutting down because it was that cold.

Michael Strahan: We had on so many body-warming creams and lotions, outfits and cold weather gear and we were still freezing. There's nothing you can do. The heaters on the bench and none of that stuff was effective. You just had to sit there and suck it up.

David Tyree: It was beyond uncomfortable. Three or four months after the game, I still had fingertips that were numb.

Regulation ended when a high snap undid Lawrence Tynes's 36-yard field-goal attempt. He had also missed a 43-yard attempt earlier in the quarter and was very much in the coach's doghouse. It was not his first trip there in the 2007 season. Coughlin had grown exasperated enough with his kicker that he auditioned replacements for him earlier in the midst of the regular season.

Green Bay won the coin toss but gave away the advantage it provided when Favre tried to hit Donald Driver—with whom he had hooked up for a 90-yard score in the second quarter—and his misfire was picked off by Corey Webster.

Corey Webster: I figured Driver has been one of his main targets he's been throwing to for years. I was able to read the route down the field, and come underneath and make a play on the ball. I was so excited, eyes wide open. I didn't feel any of the cold when the ball was on the way.

The pick gave the Giants the ball on the Green Bay 34. The Giants managed to go 5 yards on the next three downs, leaving Coughlin with the choice of going for it on fourth and 5 or sending his kicker in for a 47-yard attempt. He chose to go with Tynes's foot, and redemption came for the kicker much as it did for Joe Danelo in the playoff-clinching game of 1981. He slammed it right down the middle of the field, turned, and headed for the warmth of the locker room, his job done.

Michael Strahan: When that ball went through the uprights, all that freezing and minus-twenty-three turned into one hundred twenty-three degrees. We didn't feel any of the weather anymore.

THE GAME
Once in Arizona, the Giants stayed far from the madding crowd. They were ensconced on a reservation at the Sheraton Wild Horse Pass Resort.

David Diehl: Our team was focused on the game with a very businesslike attitude. We were very far off the strip and off the beaten path of where everybody else was staying. It was an advantage to us being so secluded. It was only players and families, and it kind of got us away from all the madness of the Super Bowl. It allowed us to really treat this as a business trip.

Corey Webster: As a secondary, we didn't do anything other than work. We didn't go out to any parties. We said to each other: "Look, we can come back to Arizona any time to visit. Now that we're here, we're working every single second to try and get better."

By now the Giants had heard every story about how they shouldn't have even been there.

Justin Tuck: We knew that they were going for history, and what better way to ruin any Boston team's chances? It wasn't that much pressure on us. No one expected us to win. We had two weeks to prepare for it and we felt very confident going into that game.

Michael Strahan: We looked at it as an opportunity to shock everybody. That was our ultimate goal.

David Tyree: We had that much more excitement playing for the coach we were playing for. When he lays it out flat, we play the game to win. That's the attitude of every player in the NFL, regardless of the choices that their coaches make for them. Every game we play we want to win. And we prepare ourselves to do that. We were excited to play one of the best teams in football history. With that said, we didn't feel there was anything magnificent or immortal about this team. We approached it that way. And we gave it everything that we had.

Amani Toomer: If you go to the Super Bowl and lose, it's the worst feeling ever. It takes most teams a year or two to get over it mentally. It's just such a draining, anticlimatic letdown. You don't even realize how special it is until you lose it. So I was like, "Are we going to go there again and lose again?" That would be the worst thing ever, so just because of that sense I had, I felt we had to go extra-hard in terms of preparing.

Steve Spagnuolo: We were very professional about it in that we just went about things like we had every other week, we weren't going to talk, we weren't going to be boisterous or anything, we let the whole focus be on the Patriots. We knew that there was an underlying confidence in our group that we knew we could beat this team. Now having said that, I felt as the coordinator going against that offense that if we could hold them under thirty that that was a good day of defense. I had a lot of confidence in our offense, that if we could find a way to score twenty-nine points we would win the game. They had so many weapons and they were so good and I have so much respect for Bill Belichick that I never thought we'd go in there and shut them down. But I didn't realize that our guys, true to form, were going to step it up another whole five notches.

David Diehl: People were counting us out of that game, saying there was no way they're gonna win—this is the dynasty team. We used that as motivation. We were the dogs throughout the playoffs. We liked being the underdogs, we liked being the ones about whom was said, "They can't do it." We used that to prove people wrong the entire year.

Justin Tuck: Before the game I told my cousin, [Patriots' linebacker] Adalius Thomas, that he wasn't beating us again. He already had a Super Bowl Ring from when the Baltimore Ravens beat the Giants. He was kind of like the biggest athlete in our area when I was coming up. We went to the same high school. I was fortunate enough to break all of his records. He was always a person I looked up to athletically all my life. To have an opportunity to play against him in the biggest game of both of our careers is something special. For a family from a small town in Alabama, it was surreal. We don't talk about it much because I know it was a heartbreaking loss for him.

Amani Toomer: I remember one of their running backs, Laurence Maroney, went to Brandon Jacobs and said, "Hey, man, why don't you come to our after party after the game?" I'm like, "What do you mean? You guys are having an after party?" Here these guys are already planning their after party and stuff. It was just like the Cowboys that season who were handing out tickets to the NFC championship the morning of their playoff game against us. The Patriots really thought we were just going to roll over and give them everything and not really try to win this game. That was more insulting than anything else. I mean, we got to the Super Bowl just like they had. Of course, we lost six more games than they did, but still, we weren't chopped liver.

Michael Strahan: The game plan was simpler than it was for us throughout the rest of the playoffs. From a defensive line standpoint, we knew we were the strong point. We knew that in order for us to win we had to make plays, we had to pressure the quarterback. When we were doing it well, it made it easier for everybody. We never wanted the quarterback to feel safe and comfortable in the pocket when he played against us. We wanted him to watch film and go, "Oh my goodness, is this what's gonna get me this week? I don't want any part of this." When we played the Patriots, we had some blitzes and they were successful. But when you go back and watch the game, we were successful with four guys rushing. We were successful with three guys rushing, we were successful with five guys rushing. It was just a flat out man-on-man, and we didn't need to blitz a ton.

THE FIRST QUARTER

No Super Bowl—and a small minority of games in general—ever had as few possessions in the first quarter as this one did. The Giants started play from their own 23 and, ten minutes later, put the finishing touch on a drive that took sixteen plays to cover 62 yards. It ended with Lawrence Tynes belting a 32-yard field goal through the uprights for a 3–0 New York lead. Although it did not produce a touchdown, it set the record for being the longest drive in the history of the Super Bowl.

Rich Seubert: We always made sure that our defense was fresh. We only came away with three points, which was kind of a downer, but we went out and proved that we could play with those guys. That drive showed that, yeah, they're the New England Patriots and they're a good team, but we were too.

The Patriots answered with a clock-eating drive of their own. It was preceded by a nice kickoff return from Laurence Maroney, who took the ball at the 1 and ran it back 43 yards before being run out of bounds by the kicker, Tynes. By the time the first quarter ended, the Patriots had run twelve plays from scrimmage and were knocking on the door. A 16-yard pass-interference call on Antonio Pierce had given them a first and goal on the 1-yard line. It was their biggest gain of the drive. Pierce, unlike 95 percent of the defenders called for interference, copped to the charge of face-guarding the tight end, Ben Watson, in the middle of the end zone.

"I looked the wrong way. I should have turned inside. I felt I was there. I might have panicked a little bit," Pierce said later.

THE SECOND QUARTER

The Patriots banged the ball over on the first play of the second quarter. Maroney took the handoff from Brady and was nearly ankle tackled in the backfield, but he blew past that attempt and into a hole that had been blasted open on the right side of the line.

The random nature of turnovers was on display in the second quarter. Manning, who had some interception problems earlier in the year, hit Steven Smith right in the numbers on a short pass in the red zone. Smith could not control the pass and it flew off his hands into the possession of Ellis Hobbs of the Patriots. Manning was charged with an interception, but the onus was really on Smith. On the Giants' next possession, Manning and Bradshaw could not connect on a handoff and linebacker Pierre Woods clearly fell on the ball. Then Bradshaw, who was wedged against Woods, rolled him over and came away with the ball in his hands. It appeared in the replays that the referees had allowed Bradshaw to continue fighting for possession long after the whistle had blown. The Giants maintained control of the ball but could not capitalize on the call.

On the ensuing possession, the Giants' defense swarmed all over Brady. With his receivers blanketed, he was sacked twice. On second down, Kawika Mitchell forced him from the pocket and he was knocked over by Michael Strahan for a 7-yard loss. On third and 17, Justin Tuck buried him. It was the second three and out in a row for the Patriots. For those who had planned on the Pats to win by 12, it was probably time to start nail-biting. This was looking like a slugging match rather than a sprint.

Ahmad Bradshaw and Brandon Jacobs tore off some real estate on the next Giants possession, but Manning had the ball slapped away on third and 4 at the Patriots' 25. Bradshaw got to the ball first but, instead of covering, he slapped it upfield, where Steve Smith grabbed it in first-down territory. Flagged for the batting violation, the Giants moved back 10 yards and, on fourth down, Jeff Feagles punted it away at the two-minute warning.

Seemingly buried at their own 11, Brady got the Patriots moving. They overcame a holding penalty and had first and 10 at their own 38. Moss shook loose from Kevin Dockery and Brady hit him for 18 yards. The Patriots were now across midfield and threatening to get into field-goal range. On first down from the Giants' 44, Brady dropped back to pass. Stepping up into the pocket, he did not see Justin Tuck come around behind him and reach in for the ball. Tuck slapped it away and players from both teams converged on the loose ball. In a struggle reminiscent of the Bradshaw-Perry ball tussle earlier in the quarter, Osi Umenyiora got possession after wrestling tackle Matt Light.

As Troy Aikman said of Tuck on the Fox broadcast of the game, "They have not been able to control him. No matter where they put him, he's been able to take advantage and get pressure on Tom Brady. They needed a play, and Justin Tuck has been able to provide it."

THE THIRD QUARTER

The Giants appeared to have the Patriots stopped on their first drive of the second half, but were caught with twelve men on the field during New England's punt, prolonging the possession.

Michael Strahan: Belichick rushed in his punting team and they caught Chase Blackburn trying to run off the field. We had twelve men on the field and the Patriots asked for that call and won the challenge. It gave them a first down, so Coach Coughlin was freaking out. You know how Coughlin can get. He was red, he was screaming. He didn't know who he was yelling at but he was yelling anyway! And I grabbed him by the shoulders with a smile on my face and I said, "Coach, don't worry about it. We got it."

True to his word, Strahan delivered a big sack that broke the back of the next phase of the drive. New England went for it on fourth and

13 from the Giants' 31, but Brady overthrew Jabar Gaffney in the end zone and the score remained 7–3.

While the first quarter had only two possessions, the third had just three—and none resulted in a score. Although Brady got into a rhythm with Welker over the middle (the Giants' game plan had the linebackers dropping deep to help contain Welker), a second-down bomb to Moss was off target and the Pats failed to convert on third and 15 from their own 46, ending the quarter.

THE FOURTH QUARTER

After Chris Hanson punted into the end zone, New York started from their own 20 and went to a new target. Kevin Boss, who had taken over at tight end for Jeremy Shockey, got away from Rodney Harrison at the Giants' 39 and Manning hit him. Boss rumbled for another 26 yards before Harrison finally caught him from behind. The 45-yard gain put the Giants in business at the Patriots' 35.

On third down, Steve Smith got underneath coverage and Manning connected with him, moving the ball to the 12. After Bradshaw made it second and 3 with a bruising 7-yard run up the middle, Manning dropped back and fired the ball toward David Tyree, who was running from right to left across the middle of the end zone. The pass was just ahead of a reaching Asante Samuel.

David Tyree: I scored a couple of touchdowns with the Giants on that exact play. It's one that I was ready for. We do it very well. It was a lot more difficult a pass to catch than it looked. Asante Samuel played it very well. Eli threw a bullet in there to go ahead.

Tyree gathered it in and pointed to the sky. The Giants led 10–7. Thirty-three minutes and fifty-two seconds had elapsed since the last score—the longest scoreless gap in Super Bowl history. The Giants were succeeding in taking the Patriots out of their high-scoring element.

Rich Seubert: We had nothing to lose. We were playing our game.

On New York's next possession, Manning scrambled free from intense pressure on second down and just overthrew Burress, who was all alone in the flat. An 8-yard pass to Toomer on the next down left them with a fourth and 1 on their own 38, and Jeff Feagles punted it to the New England 20. The Giants were just under eight minutes from upsetting the undefeated Patriots. Could they continue to keep the likes of Tom Brady, Randy Moss, and Wes Welker in check?

What followed instead was a relentless Patriots drive. With their backs to the wall—as they had often been during the second half of their pursuit of a perfect season—Brady, operating mostly from the shotgun, consistently found Moss and Welker under coverage. Laurence Maroney tore off a 9-yard run and Kevin Faulk had a key 12-yard reception that took the ball to the Giants' 6-yard line.

Bob Papa: It was all Wes Welker—it looked like the Pats from early in the season. They were just systematically taking the Giants apart. Brady was getting the ball out of his hand before any pass rush could get to him. They were never even threatened on that drive. They made it look so easy.

After two incomplete passes, Brady lined up in the shotgun once more and took the snap. The Giants had Welker double covered over the middle, but out to the right, Moss was one-on-one with Corey Webster. Moss broke inside and Webster went to follow, only to slip at the goal line. The Patriots were now up 14–10.

Corey Webster: Giving up one, especially in that crucial time of the game—I was very upset with myself. I'd like to have it back. Strahan said to me, "Come on, get up; time to cheer the offense on."

Michael Strahan: I was always that guy that would get up and walk up and down the bench and remind guys of what we had to do. Keep them alert or just joke around. One time I pulled the defensive backs together and I said, "Hey man, let me tell you guys something." And they thought I was gonna be really serious. And I said, "I have never played with an uglier group of guys in my life." [My philosophy always was] it's a game, it's a sport, it's a way to make a living, but at the same time what else would you rather be doing right now? You can either enjoy it or we can sit here and pout and hate it and when things are bad or things aren't going your way, find some joy and realize how fortunate you are and turn it around.

Steve Spagnuolo: I still wish that we had pressured them more on their last scoring drive. I've gone back and looked at it and this is still the one that haunts me. We should have pulled the trigger a couple more times on that drive.

With just 2:42 remaining, the Giants took over at their own 17-yard line. The Patriots' quest for a perfect season looked well within reach. But that's not how everyone saw it. On the New York sideline, defensive lineman Michael Strahan, playing in the last game of his long and storied career, was shouting to anyone who would listen, "Seventeen fourteen is the final. Believe it. Don't just say, it believe it! The final score is going to be seventeen fourteen!"

Michael Strahan: I felt that as a team we had come too far and too many great things had happened from winning that Dallas game with the interception in the end zone to the Green Bay game, overtime and that freaking, minus-23 weather. It was too good for it all to end without us winning. For me, I needed to let our offense know before they went on that field how it was gonna end. We have no say in it, but this is what you gotta do. Go out there and just do what you're doing. It's gonna happen. And, apparently, they believed it and made it happen.

Manning stepped onto the field with 83 yards separating him from making Strahan's sideline bravado come true.

On first down, he hit Amani Toomer in the middle of three defenders for 11 yards. This was followed by two incompletions on passes to Plaxico Burress, who had brazenly predicted a 23–17 Giants victory, a pick that had prompted Patriots quarterback Tom Brady to ask if Burress was going to be playing defense.

On the first play after the two-minute warning, Manning found Toomer for 9 yards. On fourth and 1 from the Giants' 37, Brandon Jacobs bulled into the line.

Bob Papa: Jacobs didn't make it easily. He had to make an adjustment on that run to nudge himself forward and get the first down.

Manning then scrambled for 5 yards, losing the ball in the process, although it was fairly obvious that his knee had hit the ground before the fumble. While they were sorting out the pileup, Coughlin leaned in and called time-out with 1:20 on the clock. On second and 5, Manning whipped a sideline pass to David Tyree too high; it appeared as though defender Asante Samuel mistimed his jump and the ball went off his hands.

"If I want to be known as one of the best cornerbacks in the NFL, I have to make that play," he said later.

Patriots defensive end Richard Seymour was taunting the Giants: "Hey, guys, get ready to go home!" he shouted.

"What's the sense in tempting fate like that?" thought Amani Toomer.

On third down and 5 from their own 44, the Giants went with a four-wide-out set out of the shotgun. The resulting play would become *the* highlight clip from the game. Very quickly, Manning's protection broke down and he was scrambling for freedom. He somehow eluded the grasp of Seymour and escaped the clutches of defensive end Jarvis Green, who had a fistful of his jersey. Recovering his balance, he staggered backward, away from a scrum of bodies.

Meanwhile, downfield, Tyree knew he was the last guy in the read, meaning he was the last of the receivers Manning would be looking for. There was a reason for this. The day before the Super Bowl, at the Giants' final practice, Tyree had some trouble. Manning recalled, "It was the worst practice I've ever seen at any level—I've never seen anything like it."

Amani Toomer: He was dropping everything. He dropped every ball.

Steve Spagnuolo: [During practice] Antonio Pierce whispered to Michael Strahan, "He can't catch a cold."

David Tyree: I know I dropped at least six balls. It got to the point when I caught one, everyone applauded. But Eli said, "I know you'll be ready," which speaks to the level of his growth and leadership as quarterback. I've always been there for E and it speaks to the relationship that we have.

"Before practice, I was feeling good about him," said Coughlin. "As he came off the field after practice I told him, "I give you a compliment coming out here, and now you can't catch a damn thing."

Running deep over the middle, Tyree glanced back to see his quarterback in trouble. He immediately started looking for an open area in the Patriots' coverage. "I felt them holding me," said Manning, "but I never felt anybody pull me to the ground. I stayed alive and I saw David in the middle of the field."

He let fly as Tyree, at the New England 25, got open for a moment and leapt for the ball just as Patriot safety Rodney Harrison lowered the boom on him. Because of the hit, Tyree's left hand came off the ball, but he continued trying to control it with his right. The ball descended to his helmet, with the right hand firmly pinning it to the hard plastic as he tumbled to the ground. The landing did not jolt the ball loose; it was a 32-yard completion. "It wasn't luck," Tyree would say later. "Luck is finding a fifty-dollar bill on the ground."

David Tyree: I knew I wasn't going to be open for long. I was saying to myself, "There is no way I'm letting this ball go." I knew I secured the catch, but I had no idea it was on my helmet. I give a lot of thanks and praise to God for giving me the grace to be able to pull the ball down. That's not something you can prepare for. It was a miracle.

Rich Seubert: Eli was cool and calm. All season long our two-minute drives were good. We knew we had to have guys step up and make plays. It seemed like nothing was going to stop us.

Michael Strahan: I don't know how he kept his balance because he's as clumsy as you can get sometimes. He's not real graceful even when he's just walking.

Justin Tuck: Eli was not known for his athleticism. For him to find a way to throw that ball to Tyree . . . I just knew we were going to win the game.

David Tyree: I give all the credit deservedly to Eli. I am not the kind of guy to applaud myself. It wasn't until I got back to the hotel that I saw the play and it set in that it was a historical moment.

Rich Seubert: From Tyree's play on, we knew we would get it done.

With just under a minute to play, the Giants had a first and 10 on the New England 24-yard line. The next two plays went the Patriots' way, as Manning was sacked for a loss of 1 and another pass to Tyree fell incomplete. On third down, though, Manning hooked up with rookie receiver Steve Smith, who scooted down the right sideline for 12 yards and a crucial first down, getting out of bounds to stop the clock with thirty-nine seconds left.

David Diehl: That's the one thing that you saw out of that group of '07 rookies that were drafted that year. All of them, whether it was offense, defense, special teams, those guys really stepped up and made an impact and really helped our football team win games.

It was then that Manning called the play known as 62 Café, figuring the Patriots would be blitzing and leaving Burress in one-on-one coverage. "That's a matchup we're going to take every time," said Manning. "They finally came with an all-out blitz. I'd been waiting for it all day."
It was a close-fought thing that Burress was playing at all.

Bob Papa: The hotel we were staying at in Arizona had these desert-style bricks in the shower and it was kinda slippery. I took a shower

Monday morning and I slipped a little. These stones, whatever they were, they were kinda slick. As luck would have it, Burress, on the morning of the media day, actually slipped in his shower and damaged his knee pretty badly. This situation is a lot worse than the team was letting on.

In fact, Coughlin didn't know until right before game time if Burress was a go or not. He sent Pat Hanlon, the team's vice president of communications, to get the final word from the player if he was going to be able to overcome the knee injury that had come down on top of the ankle problems he'd been battling all season.

Bob Papa: Hanlon found Plaxico at his locker on a knee praying for strength or whatever and, after he finished praying, he gave him a thumbs-up that he was going to go. They needed him in that game because he was a decoy in a lot of situations. You could see that he was not close to one hundred percent.

Ernie Accorsi: Hobbs was playing Plaxico Burress, and Burress beat him on inside moves all game. Early on, Plaxico said, "He's overplaying me inside. I can get the post corner anytime I want in the red zone." And Eli said, "Save it until we have to have it."

Burress ran a perfect corner route. An inside fake forced Hobbs to bite as Burress faded to the corner of the end zone. He found himself all alone with the ball in flight—by Manning's own admission, a "rare spiral for me."

Bob Papa: The coaches were watching tape all week getting prepared for the game. They could clearly see that Ellis Hobbs was always going to come down hard on that slant route and protect the goal line in those situations. The Giants had it diagnosed: They saw the coverage, they saw where they had Burress, and they knew that Ellis Hobbs always came down hard on that play. So they were going corner the whole way and, as Manning threw the ball, Burress was wide open.

"I was just there thinking, C'mon down," said Burress later. "I was watching my feet, to make sure they were inbounds and everything."

They were. Turning his body back to the pass, Burress made the catch, completing the comeback and rendering the Patriots' season imperfect 1,139 minutes and 26 seconds into a 1,140-minute season.

Almost. There were twenty-nine seconds remaining and the Patriots had all three time-outs left. Getting into field-goal position from their own 26 was by no means out of the question.

David Diehl: We got to the sidelines and we were cheering, all excited—but there was still time on the clock. We were saying, "It isn't over yet. There's still time, we need a defensive stop!"

Steve Spagnuolo: I can guarantee you I wasn't jumping up and down after the Tyree play. I didn't know where they were going to get the ball after the kickoff, and I knew immediately all they needed was a field goal to tie. And I knew that if they got a field goal to tie they would have all kinds of momentum. I said to myself, "Okay. Brady can throw it in the air and Moss can jump up and catch it. But if this is gonna happen, we're going down swinging." So we blitzed on the first one.

First down saw Brady throwing long to Gaffney, but it was underthrown and the ball fell into empty space at the New York 42. On second down, reserve tackle Jay Alford blew past Russ Hochstein up the middle and swallowed Brady for a 10-yard loss.

Michael Strahan: Before that play, Jay was like, "What you do want me to do, Michael?" He was a rookie, he was out there filling in, he was nervous and he wanted to stay out of my way. I said, "Go straight ahead. Just go!" And I was running around the edge and I saw Brady look like somebody hooked him up to one of those protective Hollywood stunt vests. He looked like a stunt guy when he gets hit. I said, "Oh my God!" I hadn't seen a quarterback get hit like that. After he made that hit, Jay got up and he didn't even know he had a sack. All he knew was that he ran into the quarterback. Without our rookies, we never, ever would have won the Super Bowl. It wouldn't have been close. I don't know another team that can say their rookies helped them win the Super Bowl.

It was the last of many hits and pressures that had been applied to Brady throughout the night. Justin Tuck and Michael Strahan harassed him constantly, so much so that Tuck was a strong candidate for the game's Most Valuable Player award.

On the last two plays of the game, Brady loaded up and heaved desperation bombs to Moss, both of which were deflected away by Corey Webster.

Corey Webster: I had no doubt in my mind where he was going with the ball, so I said to myself, "Not on me. Not on my clock. I can't let it happen here." I knew he was going to be able to launch the ball about sixty, seventy yards down the field. Anything I could do to get my hand in there, my foot, my pinky, to knock the ball away I wanted to do it. And I was able to get my hand in. The next one they threw, [fellow defensive back] Gibril Wilson came over and ran through me and Randy Moss. We knew where the ball was going, and we didn't want to have it happen on our clock. We had been so good throughout the game not giving up big plays, and we didn't want to give it up at the last second.

Bob Papa: One thing about Tom Brady that my broadcast partner Carl Banks pointed out was that when most quarterbacks get hit as much as he got hit in that game, they shrivel up. The fact that Brady was able to throw a seventy-five-yard strike in stride to Randy Moss on the second-to-last play of the game deserved a tip of the cap. He was a true warrior to be able to do that.

Carl Banks: I don't care what anyone says in comparing him and Peyton Manning or any of his contemporaries: Tom Brady, by far, is the best quarterback in his era, and I'll tell you why. He took a beating in that Super Bowl and then got up in their next-to-last drive and operated with the precision of a brain surgeon. You talk about a guy that shouldn't have even had the confidence that he was going to be able to get a pass off. The only thing missing was blood coming out of his mouth. That drive forever cemented the memory for me of what greatness is at that position. I don't think you could take any other quarterback in this league, subject them to what Brady had been subjected to, and say, "Okay, now go win the game for us." You won't find that anywhere else.

Steve Spagnuolo: I've got a lot of respect for Joe Montana, but Tom Brady to me is one of the all-time greatest. He's so balanced and so poised in the pocket.

The Giants killed the last second off the clock with their victory formation.

David Diehl: We knelt down and the game was over; it was a feeling like no other.

Rich Seubert: It was fun. We got to go on the field and take our one knee and have the confetti fall on us.

Michael Strahan: I remember losing [Super Bowl xxxv] and being like a zombie. They just rush you off that field and that confetti's coming down and you see the other team cheering. I said, "Don't let me feel that side of it twice." So to see that confetti falling and realize it's for us? Now I don't have to go in the locker room to have to get away from the team that's celebrating.

Corey Webster: Strahan said to me, "I told you; this is what you keep playing for, for moments like this." That's the best way to end the game: when your quarterback's kneeling down, letting the time run out. That's the best feeling ever.

Sam Madison: I was looking for my family in the stands, running around like a chicken with my head cut off.

THE AFTERMATH

Ernie Accorsi: When Eli overthrew Amani Toomer in the last drive, this guy about two rows in front of me turned around to me and said, "Well, your quarterback just blew the championship." When the game was over, the same guy came climbing over two rows of seats puckering up, trying to kiss me on the lips. But when I walked up the steps to leave, the collection of fans that was sitting around me gave me an ovation. It's hard for me to talk about it now with a dry eye. It was such a moment.

Corey Webster: Plaxico had said earlier that it was going to be 23-17. So we went out there with that on our shoulders, to tell you the truth, and said we gotta stick behind him and play. And we did play with that in the back of our minds. At the end of the game we said, "Come on Plax, you gave them too much credit. They only scored 14." So yeah, we got on him a little bit too.

Steve Spagnuolo: We said something to Plaxico like, "Thanks a lot, you didn't have any confidence!"

David Diehl: To be in the ticker-tape parade and to see the millions and millions of people that came out for it and the crowded streets and everybody going crazy . . . and just to think how presidents, war heroes, old Yankees, and all the New York teams that have gone down that path as champions—to be a part of that history—that's something that nobody can ever take away from you. I had a camcorder with me; I have it all on tape. When my daughter, who's three now, is older, I'll be able to show that to her. I'll show her everything and show her the game, so she can understand that it definitely means a lot to me. I wore my Super Bowl ring after we got them for a little bit, but now I have it put away. I barely every wear it because, as a competitor, I'm not done playing.

Michael Strahan: Trust me, every time I watch the replay of the game and I see Eli throw that ball [to Tyree], I still say, "Please catch it." It's still hard to believe he actually caught that football. I'm still screaming! And every time Eli throws the ball to Plaxico, I still say, "Did he get both feet in?"

David Diehl: Right now that's history to me, and I want to do whatever it takes to help my football team get back there, because once you have that feeling of being a champion and holding that trophy, you want to do whatever you can to get back there.

APPENDICES

The Season Spoilers

As of this writing, nearly eighteen hundred attempts have been made to achieve a perfect National Football League season, and the 1972 Dolphins remain the sole team to manage the feat. Fourteen other teams have gone through a full season with but a single blemish on their records, whether it be a win or a tie. Listed here are those teams and the team that inflicted upon them that nonvictorious exception, along with the number of wins they had at the time their perfect season was marred. Also shown is the record of the team that spoiled perfection at both the time of their win/tie as well as their final record.

The achievements of the 2007 and 1934 Giants are both quite similar. Both were teams of modest accomplishment during the regular season that found themselves in the championship against teams of apparent destiny, and both responded with upset wins. The 2007 Giants pulled the neat trick of running up the highest score against the Patriots in one game (35) and holding them to their lowest score in another (14). The '34 Giants ruined the Chicago Bears' perfect season when they scored 27 points in the fourth quarter of the famous Sneaker Game. The '42 Bears also had their season wrecked in the championship game, this time by the Redskins—a team that was itself just one win from perfection save for the efforts of the Giants.

Year	Team	Total wins	Wins when lost/tied	Spoiler, score	Spoiler's record at time of game	Final record
2007	New England Patriots	18	18	New York Giants, 17–14	13–6	10–6 (14–6 w/playoffs)
1934	Chicago Bears	13	13	New York Giants, 30–13	8–5	8–5 (9–5 w/playoffs)
1985	Chicago Bears	18	12	Miami Dolphins, 38–24	8–4	12–4 (13–5 w/playoffs)
1942	Chicago Bears	11	11	Washington Redskins, 14–6	10–1	10–1 (11–1 w/playoffs)

Year	Team	Total wins	Wins when lost/tied	Spoiler, score	Spoiler's record at time of game	Final record
1962	Green Bay Packers	14	10	Detroit Lions, 26–14	8–2	11–3
1929	Green Bay Packers	12	10	Frankford Yellow Jackets, 0–0	8–2–2	9–2–3
1984	San Francisco 49ers	18	6	Pittsburgh Steelers, 20–17	3–3	9–7 (10–8 w/playoffs)
1923	Canton Bulldogs	11	6	Buffalo All-Americans, 3–3	3–2–1	5–4–3
1941	Chicago Bears	12	5	Green Bay Packers, 14–6	6–1	10–1 (10–2 w/tiebreaker)
1945	Cleveland Rams	10	4	Philadelphia Eagles, 28–14	1–2	7–3
1982	Washington Redskins	12	4	Dallas Cowboys, 24–10	3–1	6–3 (8–4 w/playoffs)
1949	Philadelphia Eagles	12	3	Chicago Bears, 38–21	2–1	9–3
1976	Oakland Raiders	16	3	New England Patriots, 48–17	2–1	11–3 (11–4 w/playoffs)
1942	Washington Redskins	11	1	New York Giants, 14–7	0–0	5–5–1

The Duluth Kelleys were 5–1 in 1924, losing only to the Green Bay Packers, 13–0.

As you can see, the teams that wrecked the perfect seasons were, in the majority, fine squads themselves. Only the '42 Giants and '23 Buffalo All-Americans finished at or slightly above .500. When combined, the spoiling teams had an impressive 132–55–7 final record.

Super Bowl Champions Beaten Twice by the Same Team

The 2007 Giants were not the first Super Bowl winner to have lost two games to one team in the same season. They were the first to lose by as much as a combined margin of 21 points, however. Like two of the previous twice-beaten champions, they got their revenge when it counted: in the playoffs.

THE MOST MEMORABLE GAMES IN GIANTS HISTORY

Year	Champ	Victorious opponent	Scores	Notes
1969	Kansas City Chiefs	Oakland Raiders	27–24 and 10–6	Kansas City beat Oakland for AFL title, 17–7
1983	L.A. Raiders	Seattle Seahawks	38–36 and 34–21	Los Angeles beat Seattle for AFC title, 30–14
1995	Dallas Cowboys	Washington Redskins	27–23 and 24–17	The Redskins were 4–10 in their other games
2002	Tampa Bay Buccaneers	New Orleans Saints	26–20 and 23–20	The Saints were 7–7 otherwise
2007	New York Giants	Dallas Cowboys	45–35 and 31–20	New York beat Dallas in divisional round, 21–17

Acknowledgments

The person we must thank first and foremost is Peter Thomas Fornatale. Pete brought us together in the earliest stages of the book and got it off the ground. In the latter stages, he came in near deadline and contributed heavily to the chapters on the 1990 and 2000 playoff games. Our editor at Bloomsbury USA, Benjamin Adams, took our original idea and sent it in a much better direction and was very helpful throughout the process.

We assembled a team of researchers who also helped out with the transcription of the interviews. In Boston, Kevin Edelson proved invaluable; while in Austin, R. J. LaForce, Mark Collins, and Christopher Bond put in many hours helping to make this book what it is. Our hope for all four is that this is just their first foray into publishing.

Early on and throughout the project, Dave Ringel offered insight and guidance on Giants history, while Rob Neyer proved an asset with his expertise and resources. We'd also like to thank our agent, Frank Scatoni of Venture Literary, Inc., for getting behind us from day one. Cristina Zizza and Kathy Hussey were key components in transcribing the interviews. Nate Knaebel at Bloomsbury USA would be an asset to any book.

Tracking down and contacting all these football greats was not something we could have done by ourselves. In this regard, we are indebted to Peter-John Baptiste, the Giants' Director of Public Relations; Tom Scott, Harold Carmichael, Greg Ferguson, Jack Mahoney, and Robin Brendle, of CBS Sports; Steve Thurlow—one of the original Baby Bulls—Dan Margarita, Jeff Jeffers, John Painter, and Dianne Shabat of the Chicago Bears; Julie Faron of the St. Louis Rams, Ryan Moore of the San Francisco 49ers, Pete Noyes, Jeff Jeffers, and John Painter.

Others who offered insight and assistance include Ernie Accorsi, Ed Croke, Robert Korpeles, Mike Malarkey, Lynn Byckog, Vern Morrison, Allen Barra, Chuck Kaufman, David Schoenfield, Jack Cavanaugh, Jack Clary, William N. Wallace, Upton Bell, Todd Schmidt at NFL Films, and Michael Pehanich, the Washington Redskins' Director of Communications.

Our eternal gratitude is also extended to all of the players, coaches, broadcasters, and writers who were gracious enough to share their recollections with us. A book of this sort cannot exist without the buy-in of these talented people and we were very fortunate to have so many of them participate.

The Voices

Ernie Accorsi: The Giants' general manager form 1998 to 2007. Prior to that, he was the team's assistant GM and also served general manager stints with the Colts and Browns.

Dave Anderson: Award-winning (including the Pulitzer) journalist who wrote about the Giants throughout his career, first with the *New York Journal-American* and then with the *New York Times.*

Billy Ard: The Giants' left guard from 1981 to 1988. He finished his career with three seasons in Green Bay.

Jessie Armstead: A member of the New York linebacking corps from 1993 to 2001 and a five-time Pro Bowler.

Doug Atkins: The Hall of Fame defensive end of the famed 1963 Bears defensive unit, he also played for the Browns and Saints. An eight-time Pro Bowler.

Carl Banks: Played 126 games at linebacker for the Giants between 1984 and 1993 and was the defensive star of their victory in Super Bowl XXI. He made the Pro Bowl the following season. He played an additional forty-seven games with Washington and Cleveland. He is an analyst for the Giants' radio broadcasts, a position he's held since 2007.

Al Barry: The starting left guard on the Eastern Division championship teams of 1958 and 1959.

Upton Bell: Broadcaster, executive, and the son of former NFL commissioner Bert Bell. He was the personnel director of the Baltimore Colts and the general manager of the New England Patriots.

Brad Benson: An offensive lineman who spent his entire ten-year career with the Giants, making the Pro Bowl in the championship season of 1986.

Bill Bergey: Outstanding linebacker with the Bengals and Eagles, he made the Pro Bowl five times and was twice named All-Pro.

Lomas Brown: The sixth player taken in the 1985 draft, he went on to an eighteen-year career in which he played 263 games (second among offensive linemen) and made seven Pro Bowls. He came to the Giants after a long stint with the Lions and a stop in Arizona and was New York's left tackle in 2000 and 2001.

Jim Burt: The Giants' nose tackle from 1981 to 1988 who then went on to the 49ers for three seasons where he faced New York in the play-offs. He is the author of *Hard Nose: The Story of the 1986 Giants.*

Harry Carson: Was inducted into the Hall Of Fame in 2006 after a thirteen-year linebacking career in which he made the Pro Bowl nine times.

Jack Cavanaugh: The author of the much-praised *Giants Among Men,* a book about the Giants' golden age of 1956 to 1963.

Mike Ciccolella: The New York Giants' middle linebacker from 1966 to 1968.

Jack Clary: A highly regarded football historian and the author of sixty-eight books and more than four hundred magazine articles. Among his titles are a history of Navy football and a biography of Paul Brown.

Kerry Collins: His long NFL career began in 1995 with the Carolina Panthers who went to the NFC championship game in their second year of existence with him as their quarterback. He came to the Giants in 1999 and was their starter from 2000 to 2003. Since then, he's been with the Raiders and Titans.

Greg Comella: A free-agent out of Stanford who made the roster in 1998, he became the Giants' starting fullback in 2000 and 2001.

Don Criqui: Has been calling NFL games on the national stage for over four decades. He was at the microphone for CBS during the Miracle at the Meadowlands.

Ed Croke: The New York Giants' director of public relations for over three decades.

Howard Cross: The tight end's long career with New York began in 1989 and ended in 2001 with him having played the second-most games in team history at 207.

Dan Daly: A columnist with the *Washington Times* and author of *The Pro Football Chronicle.*

Joe Danelo: Spent six years of his nine-year NFL career kicking for the Giants, for whom he had 103 points in 1981.

Steve DeOssie: A linebacker with a twelve-year NFL career, he was with the Giants from 1989 to 1993. He is the father of Zak DeOssie, a linebacker on the Super Bowl XLII-winning Giants team.

David Diehl: A starter on the offensive line from the opening game of his rookie year in 2003, Diehl is known for never missing a game.

Bob Dobelstein: Was a rookie guard on the 1946 Eastern Division champion team that met the Bears in the title game. He played until 1949.

Dale Dodrill: A four-time Pro Bowler with the Steelers who became an assistant coach under Frank Filchock at Denver in 1960 in the fledgling American Football League.

Fred Dryer: Was the Giants' first-round pick in the 1969 draft and was their starting defensive end for the three seasons. He spent the next ten years with the Los Angeles Rams where he developed an interest in acting and was the star of the hit TV show *Hunter* and also had recurring roles on *Cheers* and *Land's End.*

Monk Edwards: A lineman out of Baylor, William "Monk" Edwards was a late-round draft pick of the Giants in 1940, but made the team and stuck for three seasons. He returned from World War II and played one more season for New York.

Jim Fassel: The head coach of the Giants from 1997 to 2003, he took them to Super Bowl XXXV. As a player, he threw the last pass in the World Football League and coaches Las Vegas in the United Football League.

George Franck: Taken out of Minnesota by the Giants in the first round of the 1941 draft and the sixth player picked overall, he is in the College Football Hall of Fame. He played for the Giants in 1941 and from 1945 to 1947; he was pressed into service as starting fullback in the 1946 title game because of the suspension of Merle Hapes.

Joe Fortunato: The career Bears linebacker made the Pro Bowl five times in his twelve seasons and was also All-Pro three times.

Tucker Frederickson: The number one pick overall in the 1965 draft, his career lasted until 1971, constantly threatened by injuries. In 1970, he was the Giants' starter at fullback.

Joe Galat: The linebacker coach for the Giants in 1977 and 1978, he was present in the coaches booth for the Miracle at the Meadowlands. He was later the head coach of the Canadian Football League's Montreal Allouettes. He is currently the president of American Youth Football.

Frank Gifford: One of the most versatile players in NFL history, his number 16 jersey was retired by the Giants after a twelve-year career. He was an eight-time Pro Bowler at three different positions. After retirement, he became one of the most familiar personalities in sports broadcasting.

Charlie Gogolak: Drafted by the Redskins in the first round of the 1966 draft, he was the first pure kicker ever to be so chosen. He was part of the first wave of soccer-style kickers who changed the kicking game in professional football.

Pete Gogolak: The older brother of Charlie, he was the very first soccer-style kicker in professional football. He started with the Buffalo Bills of the AFL and joined the Giants prior to the 1966 season. He would remain their kicker through 1974.

Gordon Gravelle: The Giants' starting left tackle in 1977 and 1978. He also played with the Rams and the Super Bowl champion Steelers.

Rosey Grier: A member of two different quartets of down linemen called the "Fearsome Foursome"; the first with the Giants and the second with the Los Angeles Rams. He became a popular entertainer while still active, and continued singing and acting after his eleven-year playing career came to an end.

Keith Hamilton: He played both defensive end and tackle, and totaled 173 games in his twelve-year Giants career, seventh all-time in team history.

Jerry Hillebrand: The thirteenth player taken in the 1962 draft, he played linebacker for the Giants from 1963 to 1966. He also played for the Cardinals and Steelers in his eight-year career.

Ike Hilliard: One of the most prolific pass catchers in Giants history, he was a first-round pick of Big Blue in 1997. He played with them through 2004, after which he spent four years with the Buccaneers.

Joe Horrigan: The vice president of Communications/Exhibits at the Pro Football Hall of Fame.

Jeff Hostetler: A backup quarterback to Phil Simms for the better part of five seasons, he got the call and made the most of it when Simms went down late in the 1990 campaign. The author of *One Giant Leap,* which details that season, he also helmed the Raiders offense for four seasons.

Erik Howard: The Giants' starter at nose tackle in 1989, 1990, and 1992 through 1994. His best season was 1990 when he helped New York go all the way, making the Pro Bowl in the process.

Sam Huff: Perhaps the most famous defensive player of his era, he was a four-time Pro Bowler with the Giants and made it once more after being traded to the Redskins prior to the 1964 season. He was elected to the Pro Football Hall of Fame in 1982.

Greg Jackson: In his first year as a starter, the safety contributed four sacks and five interceptions to the Giants' championship cause in 1990. He spent five years in New York and played another seven in Philadelphia, New Orleans, and San Diego.

Stan Jones: He was perennial Pro Bowler and eventual Hall of Famer as a Bears offensive lineman who was switched to the defensive line before the 1963 season in which they allowed just 144 points in fourteen games.

Jim Keane: An end and defensive end with the Bears from 1946 to 1951 and a player with the Packers in 1952. Keane led the NFL in receptions in 1947 and was a UPI All-NFL Second Team selection in that year and in 1949.

Brian Kelley: Long-time Giants linebacker, whose career lasted from 1973 to 1983. In New York's 3–4 defense, he was a member of the Crunch Bunch with fellow linebackers Lawrence Taylor, Harry Carson, and Brad Van Pelt.

Greg Larson: The New York center's long career spanned two eras in team history. He began at the dawn of the Allie Sherman coaching regime in 1961 and ended in Alex Webster's last season as coach.

Marv Levy: The man who coached the Bills against New York in Super Bowl XXV. He compiled a 143–112 record in his seventeen-year coaching career with Kansas City and Buffalo. He is a member of the Pro Football Hall of Fame's Class of 2001.

Bob Lurtsema: In spite of his nickname "Benchwarmer Bob" (or "The Old Benchwarmer") he was actually a starter on the Giants' defensive line from 1967 to 1970. He was traded to the Vikings in the middle of the 1971 season and went on to become a local hero in his four seasons there.

Sam Madison: A four-time Pro Bowl selection and two-time All Pro while with the Miami Dolphins, he came to the Giants as a free agent prior to the 2006 season and helped shore up the defensive backfield.

Bob Margarita: He was a *Chicago Herald-American* and *New York Daily News* selection for All-Pro halfback in 1945 and was third in the NFL in rushing that season. He played with the Bears from 1944 to 1946.

Leonard Marshall: A hard-rushing defensive end who recorded 83.5 sacks in his career, he was with New York from 1983 to 1992. His peak seasons were 1985 and 1986, and he made the Pro Bowl in both years.

George Martin: A feared pass rusher and prolific scorer for a defensive lineman (seven career touchdowns). With 201, he played the third-most games in Giants history.

Clifton McNeil: The wide receiver spent all of 1970 and part of 1971 with the Giants in the midst of a ten-year career. He caught 66 passes in his twenty games with New York.

Chuck Mercein: A high draft pick out of Yale in 1965, he played fullback for New York from 1965 to 1967. He next went to Green Bay where he played in the "Ice Bowl" and Super Bowl II.

Dick Modzelewski: Came to the Giants in his fourth year in the NFL, in time to contribute to the 1956 championship. He was a starter at defensive tackle through 1963 before finishing his career in Cleveland.

Joe Morris: A Giants running back from 1982 to 1989. He scored 21 touchdowns in 1985 and, in the next season, set the team mark for most rushing yards in a season with 1,516.

Karl Nelson: The Giants' starting offensive right tackle form 1984 to 1986. He now works as the color analyst on Giants radio broadcasts.

Ed O'Bradovich: Spent ten years as a defensive end with the Chicago Bears. He is known to modern fans in the Chicago area as the host of the Bears postgame radio show.

Bart Oates: After cutting his teeth in the USFL, he was the Giants' starting center from 1985 to 1993. He went to three Pro Bowls as a

Giant and two more as a 49er, with whom he won a third Super Bowl ring in Super Bowl XXIX.

Brig Owens: Redskins safety who enjoyed a long career that included 36 interceptions and 5 defensive touchdowns.

Bob Papa: The radio voice of the New York Giants since 1995.

Vince Papale: Eagles special-teams player extraordinaire and Philadelphia folk hero who played for both the WFL and NFL without benefit of college experience. He inspired the 2006 movie *Invincible*.

Ray Perkins: The Giants' head coach from 1979 to 1982 and one of the men credited with helping the team turn the corner after years of losing and the disaster of 1978.

Luke Petitgout: Drafted as a guard with the Giants' first pick in the 1999 draft, he moved to tackle and started there for New York until 2005.

Don Pierson: A long-time *Chicago Tribune* columnist and contributor to *Pro Football Weekly*.

Joe Pisarcik: The Giants' starting quarterback in 1977 and 1978. He was later a backup with the Philadelphia Eagles.

Bill Romanowski: A two-time Pro Bowl linebacker who did not miss a single game between 1988 and 2002. He played for the 49ers when they met the Giants in the 1990 NFC championship.

Bob Schnelker: The Giants' starting end from 1954 to 1960, he caught 183 passes in his Giants career and made the Pro Bowl twice.

Tom Scott: A Pro Bowl linebacker with the Eagles, he continued as a linebacker with the Giants where he was a starter from 1961 to 1964. He went on to become the team's linebacker coach.

Rich Seubert: An offensive guard with the Giants since 2001, when he made the team as an undrafted free agent. He made a long and arduous return from having his leg destroyed in a game against Philadelphia in 2003.

Del Shofner: After coming over from the Rams in 1961, "The Blade" became Y. A. Tittle's favorite target. He was a five-time first-team All-Pro, including three times with New York.

Phil Simms: He was with the Giants from 1979 to 1993 and quarterbacked 164 regular season games. He was twice named to the Pro Bowl and had his number 11 retired by the Giants in 1995. His broadcast career began the year after his retirement and he was soon regarded as one of the best color analysts in the game. He served on the lead NFL broadcast team for NBC and, is currently with CBS.

Steve Spagnuolo: After twenty-five years of coaching, the Giants hired him as their defensive coordinator in 2007, and his superlative work with them resulted in his being hired as head coach of the St. Louis Rams.

Ed Sprinkle: He had a twelve-year career with the Bears from 1944 to 1955, playing the line on both sides of the ball. He was named to four Pro Bowls.

Michael Strahan: One of the most dominant players of his era, Strahan was named to seven Pro Bowls and four All-Pro teams at defensive end. Long a presence in the media, he became an analyst for Fox Sports when he retired after Super Bowl XLII.

Pat Summerall: He was the Giants' placekicker from 1958 to 1961, scoring 90 points in 1959. When his career ended, he entered broadcasting and thrived, being elected to the National Sporstcasters and Sportswriters Association Hall of Fame in 1994.

Aaron Thomas: After starting his career with the 49ers, he came to the Giants in mid-1962 and spent eight-plus seasons with the team, mostly as a tight end. He led the NFL in yards per reception in 1965 and made the Pro Bowl in 1964.

Steve Thurlow: A running back from Stanford who was the Giants' pick in the second round of the 1964 draft, he was surprised to find himself traded to the Redskins one game into the 1966 season.

Y. A. Tittle: After a long career in Baltimore and San Francisco, he was traded to the Giants prior to the 1961 season. Although only with the team for four years, the Giants retired his number, 14. He was first-team All-Pro in both 1962 and 1963 and was elected to the Pro Football Hall of Fame in 1971.

Amani Toomer: He spent his entire twelve-year career with the Giants and retired as their all-time pass reception yardage leader. He scored 58 touchdowns and was also a fine return man before becoming a starting wide receiver.

Justin Tuck: A defensive end out of Notre Dame who many feel should have been the MVP of Super Bowl XLII, he is known for his tireless philanthropic efforts.

Bob Tucker: A tight end with the Giants from 1970 to 1977, during which time he caught 327 passes before finishing his career with the Vikings.

J. T. Turner: He came to the Giants in 1977 and became their starting right guard the following season, a position he held until 1983.

David Tyree: He joined the Giants in 2003 and quickly became the most dynamic man on their special-teams units. He was selected for the Pro Bowl in 2005 in this role. Used sparingly on scrimmage play, he came to national attention with his performance in Super Bowl XLII. He has since played for the Baltimore Ravens.

Doug Van Horn: An All-American at Ohio State, he was a mainstay of the Giants' offensive line from 1969 to 1979.

Joe Walton: After being acquired from the Redskins after four seasons in Washington, he caught 95 passes in his three years playing tight end for the Giants, starting in 1961. He later became the head coach of the New York Jets from 1983 to 1989.

Allan Webb: He was a defensive back with the Giants from 1961 to 1965. After his playing career, he got into coaching and was on the Giants staff in 1978, sitting next to offensive coordinator Bob Gibson in the coaches' booth for the Miracle at the Meadowlands.

Alex Webster: "Red" was in the Giants backfield from 1955 to 1964, during which time he scored 56 touchdowns and was named to two Pro Bowls. When he retired, he became an assistant coach with the team and was the surprise choice to take over the coaching reigns when Allie Sherman was fired just prior to the 1969 season. He was named UPI NFL Head Coach of the Year in 1970.

Corey Webster: He was taken by the Giants in the second round of the 2005 draft out of Louisiana State University and has played both left and right cornerback for New York. He had been reduced to reserve status in the 2007 season, but came back strong down the stretch, regaining his starting job and starring in the playoffs. He signed a five-year contract with the Giants a year later.

Perry Williams: A career Giant who played with the team for a decade, beginning in 1984. He did most of his duty at right corner back.

INDEX